A Country Christmas

FESTIVE FOODS • GIFTS & GIVING • CHRISTMAS DECORATING

LORENZ BOOKS

LONDON • NEW YORK • SYDNEY • BATH

A Country Christmas

First published in 1996 by Lorenz Books

© Anness Publishing Limited 1996

Lorenz Books is an imprint of
Anness Publishing Limited
Hermes House
88-89 Blackfriars Road
London SE1 8HA

ISBN 1 85967 304 X

A CIP catalogue record is available from the British Library

Publisher: Joanna Lorenz
Contributors: Pamela Westland, Janice Murfitt, Elizabeth Wolf-Cohen,
Sally Walton, Sue Maggs, Tessa Evelegh
Photographers: Karl Adamson, Nelson Hargreaves, Debbie Patterson, Michelle Garrett,
James Duncan, Madelaine Brehaut, Edward Allwright, Amanda Heywood

Measurements
Three sets of measurements have been provided, in the following order:
metric, imperial and US cups. It is essential that one set of
measurements is followed throughout each recipe. Where conversions
result in an awkward number, these have been rounded for convenience
but will still provide a successful result.

Printed and bound in Hong Kong

A Country Christmas

CONTENTS

INTRODUCTION

As we warm to the annual ritual of filling our kitchens with the homely smell of rich, spicy baking; as we welcome carol singers to the door with a glass of steaming hot mull, and gather the branches of evergreens to decorate our homes; as we write Christmas card messages to friends and relatives, and wrap presents for family and those we love; as we light candles, hang glittering ornaments on the tree and assemble for midnight mass; as we gather around the table for Christmas dinner, and later join in party games, we are carrying on traditions that have been perpetuated over two thousand years and have evolved, with remarkable similarities still, in many parts of the Christian world.

The festival of Christmas as it is celebrated today has its origins in pagan times, when ancient peoples in countries throughout the northern hemisphere gathered together to feast and frolic at the winter solstice.

The transition from a string of pagan festivals to the festival of Christmas was gradual. In the early days of Christianity the birth of Christ was not only not celebrated; it was not even marked by a specific date. It was only in the fourth century that the church fixed the date of Christ's birth as December 25. Then, when St Augustine arrived in Britain, he instructed the faithful to adopt many of the existing customs, applying new meanings and Christian standards to the ancient rituals. In that way, followers were not asked to forego traditional pleasures.

In medieval Britain the emphasis fell heavily on the merrymaking aspect of the festival. Groups of masked mummers, usually men, performed plays in local villages and towns throughout England, receiving money, fruit and other seasonal foods in return for their entertainment. The plays usually centred on a fight between a hero and villain, with a quack doctor arriving in the nick of time to revive the fallen hero with magic potion.

With the rise of Puritanism in the seventeenth century, the merrymaking and, indeed, the celebration of Christmas had to stop. The Puritans denounced the festival and passed an Act of

Parliament prohibiting any celebrations, announcing that the only fitting way to commemorate the birth of Christ was to fast. They even employed troops to patrol the streets and ensure that no-one broke the law and cooked lunch. In New England the Pilgrims and Puritans, in protest against what they saw as the laxity of the Church of England, refused to recognize Christmas Day as a holiday and eschewed all those customs with pagan origins.

With the Restoration of the Monarchy in Great Britain in 1660, Christmas feasting became increasingly lavish, and a journal of the time records that a London merchant's table was set with '... turkies, geese, capons, puddings of a dozen sorts ... besides brawn, roast beef and many things ... minc'd pies and a thing called plumb pottage'

Although the turkey, after having been discovered in South America, had been brought to England in the sixteenth century, it did not become widely popular until the nineteenth century when Mrs Beeton, the Victorian writer on household management, pronounced it as 'one of the most glorious presents made by the New World to the Old'. It was in Victorian Britain that many existing Christmas customs were practised

with renewed enthusiasm, and many innovations were introduced, customs that are now deeply woven into the fabric of Christmas as it is celebrated today.

With marked lack of restraint, the Victorians covered their homes with evergreens, draping boughs across mirrors and picture frames, over mantels and furniture and weaving them in and out of the banisters. Those who could not gather greenery for themselves bought it from street vendors whose barrows were piled high with holly and mistletoe.

Then, in 1841, came the Christmas tree, which had played a prominent role in German festivities since the fifteenth century. When Queen Charlotte, wife of King George III, erected a tree at Windsor Castle in the late eighteenth century, its introduction had passed largely unnoticed. But

when Prince Albert, consort of Queen Victoria, reintroduced the custom, decorating the tree with glittering trinkets and baubles, from his native Germany, it was as if everyone had been waiting for the moment. A photograph of the Royal Family

gathered around their tree appeared in a London journal and from then on a decorated and illuminated tree became the focal point of the festivities in Britain and, shortly afterwards, in the United States.

Although many tree decorations were made at home, manufacturers became more and more inventive, creating delicate and exquisite glass bells, balls, stars and other fancy, festive shapes, as well as twisted candles that fitted into 'safety' holders.

The idea of decorating a tree with lighted candles is thought to have originated with Martin Luther, professor of theology at the Saxon University of Wittenburg in the early sixteenth century, as a way of reminding children that the birth of the infant Jesus brought light into the world. The first electric tree lights appeared in New York in 1882 when an associate of Thomas Edison used strings of coloured lights to illuminate his tree. A decade later, when they were manufactured commercially by The General Electric Company, this form of safety lighting became generally available.

The 1840s heralded the introduction to Victorian Britain not only of the Christmas tree,

but of Christmas cards and Christmas crackers as well. Christmas greetings cards evolved over several decades from an eighteenth-century school practice in Britain of writing 'Christmas pieces' and reports which were given by children to their parents to indicate what progress they had made at school. It was this custom, and the fact that the pieces became ever more elaborate, that prompted Henry (later Sir Henry) Cole, the first director of the Victoria & Albert Museum in London, to commission in 1843 the first known Christmas card. The hand-coloured and printed card, designed by his friend Sir John Callcot Horsley, R.A., showed a close family group seated at a table drinking red wine, and is flanked on either side by allegorical sketches depicting kindly, charitable acts. Surrounded by a rustic vine entwined with ivy, a coloured panel carries the seasonal message 'A Merry Christmas and a Happy New Year to you'.

Later designs depicted scenes of the typical Victorian Christmas: children dancing around a tree, gathering foliage, and playing games; families expressing delight at the entry of the Christmas pudding; skating on ponds, and playing with snowballs. The romantic idea of a white Christmas emanates from this time, a period of particularly harsh winters and deep snow, and persists long after the weather pattern has changed.

'Christmas won't be Christmas without presents', begins Louisa May Alcott's Victorian novel, *Little Women*, expressing a sentiment that would be echoed throughout the Christian world if Father Christmas, Santa Claus, St Nicholas, St Basil, Christkindl, La Befana, Grandfather Frost, Julenisse or any of the other benefactors were to fail in their customary distribution of gifts in December or January.

The familiar figure of Santa Claus or Father Christmas, red-robed, white-haired and jolly, has a somewhat confused ancestry. The distribution of gifts at that time of the year was part of many pagan rituals – Norsemen, for example, believed that their god Woden brought them gifts in honour of the winter solstice. And then, in the Christian church, a number of legends built up around St Nicholas, a fourth-century bishop of a Turkish See. He is said to have distributed baskets of grain, fruit and honey cakes to poor children, thrown bags of gold into a house where there were three young girls, and even brought back to life three boys who had been murdered. With so much good work to his credit, early churchmen conferred on St Nicholas the honour of being the distributor of Christmas gifts.

The legend of the bags of gold had far-reaching consequences. It is said that the gold landed in the girls' stockings which were hung up by the fire to dry, and this gave rise to the custom that is dear to children's hearts today. One of the traditional tokens placed in children's stockings, gold-wrapped chocolate coins, commemorates the wealthy prelate's gift. And the fact that the stockings were hung by the fire prompted St Nicholas – Father Christmas or Santa – to enter the house by the most direct route – down the chimney.

Originally the stockings hung up in eager anticipation would have been workaday ones, perhaps outgrown by the youngest child, but gradually they became an art form in themselves, ranging from those made of homespun gingham in the Shaker community of Pennsylvania – where sugar plums and molasses toffee were customary fillers – to the elaborate petit-point designs of the Victorians, where clove-studded oranges and nuts were obligatory gifts.

Festive Foods

TRADITIONAL COOKING

In country communities all over the world,
families and friends gather to create
and share their own traditions. Here are
wholesome, failsafe recipes to ensure that
the heart of your festival glows with natural
warmth and goodwill.

Christmas Salad

A light first course that can be prepared ahead and assembled just before serving.

Serves 8

INGREDIENTS
mixed red and green lettuce leaves
2 sweet pink grapefruit
1 large or 2 small avocados, peeled
   and cubed

FOR THE DRESSING
90 ml/6 tbsp light olive oil
30 ml/2 tbsp red wine vinegar
1 garlic clove, crushed
5 ml/1 tsp Dijon mustard
salt and freshly ground black pepper

FOR THE CARAMELIZED ORANGE PEEL
4 oranges
50 g/2 oz/4 tbsp caster sugar
60 ml/4 tbsp cold water

lettuce leaves

red wine vinegar

oranges

avocados

grapefruit

olive oil

1 To make the caramelized peel, using a vegetable peeler, remove the rind from the oranges in thin strips and reserve the fruit. Scrape away the white pith from the underside of the rind with a sharp knife, and cut the rind in fine shreds.

2 Put the sugar and water in a small pan and heat gently until the sugar has dissolved. Then add the shreds of orange rind, increase the heat and boil steadily for 5 minutes, until the rind is tender. Using two forks, remove the orange rind from the syrup and spread it out on a wire rack to dry. (This can be done the day before.) Reserve the syrup to add to the dressing.

3 Wash and dry the lettuce and tear the leaves into bite-sized pieces. Wrap them in a clean, damp tea towel and keep them in the fridge. Cut the pith off the oranges and grapefruit. Holding the fruit over a bowl to catch any juice, cut them into segments, removing all the pith.

4 Put all the dressing ingredients into a screw-top jar and shake the jar vigorously to emulsify the dressing. Add the reserved orange-flavoured syrup and adjust the seasoning to taste. Arrange the salad ingredients on individual plates with the avocados, spoon over the dressing and scatter on the caramelized peel.

Warm Prawn Salad with Spicy Marinade

The ingredients can be prepared in advance; if you do this, cook the prawns and bacon just before serving, spoon over the salad and serve with hot herb and garlic bread.

Serves 8

INGREDIENTS
225 g/8 oz large, cooked, shelled prawns
225 g/8 oz smoked streaky bacon, chopped
mixed lettuce leaves
30 ml/2 tbsp snipped fresh chives

FOR THE LEMON AND CHILLI MARINADE
1 garlic clove, crushed
finely grated rind of 1 lemon
15 ml/1 tbsp lemon juice
60 ml/4 tbsp olive oil
¼ tsp chilli paste, or a large pinch dried ground chilli
15 ml/1 tbsp light soy sauce
salt and freshly ground black pepper

prawns
chilli paste
lettuce leaves
chives
lemon
soy sauce
garlic
bacon

1 In a glass bowl, mix the prawns with the garlic, lemon rind and juice, 45 ml/ 3 tbsp of oil, the chilli paste and soy sauce. Season with salt and pepper. Cover with clear film and leave to marinate for at least one hour.

2 Gently cook the bacon in the remaining oil until crisp. Drain on a kitchen towel.

3 Wash and dry the lettuce, tear the leaves into bite-sized pieces and arrange them in individual bowls or on plates.

4 Just before serving, put the prawns with their marinade into a large frying-pan, bring to the boil, add the bacon and cook for one minute. Spoon over the salad and sprinkle with snipped chives. Serve immediately.

Baked Gammon with Cumberland Sauce

Serve this delicious cooked meat and sauce either hot or cold. The gammon must be soaked overnight before cooking to remove any strong salty flavour resulting from the curing process.

Serves 8–10

INGREDIENTS
2.25 kg/5 lb smoked or unsmoked
    gammon joint
1 onion
1 carrot
1 celery stick
bouquet garni sachet
6 peppercorns

FOR THE GLAZE
whole cloves
2 oz/50 g/4 tbsp soft light brown or
    demerara sugar
30 ml/2 tbsp golden syrup
5 ml/1 tsp English mustard powder

FOR THE CUMBERLAND SAUCE
juice and shredded rind of 1 orange
30 ml/2 tbsp lemon juice
120 ml/4 fl oz/½ cup port or red wine
60 ml/4 tbsp redcurrant jelly

1 Soak the gammon overnight in a cool place in plenty of cold water to cover. Discard this water. Put the joint into a large pan and cover it again with more cold water. Bring the water to the boil slowly and skim any scum from the surface with a slotted spoon.

2 Add the vegetables and seasonings, cover and simmer very gently for 2 hours. (The meat can also be cooked in the oven at 180°C/350°F/Gas 4. Allow 30 minutes per 450 g/1 lb.)

3 Leave the meat to cool in the liquid for 30 minutes. Then remove it from the liquid and strip off the skin neatly with the help of a knife (use rubber gloves if the gammon is too hot to handle).

4 Score the fat in diamonds with a sharp knife and stick a clove in the centre of each diamond.

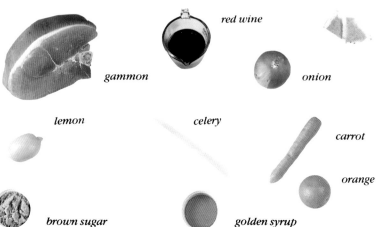

gammon

red wine

bouquet garni

onion

lemon

celery

carrot

orange

brown sugar

golden syrup

5 Preheat the oven to 180°C/350°F/ Gas 4. Put the sugar, golden syrup and mustard powder in a small pan and heat gently to melt them. Place the gammon in a roasting tin and spoon over the glaze. Bake it until golden brown, about 20 minutes. Put it under a hot grill, if necessary, to get a good colour. Allow to stand in a warm place for 15 minutes before carving (this allows the flesh to relax and makes carving much easier).

6 For the sauce, put the orange and lemon juice into a pan with the port and redcurrant jelly, and heat gently to melt the jelly. Pour boiling water on to the orange rind, drain, and add to the sauce. Cook gently for 2 minutes. Serve the sauce hot, in a sauce boat.

Roast Turkey

Serve with stuffing balls, bacon rolls, roast potatoes, Brussels sprouts and gravy.

Serves 8

INGREDIENTS

4.5 kg/10 lb oven-ready turkey, with giblets (thawed overnight if frozen)
1 large onion, peeled and stuck with 6 whole cloves
50 g/2 oz/4 tbsp butter, softened
10 chipolata sausages
salt and freshly ground black pepper

FOR THE STUFFING

225 g/8 oz rindless, streaky bacon, chopped
1 large onion, finely chopped
450 g/1 lb pork sausagemeat
25 g/1 oz/⅓ cup rolled oats
30 ml/2 tbsp chopped fresh parsley
10 ml/2 tsp dried mixed herbs
1 large egg, beaten
115 g/4 oz dried apricots, finely chopped

FOR THE GRAVY

25 g/1 oz/2 tbsp plain flour
450 ml/¾ pint/1⅞ cups giblet stock

bacon

turkey

onion

parsley

apricots   oats

1 Preheat the oven to 200°C/400°F/Gas 6. Adjust the oven shelves to allow for the size of the turkey. For the stuffing, cook the bacon and onion gently in a pan until the bacon is crisp and the onion tender. Transfer to a large bowl and mix in all the remaining stuffing ingredients. Season well with salt and pepper.

4 Spread the turkey with the butter and season it with salt and pepper. Cover it loosely with foil and cook it for 30 minutes. Baste the turkey with the pan juices. Then lower the oven temperature to 180°C/350°F/Gas 4 and cook for the remainder of the calculated time (about 3½ hours for a 4.5 kg/10 lb bird). Baste it every 30 minutes or so.

2 Stuff the neck-end of the turkey only, tuck the flap of skin under and secure it with a small skewer or stitch it with thread (do not over-stuff the turkey or the skin will burst during cooking). Reserve any remaining stuffing.

5 With wet hands, shape the remaining stuffing into small balls or pack it into a greased ovenproof dish. Cook in the oven for 20 minutes, or until golden brown and crisp. About 20 minutes before the end of cooking put the chipolata sausages into an ovenproof dish and put them in the oven. Remove the foil from the turkey for the last hour of cooking and baste it. The turkey is cooked if the juices run clear when the thickest part of the thigh has been pierced with a skewer.

3 Put the whole onion studded with cloves in the body cavity of the turkey and tie the legs together. Weigh the stuffed bird and calculate the cooking time; allow 15 minutes per 450 g/1 lb plus 15 minutes over. Place the turkey in a large roasting tin.

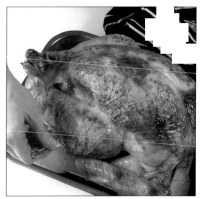

6 Transfer the turkey to a serving plate, cover it with foil and let it stand for 15 minutes before carving. To make the gravy, spoon off the fat from the roasting pan, leaving the meat juices. Blend in the flour and cook for 2 minutes. Gradually stir in the stock and bring to the boil. Check the seasoning and pour into a sauce boat. Remove the skewer or string and pour any juices into the gravy. To serve, surround the turkey with chipolata sausages, bacon rolls and stuffing balls.

Filo Vegetable Pie

This stunning pie makes a delicious main course for vegetarians or is an excellent accompaniment to cold sliced turkey or other meat dishes.

Serves 6–8

INGREDIENTS
225 g/8 oz leeks
165 g/5½ oz/11 tbsp butter
225 g/8 oz carrots, cubed
225 g/8 oz mushrooms, sliced
225 g/8 oz Brussels sprouts, quartered
2 garlic cloves, crushed
115 g/4 oz cream cheese
115 g/4 oz Roquefort or Stilton cheese
150 ml/¼ pint/⅔ cup double cream
2 eggs, beaten
225 g/8 oz cooking apples
225 g/8 oz/1 cup cashew nuts or pine nuts, toasted
350 g/12 oz frozen filo pastry, defrosted
salt and freshly ground black pepper

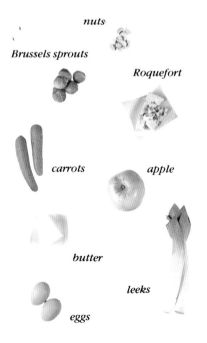

1 Preheat the oven to 180°C/350°F/Gas 4. Cut the leeks in half through the root and wash them to remove any soil, separating the layers slightly to check they are clean. Slice into 1 cm/½ in pieces, drain and dry on kitchen paper.

2 Heat 40 g/1½ oz/3 tbsp of the butter in a large pan and cook the leeks and carrots covered over a medium heat for 5 minutes. Add the mushrooms, sprouts and garlic and cook for another 2 minutes. Turn the vegetables into a bowl and let them cool.

3 Whisk the cream cheese and blue cheese, cream, eggs and seasoning together in a bowl. Pour them over the vegetables. Peel and core the apples and cut into 1 cm/½ in cubes. Add them to the vegetables, with the toasted nuts.

4 Melt the remaining butter. Brush the inside of a 23 cm/9 in loose-based springform cake tin with melted butter. Brush two-thirds of the filo pastry sheets with butter, one at a time and use them to line the base and sides of the tin, overlapping the layers so that there are no gaps.

5 Spoon in the vegetable mixture and fold over the excess filo pastry to cover the filling.

6 Brush the remaining filo sheets with butter and cut them into 2.5 cm/1 in strips. Cover the top of the pie with these strips, arranging them in a rough mound. Bake for 35–45 minutes until golden brown all over. Allow to stand for 5 minutes, and then remove the cake tin and transfer to a serving plate.

Turkey and Cranberry Pie

The cranberries add a tart layer to this turkey pie. Cranberry sauce can be used if fresh cranberries are not available. The pie freezes well.

Serves 8

INGREDIENTS
450 g/1 lb pork sausagemeat
450 g/1 lb lean minced pork
15 ml/1 tbsp ground coriander
15 ml/1 tbsp dried mixed herbs
finely grated rind of 2 large oranges
10 ml/2 tsp grated fresh root ginger or
    2.5 ml/½ tsp ground ginger
10 ml/2 tsp salt
450 g/1 lb turkey breast fillets, thinly
    sliced
115 g/4 oz fresh cranberries
freshly ground black pepper

FOR THE PASTRY
450 g/1 lb/4 cups plain flour
5 ml/1 tsp salt
150 g/5 oz/⅔ cup lard
150 ml/¼ pint/⅔ cup mixed milk and
    water

TO FINISH
1 egg, beaten
300 ml/½ pint/1¼ cups aspic jelly,
    made up as packet instructions

cranberries

turkey fillets

pork

ginger

herbs

orange

coriander

1 Preheat the oven to 180°C/350°F/ Gas 4. Place a baking tray in the oven to preheat. In a bowl, mix together the sausagemeat, pork, coriander, herbs, orange rind, ginger and salt and pepper.

2 To make the pastry, put the flour into a large bowl with the salt. Heat the lard in a small pan with the milk and water until just beginning to boil. Draw the pan aside and allow to cool slightly.

3 Using a wooden spoon, quickly stir the liquid into the flour until a very stiff dough is formed. Turn on to a work surface and knead until smooth. Cut one-third off the dough for the lid, wrap it in clear film and keep it in a warm place.

4 Roll out the large piece of dough on a floured surface and line the base and sides of a well-greased 20 cm/8 in loose-based, springform cake tin. Work with the dough while it is still warm, as it will crack and break if it is left to get cold.

5 Put the turkey breast fillets between two pieces of cling film and flatten with a rolling pin to a 3 mm/⅛ in thickness. Spoon half the pork mixture into the base of the tin, pressing it well into the edges. Cover with half of the turkey slices and then the cranberries, followed by the remaining turkey and finally the rest of the pork mixture.

6 Roll out the rest of the dough and cover the filling, trimming any excess and sealing the edges with a little beaten egg. Make a steam hole in the centre of the lid and decorate the top by cutting pastry trimmings into leaf shapes. Brush with beaten egg. Bake for 2 hours. Cover the pie with foil if the top gets too brown. Place the pie on a wire rack to cool. When cold, use a funnel to fill the pie with liquid aspic jelly. Leave to set for a few hours or overnight, before unmoulding the pie to serve it.

Brussels Sprouts with Chestnuts and Carrots

Be sure to allow plenty of time to peel the chestnuts; they are very fiddly but well worth the effort.

Serves 8

INGREDIENTS
450 g/1 lb fresh chestnuts
450 ml/¾ pint/1⅞ cups vegetable
   stock
450 g/1 lb Brussels sprouts
450 g/1 lb carrots
25 g/1 oz/2 tbsp butter
salt and freshly ground black pepper

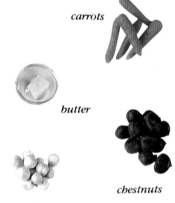

carrots

butter

chestnuts

Brussels sprouts

1 Using a sharp knife, peel the raw chestnuts, leaving the brown papery skins intact. Bring a small pan of water to the boil, drop a handful of chestnuts into the water for a few minutes, and remove with a slotted spoon. The brown papery skins will slip off easily.

2 Put the peeled chestnuts in a pan with the stock. Cover the pan and bring to the boil. Simmer for 5–10 minutes, until tender. Drain.

3 Remove the outer leaves from the sprouts, if necessary, and trim the stalks level. Cook in a pan of boiling, salted water for about 5 minutes, or until just tender. Drain and rinse under cold running water to stop the cooking.

4 Peel the carrots and cut them in 1 cm/½ in diagonal slices. Put them in a pan with cold water to cover, bring to the boil and simmer until just tender, 5–6 minutes. Drain and rinse under cold running water. Melt the butter in a heavy-based pan, add the chestnuts, sprouts and carrots and season with salt and pepper. Cover with a lid and reheat, occasionally stirring the vegetables in the pan.

Sweet and Sour Red Cabbage

The cabbage can be cooked the day before and reheated for serving. It is a good accompaniment to goose, pork or strong-flavoured game dishes. The crispy bacon added at the end of cooking is optional and can be omitted.

Serves 8

INGREDIENTS
900 g/2 lb red cabbage
30 ml/2 tbsp olive oil
2 large onions, sliced
2 large cooking apples, peeled, cored
    and sliced
30 ml/2 tbsp cider vinegar
30 ml/2 tbsp soft brown sugar
225 g/8 oz rindless streaky bacon
    (optional)
salt and freshly ground black pepper

apples
olive oil
cider vinegar
cabbage
brown sugar
streaky bacon
onions

1 Preheat the oven to 180°C/350°F/Gas 4. Cut the cabbage into quarters through the stalk and shred it finely with a sharp knife or in a food processor, discarding the hard core.

2 Heat the oil in a large ovenproof casserole. Cook the onion over a gentle heat for 2 minutes.

3 Stir the cabbage, apples, vinegar, sugar and seasoning into the casserole. Cover with a tight-fitting lid and cook for about 1 hour, or until very tender. Stir half-way through cooking.

4 Chop the bacon, if using, and fry it gently in a pan until crisp. Stir it into the cabbage just before serving.

Carving a Turkey

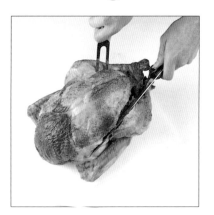

1 First remove the leg, by cutting the skin between the breast and leg. Press the leg flat, to expose the joint. Cut between the bones through the joint.

2 Cut the leg in two, through the joint.

3 Carve the leg into slices.

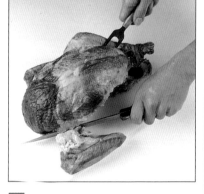

4 Remove the wing, cutting through the joint in the same way as for the leg.

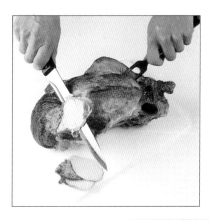

5 Carve the breast in thin slices, starting at the front of the breast. Then carve slices from the back of the breast, alternating the slices between front and back, until all the breast has been carved.

Times for Roasting Turkey

When choosing a turkey for Christmas, you should allow about 450 g/1 lb of dressed (plucked and oven-ready) bird per head. A good sized turkey to buy for Christmas is 4.5 kg/10 lb. This will serve about 12 people, with leftovers for the following day.

Thaw a frozen turkey, still in its bag, on a plate at room temperature (18–21°C/65–70°F) until the legs are flexible and there are no ice crystals in the cavity of the bird. Remove the giblets from the cavity as soon as the bird has thawed enough.

Oven-ready weight	Thawing time	Number of servings	Cooking time
3.5 kg/8 lb	18 hours	8–10 people	2½–3½ hours
4.5 kg/10 lb	19 hours	12–14 people	3½–4 hours
5.5 kg/12 lb	20 hours	16–18 people	3¾–4½ hours
6.3 kg/14 lb	24 hours	18–20 people	4–5 hours

These times apply to a turkey weighed after stuffing and at room temperature. Cook in a moderate oven, 180°C/350°F/Gas 4, covered with butter and bacon rashers and loosely covered with foil.

To test whether the turkey is fully cooked, push a skewer into the thickest part of the leg and press the flesh; the juices should run clear and free from any blood. The legs take longer than the breast to cook; keep the breast covered with foil until the legs are cooked. The foil can be removed for the final hour of cooking, to brown and crisp the skin. The turkey should be basted with the juices from the roasting tin, every hour of cooking.

Plan for the turkey to be ready 15–20 minutes before you want to serve dinner. Remove it from the oven and allow the flesh to relax before carving it.

Curried Fruit Chutney

Make this well ahead of Christmas, to serve with cold sliced turkey and ham.

Makes about 1.2 kg/2½ lb

INGREDIENTS
225 g/8 oz dried apricots
225 g/8 oz dried peaches
225 g/8 oz dates, stoned
225 g/8 oz/1⅓ cups raisins
1–2 garlic cloves, crushed
225 g/8 oz/1 generous cup soft light brown sugar
300 ml/½ pint/1¼ cups white malt vinegar
300 ml/½ pint/1¼ cups water
5 ml/1 tsp salt
10 ml/2 tsp mild curry powder

2 Chop or mince the mixture coarsely in batches in a food processor.

1 Put all the ingredients in a large pan, cover and simmer very gently for 10–15 minutes, or until tender.

3 Spoon into clean jam jars. Seal the jars and label them. Store in a cool place for 4 weeks before using.

Ginger, Date, and Apple Chutney

Make this well ahead and store it in airtight jars. Serve with cold sliced meats or pies.

Makes about 1.5 kg/3½ lb

INGREDIENTS
450 g/1 lb cooking apples
450 g/1 lb dates
225 g/8 oz dried apricots
115 g/4 oz glacé ginger, chopped
1–2 garlic cloves, crushed
225 g/8 oz/1⅓ cups sultanas
225 g/8 oz/1 generous cup soft light brown sugar
5 ml/1 tsp salt
300 ml/½ pint/1¼ cups white malt vinegar

2 Put all the fruit together in a large pan, with the remaining ingredients. Cover and simmer gently for 10–15 minutes, or until tender.

1 Peel, core and chop the apples. Stone the dates and chop them roughly. Chop the apricots.

3 Spoon into clean jam jars. Seal the jars and label them. Store in a cool place for 4 weeks before using.

Prune, Orange and Nut Stuffing

You could also finely chop the reserved turkey liver and mix it into this stuffing.

Serves 8 (enough to stuff a 4.5 kg/10 lb turkey)

INGREDIENTS
115 g/4 oz/1 cup stoned prunes
60 ml/4 tbsp red wine or sherry
1 onion, finely chopped
25 g/1 oz/2 tbsp butter
225 g/8 oz/5 cups fresh white
    breadcrumbs
finely grated rind of 1 orange
2 eggs, beaten
30 ml/2 tbsp chopped fresh parsley
15 ml/1 tbsp mixed dried herbs
large pinch of ground allspice
large pinch of grated nutmeg
115 g/4 oz/1 cup chopped walnuts
    or pecans
2 celery sticks, finely chopped
salt and freshly ground black pepper

1 Put the prunes and red wine or sherry in a small pan, cover and simmer gently until tender. Set aside to cool.

2 Cook the onion gently in the butter until tender, about 10 minutes.

3 Cut each prune into four pieces. Mix all the ingredients in a large bowl and season well with salt and pepper.

Rice, Mushroom and Leek Stuffing

The rice gives this stuffing a crumbly, light texture.

Serves 8 (enough to stuff a 4.5 kg/10 lb turkey)

INGREDIENTS
115 g/4 oz/½ cup rice
25 g/1 oz/2 tbsp butter
225 g/8 oz leeks, washed and sliced
225 g/8 oz mushrooms, chopped
2 celery sticks, finely chopped
50 g/2 oz/½ cup chopped walnuts
1 egg, beaten
60 ml/4 tbsp chopped fresh parsley
10 ml/2 tsp dried thyme
finely grated rind of 1 lemon
225 g/8 oz apple, peeled, cored
    and diced
salt and freshly ground black pepper

2 Mix all the remaining ingredients thoroughly together in a large bowl and season with salt and pepper.

1 Cook the rice in plenty of boiling, salted water for 12 minutes until tender. Drain the rice thoroughly and let it cool. Melt the butter in a frying-pan and cook the leeks and mushrooms until tender. Increase the heat and cook to evaporate any remaining moisture in the pan. Set aside to cool.

3 Add the rice, and the leek and mushroom mixture to the bowl and mix together thoroughly.

Making Bacon Rolls

If you want to wrap stoned prunes or chicken livers inside each rasher cut the bacon rashers in half after stretching them.

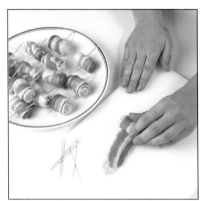

1 Remove the rind from the rashers of bacon and stretch them with the back of a large knife.

2 Roll the rashers up neatly.

3 Skewer the bacon rolls with cocktail sticks. Grill the rolls until crisp, turning them half-way through cooking.

Roasting Potatoes

Floury potatoes make the best crisp roast potatoes. Garlic or rosemary can be added to the oil, to flavour the potatoes during cooking.

1 Preheat the oven to 200°C/400°F/ Gas 6. Peel the potatoes and cut large potatoes in half. Parboil them for 10 minutes. Drain. Score the surface of each potato with a fork. Roll them in flour and tap them to remove any excess. Heat 2.5 cm/1 in olive oil in a shallow roasting tin until smoking hot.

2 Put the potatoes in the hot oil and baste them to coat them in oil. Roast for about an hour.

3 Baste and turn the potatoes twice during cooking. Drain them on kitchen paper and sprinkle them with salt.

CHRISTMAS CAKES AND BAKES

These recipes for pudding, a classic cake,
a mince tart, a yule log, biscuits and
a country-style gingerbread house will
satisfy all your baking needs this
Christmas – for giving, entertaining or
treating your family.

Christmas Pudding

This recipe makes enough to fill one 1.2 litre/2 pint/ 5 cup basin or two 600 ml/1 pint/2½ cup basins. It can be made up to a month before Christmas and stored in a cool, dry place. Steam the pudding for 2 hours before serving. Serve with brandy or rum butter, whisky sauce, custard or whipped cream, topped with a decorative sprig of holly.

Serves 8

INGREDIENTS
115 g/4 oz/½ cup butter
225 g/8 oz/1 heaped cup soft dark
  brown sugar
50 g/2 oz/½ cup self-raising flour
5 ml/1 tsp ground mixed spice
¼ tsp grated nutmeg
2.5 ml/½ tsp ground cinnamon
2 eggs
115 g/4 oz/2 cups fresh white
  breadcrumbs
175 g/6 oz/1 cup sultanas
175 g/6 oz/1 cup raisins
115 g/4 oz/½ cup currants
25 g/1 oz/3 tbsp mixed candied peel,
  chopped finely
25 g/1 oz/¼ cup chopped almonds
1 small cooking apple, peeled, cored
  and coarsely grated
finely grated rind of 1 orange
  or lemon
juice of 1 orange or lemon, made up
  to 150 ml/¼ pint/⅔ cup with
  brandy, rum or sherry

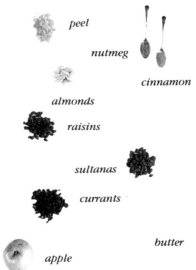

breadcrumbs

peel

nutmeg

cinnamon

almonds

raisins

sultanas

currants

brown sugar

orange

apple

butter

2 Whisk the butter and sugar together until soft. Beat in the flour, spices and eggs. Stir in the remaining ingredients thoroughly. The mixture should have a soft dropping consistency.

3 Turn the mixture into the greased basin(s) and level the top.

1 Cut a disc of greaseproof paper to fit the base of the basin(s) and butter the disc and basin(s).

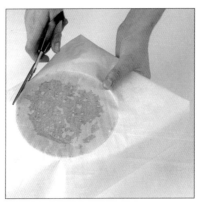

4 Cover with another disc of buttered greaseproof paper.

5 Make a pleat across the centre of a large piece of greaseproof paper and cover the basin(s) with it, tying it in place with string under the rim. Cut off the excess paper. Pleat a piece of foil in the same way and cover the basin(s) with it, tucking it around the bowl neatly, under the greaseproof frill. Tie another piece of string around the basin(s) and across the top, as a handle.

6 Place the basin(s) in a steamer over a pan of simmering water and steam for 6 hours. Alternatively, put the basin(s) into a large pan and pour round enough boiling water to come halfway up the basin(s) and cover the pan with a tight-fitting lid. Check the water is simmering and top it up with boiling water as it evaporates. When the pudding(s) have cooked, leave to cool completely. Then remove the foil and greaseproof paper. Wipe the basin(s) clean and replace the greaseproof paper and foil with clean pieces, ready for reheating.

To Serve

Steam for 2 hours. Turn on to a plate and leave to stand for 5 minutes, before removing the pudding basin (the steam will rise to the top of the basin and help to loosen the pudding).

Moist and Rich Christmas Cake

The cake can be made 4–6 weeks before Christmas. During this time, pierce the cake with a fine needle and spoon over 30–45 ml/2–3 tbsp brandy.

Makes 1 cake

INGREDIENTS
225 g/8 oz/1⅓ cups sultanas
225 g/8 oz/1 cup currants
225 g/8 oz/1⅓ cups raisins
115 g/4 oz/1 cup prunes, stoned and chopped
50 g/2 oz/¼ cup glacé cherries, halved
50 g/2 oz/⅓ cup mixed candied citrus peel, chopped
45 ml/3 tbsp brandy or sherry
225 g/8 oz/2 cups plain flour
pinch of salt
2.5 ml/½ tsp ground cinnamon
2.5 ml/½ tsp grated nutmeg
15 ml/1 tbsp cocoa powder
225 g/8 oz/1 cup butter
225 g/8 oz/1 generous cup soft dark brown sugar
4 large eggs
finely grated rind of 1 orange or lemon
50 g/2 oz/⅔ cup ground almonds
50 g/2 oz/½ cup chopped almonds

TO DECORATE
60 ml/4 tbsp apricot jam
25 cm/10 in round cake board
450 g/1 lb almond paste
450 g/1 lb white fondant icing
225 g/8 oz royal icing
1½ m/1½ yd ribbon

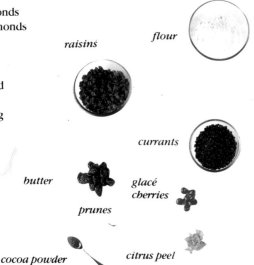

raisins

flour

almonds

butter

glacé cherries

currants

prunes

nutmeg

cinnamon

cocoa powder

citrus peel

1 The day before you want to bake the cake, put all the dried fruit to soak in the brandy or sherry, cover it with clear film and leave overnight. Grease a 20 cm/8 in round cake tin and line it with a double thickness of greaseproof paper.

2 The next day, preheat the oven to 170°C/325°F/Gas 3. Sift together the flour, salt, spices and cocoa powder. Whisk the butter and sugar together until light and fluffy and beat in the eggs gradually. Finally mix in the orange or lemon rind, the ground and chopped almonds, dried fruits (with any liquid) and the flour mixture.

4 Warm then sieve the apricot jam to make a glaze. Remove the paper from the cake and place it in the centre of the cake board and brush it with hot apricot glaze. Cover the cake with a layer of almond paste and then a layer of fondant icing. Pipe a border around the base of the cake with royal icing. Tie a ribbon around the sides.

3 Spoon into the prepared cake tin, level the top and give the cake tin a gentle tap on the work surface to settle the mixture and disperse any air bubbles. Bake for 3 hours, or until a fine skewer inserted into the middle comes out clean. Transfer the cake tin to a wire rack and let the cake cool in the tin for an hour. Then carefully turn the cake out on to the wire rack, but leave the paper on, as it will help to keep the cake moist during storage. When the cake is cold, wrap it tightly in foil and store it in a cool place.

5 Roll out any trimmings from the fondant icing and stamp out 12 small holly leaves with a cutter. Make one bell motif with a biscuit mould, dusted first with sifted icing sugar. Roll 36 small balls for the holly berries. Leave on greaseproof paper to dry for 24 hours. Decorate the cake with the leaves, berries and bell, attaching them with a little royal icing.

Chocolate Christmas Log

Begin preparations for this cake at least one day ahead. It is easy to prepare, but has several components. Make the mushrooms by sandwiching small meringues together with ganache frosting.

Serves 12–14

INGREDIENTS
5 eggs, separated
20 g/¾ oz/3 tbsp unsweetened cocoa plus extra for dusting
⅛ tsp cream of tartar
115 g/4 oz/1 cup icing sugar

CHOCOLATE GANACHE FROSTING
300 ml/10 fl oz/1¼ cups double or whipping cream
350 g/12 oz bittersweet chocolate, chopped
30 ml/2 tbsp brandy or chocolate-flavour liqueur

CRANBERRY CHRISTMAS SAUCE
450 g/1 lb fresh or frozen cranberries, rinsed and picked over
285 g/10 oz/1 cup seedless raspberry preserve, melted
100 g/3½ oz/½ cup granulated sugar, or to taste

WHITE CHOCOLATE CREAM FILLING
200 g/7 oz fine quality white chocolate, chopped
450 ml/16 fl oz/2 cups double cream
30 ml/2 tbsp brandy or chocolate-flavour liqueur (optional)

raspberry preserve

bittersweet chocolate

cranberries

COOK'S TIP

Small decorative 'mushrooms' are traditionally used to enhance the chocolate yule log. These can be made from meringue. Pipe the 'caps' and 'stems' separately, and when dry and hard, stick together using a little ganache or melted chocolate. You may lightly dust them with cocoa after assembling.

1 Prepare ganache frosting. In a medium saucepan over medium heat, bring the cream to a boil. Remove from heat and add chocolate all at once, stirring constantly until melted and smooth. Stir in liqueur if using, then strain into a medium bowl and cool to room temperature. Remove 125 ml/4 fl oz/½ cup at room temperature, then refrigerate remaining ganache for 6–8 hours or overnight.

2 Prepare sauce. In a food processor fitted with a metal blade, process the cranberries until liquid. Press through a sieve into a small bowl, discard pulp. Stir in melted raspberry preserve and sugar to taste. If sauce is too thick, add a little water to thin. Refrigerate until needed.

3 Prepare cake. Preheat oven to 200°C/400°F/Gas 6. Grease 39 cm × 26 cm/15½ × 10½ in Swiss roll tin, line with non-stick baking paper, overlapping edge by 2.5 cm/1 in.

In a bowl with electric mixer, beat egg yolks until thick and creamy. Reduce speed and beat in cocoa and half the sugar. In large bowl with electric mixer with cleaned beaters, beat egg whites. Add cream of tartar and beat on high speed until soft peaks form. Add remaining sugar 30 ml/2 tbsp at a time, beating well after each addition until stiff and glossy. Gently fold beaten yolk mixture into the whites. Spread batter in tin and bake for 15–20 minutes.

Lay a clean dish towel on a work surface and cover with non-stick baking paper; dust with cocoa or sugar. When cake is done, immediately turn out on to paper. Peel off lining paper. Cut off crisp edges and, starting from one narrow end, roll cake with the paper and towel, Swiss roll fashion. Cool cake.

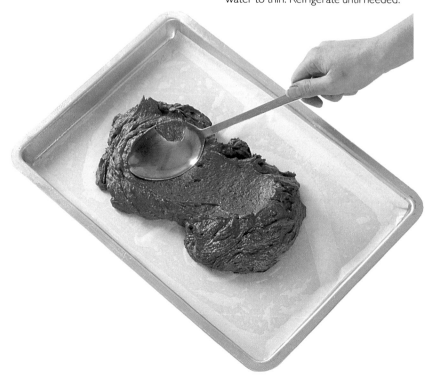

4 Prepare filling. In a saucepan over low heat, melt white chocolate with 125 ml/4 fl oz/½ cup cream until melted, stirring frequently. Strain into a bowl and cool to room temperature. In another bowl with electric mixer, beat remaining cream and brandy until soft peaks form. Stir a spoonful of cream into white chocolate mixture to lighten it, then fold in remaining cream. Unroll cooled cake and spread with chocolate cream. Starting from the same end, re-roll cake without paper (it doesn't matter if it cracks). Cut off one-quarter at an angle. Place against the long piece to resemble a branch.

5 Allow frosting to soften at room temperature. With an electric mixer, beat the ganache until it begins to lighten in colour and texture, about 30–45 seconds. It should have a soft spreading consistency; do not over-beat as chocolate will become stiff and grainy. Using a metal palette knife, spread ganache over the cake surface. Using a fork, mark the ganache lengthwise to resemble tree bark. Dust cake with icing sugar and serve with cranberry sauce.

De Luxe Mincemeat Tart

The mincemeat can be made up and kept in the fridge for up to two weeks. It can also be used to make individual mince pies.

Serves 8

INGREDIENTS
225 g/8 oz/2 cups plain flour
10 ml/2 tsp ground cinnamon
50 g/2 oz/⅔ cup walnuts, finely ground
115 g/4 oz/½ cup butter
50 g/2 oz/4 tbsp caster sugar, plus
    extra for dusting
1 egg
2 drops vanilla essence
15 ml/1 tbsp cold water

FOR THE MINCEMEAT
2 dessert apples, peeled, cored and
    coarsely grated
225 g/8 oz/1⅓ cups raisins
115 g/4 oz no-soak dried apricots,
    chopped
115 g/4 oz no-soak dried figs or
    prunes, chopped
225 g/8 oz green grapes, halved and
    seeded
50 g/2 oz/½ cup chopped almonds
finely grated rind of 1 lemon
30 ml/2 tbsp lemon juice
30 ml/2 tbsp brandy or port
¼ tsp ground mixed spice
115 g/4 oz/generous ½ cup soft light
    brown sugar
25 g/1 oz/2 tbsp butter, melted

1 To make the pastry, put the flour, cinnamon and walnuts in a food processor. Add the butter and process until the mixture resembles fine breadcrumbs. Turn into a bowl and stir in the sugar. Using a fork, beat the egg with the vanilla essence and water. Gradually stir the egg mixture into the dry ingredients. Gather together with your fingertips to form a soft, pliable dough. Knead briefly on a lightly floured surface until smooth; then wrap the dough in clear film and chill it for 30 minutes.

2 Mix all the mincemeat ingredients together thoroughly in a bowl.

3 Cut one-third off the pastry and reserve it for the lattice. Roll out the remainder and use it to line a 23 cm/9 in, loose-based flan tin. Take care to push the pastry well into the edges and make a 5 mm/¼ in rim around the top edge.

4 With a rolling pin, roll off the excess pastry to neaten the edge. Fill the pastry case with the mincemeat.

almonds

brandy

raisins

grapes

brown sugar

walnuts

lemon

flour

apple

butter

apricots

figs

5 Roll out the remaining pastry and cut it into 1 cm/½ in strips. Arrange the strips in a lattice over the top of the pastry, wet the joins and press them together well. Chill for 30 minutes.

6 Preheat the oven to 190°C/375°F/ Gas 5. Place a baking sheet in the oven to preheat. Brush the pastry with water and dust it with caster sugar. Bake it on the baking sheet for 30–40 minutes. Transfer to a wire rack and leave to cool for 15 minutes. Then carefully remove the flan tin. Serve warm or cold, with sweetened, whipped cream.

Christmas Biscuits

These are great fun for children to make as presents. Any shape of biscuit cutter can be used. Store them in an airtight tin. For a change, omit the lemon rind and add 25 g/1 oz/⅓ cup of ground almonds and a few drops of almond essence.

Makes about 12

INGREDIENTS
75 g/3 oz/6 tbsp butter
50 g/2 oz/generous ½ cup icing sugar
finely grated rind of 1 small lemon
1 egg yolk
175 g/6 oz/1½ cups plain flour
pinch of salt

TO DECORATE
2 egg yolks
red and green edible food colouring

1 In a large bowl, beat the butter, sugar and lemon rind together until pale and fluffy. Beat in the egg yolk, and then sift in the flour and the salt. Knead together to form a smooth dough. Wrap in clear film and chill for 30 minutes.

2 Preheat the oven to 190°C/375°F/ Gas 5. On a lightly floured surface, roll out the dough to 3 mm/⅛ in thick. Using a 6 cm/2½ in fluted cutter, stamp out as many biscuits as you can, with the cutter dipped in flour to prevent it from sticking to the dough.

3 Transfer the biscuits on to lightly greased baking trays. Mark the tops lightly with a 2.5 cm/1 in holly leaf cutter and use a 5 mm/¼ in plain piping nozzle for the berries. Chill for 10 minutes, until firm.

flour

icing sugar

butter

eggs

food colouring   *lemon*

4 Meanwhile, put each egg yolk into a small cup. Mix red food colouring into one and green food colouring into the other. Using a small, clean paintbrush, carefully paint the colours on to the biscuits. Bake the biscuits for 10–12 minutes, or until they begin to colour around the edges. Let them cool slightly on the baking trays, and then transfer them to a wire rack to cool completely.

Gingerbread House

This gingerbread house makes a memorable family gift, especially if filled with lots of little gifts and surprises.

Makes 1

INGREDIENTS
90 ml/6 tbsp golden syrup
30 ml/2 tbsp black treacle
75 g/3 oz/⅓ cup light soft brown
  sugar
75 g/3 oz/5 tbsp butter
450 g/1 lb/4 cups plain flour
15 g/1 tbsp ground ginger
15 g/1 tbsp bicarbonate of soda
2 egg yolks
225 g/8 oz barley sugar sweets

ICING AND DECORATION
1 quantity Royal Icing (see
  Introduction)
25 cm/10 in square silver cake board

black treacle

biscuit cutters

barley sugar sweets

eggs

golden syrup

1 Preheat the oven to 190°C/375°F/Gas 5. Line several baking sheets with non-stick baking paper. Cut out the templates. Place the syrup, treacle, sugar and butter in a saucepan and heat gently, stirring occasionally until melted.

2 Sift the flour, ginger and bicarbonate of soda into a bowl. Add the egg yolks and pour in the treacle mixture, stirring with a wooden spoon to form a soft dough. Knead on a lightly floured surface until smooth and place in a polythene bag. Cut off ⅓ of the dough and roll out thinly.

3 Place the template for the end walls at one end and cut neatly around the shape using a sharp knife. Repeat to cut another end wall. Using a 2.5 cm/1 in round cutter, stamp out 1 round window on each end piece. Cut a door shape on each end piece using a 2.5 cm/1 in square cutter and rounding off the tops. Place a sweet in each opening and bake in the oven for 8–10 minutes until the sweet has filled the frame and the gingerbread is golden. Cool on the baking sheet.

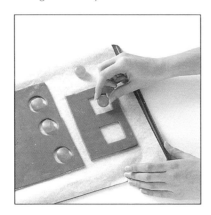

4 Repeat the above instructions using the remaining dough for the 2 side walls and the two roof pieces. Using the 2.5 cm/1 in square cutter, stamp out 2 window shapes for each wall piece. Using the 2.5 cm/1 in round cutter, stamp out 3 round windows on each roof piece. Place sweets in the openings and bake as before.

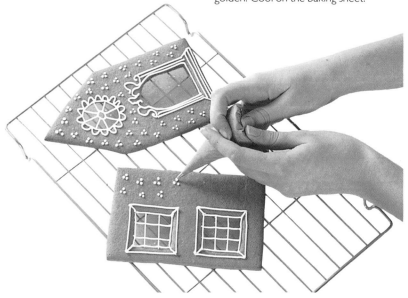

5 Make the Royal Icing. Place some of the icing in a greaseproof paper piping bag fitted with a No. 2 plain writing nozzle. Pipe lines, loops and circles around the windows, doors and on the walls and roof to decorate. Pipe beads of icing in groups of 3 all over the remaining spaces and leave flat to dry.

TEMPLATES FOR THE GINGERBREAD HOUSE

1 For the side wall, measure and cut out a rectangle 15 cm × 10 cm (6 in × 4 in) from stiff card.

2 For the pitch of the roof, measure and cut out a rectangle 18 cm × 10 cm (7 in × 4 in). Measure 10 cm (4 in) up each long side and mark these points. Mark a centre point at the top of the short edge. Draw a line from each of the side points to the top point. Cut out.

3 For the roof, measure and cut out a rectangle 20 cm × 10 cm (8 in × 6 in) from stiff card.

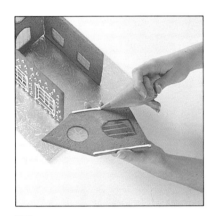

6 To assemble the house, pipe a line of icing on the side edges of the walls and side pieces. Stick them together to form a box shape on the cake board. Pipe a line of icing following the pitch of the roof on both end pieces and along the top of the 2 roof pieces. Press gently in position and support the underneath of each roof while the icing sets. Pipe the finishing touches to the roof and base of the house. Dust the cake board with icing sugar to look like snow. Wrap ribbon around the edges of the board.

CHRISTMAS TREATS

Delight visitors, friends and family with
these really special indulgences – individual
ideas that reflect the thoughts and feelings
you have for your loved ones.

Festive Gingerbread

These brightly decorated gingerbread biscuits are fun to make and may be used as edible Christmas tree decorations.

Makes 20

INGREDIENTS
30 ml/2 tbsp golden syrup
15 ml/1 tbsp black treacle
50 g/2 oz/¼ cup light soft brown
 sugar
25 g/1 oz/2 tbsp butter
175 g/6 oz/1½ cups plain flour
¾ tsp bicarbonate of soda
½ tsp ground mixed spice
1½ tsp ground ginger
1 egg yolk

ICING AND DECORATION
½ quantity Royal Icing (see
 Introduction)
red, yellow and green food colourings
brightly coloured ribbons

biscuit cutters

ginger

egg

1 Preheat the oven to 190°C/375°F/ Gas 5. Line several baking sheets with non-stick baking paper. Place the syrup, treacle, sugar and butter into a saucepan. Heat gently, stirring occasionally, until the butter has melted.

2 Sift the flour, bicarbonate of soda, mixed spice and ginger into a bowl. Using a wooden spoon stir in the treacle mixture and the egg yolk and mix to a soft dough. Knead on a lightly floured surface until smooth.

3 Roll out the dough thinly and using a selection of festive cutters, stamp out as many shapes as possible, kneading and re-rolling the dough as necessary. Arrange the shapes well spaced apart on the baking sheets. Make a hole in the top of each shape using a drinking straw if you wish to use the biscuits as hanging decorations.

4 Bake in the oven for 15–20 minutes or until risen and golden and leave to cool on the baking sheets before transferring to a wire rack using a palette knife.

5 Divide the Royal Icing into 4 and colour ¼ red, ¼ yellow and ¼ green using the food colourings. Make 4 greaseproof paper piping bags and fill each one with the different coloured icings. Fold down the tops and snip off the points.

6 Pipe lines, dots, and zigzags on the gingerbread biscuits using the coloured icings. Leave to dry. Thread ribbons through the holes in the biscuits.

Hogmanay Shortbread

Light, crisp shortbread looks so professional when shaped in a mould, although you could also shape it by hand.

Makes 2 large or 8 individual shortbreads

INGREDIENTS
175 g/6 oz/¾ cup plain flour
50 g/2 oz/¼ cup cornflour
50 g/2 oz/¼ cup caster sugar
115 g/4 oz/½ cup unsalted butter

flour

sugar

butter

1 Preheat the oven to 160°C/325°F/ Gas 3. Lightly flour the mould and line a baking sheet with non-stick baking paper. Sift the flour, cornflour and sugar into a mixing bowl. Cut the butter into pieces and rub into the flour mixture until it binds together and you can knead it into a soft dough.

2 Place the dough into the mould and press to fit neatly. Invert the mould onto the baking sheet and tap firmly to release the dough shape. Bake in the oven for 35–40 minutes or until pale golden.

3 Sprinkle the top of the shortbread with a little caster sugar and cool on the baking sheet. Wrap in cellophane paper or place in a box tied with ribbon.

Christmas Tree Biscuits

These biscuits make an appealing gift. They look wonderful hung on a Christmas tree or in front of a window to catch the light.

Makes 12

INGREDIENTS
175 g/6 oz/1½ cups plain flour
75 g/3 oz/5 tbsp butter
40 g/1½ oz/3 tbsp caster sugar
1 egg white
30 ml/2 tbsp orange juice
225 g/8 oz coloured fruit sweets

DECORATION
coloured ribbons

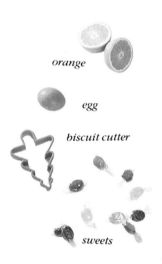

orange

egg

biscuit cutter

sweets

1 Preheat the oven to 180°C/350°F/Gas 4. Line 2 baking sheets with non-stick baking paper. Sift the flour into a mixing bowl. Cut the butter into pieces and rub into the flour until the mixture resembles fine breadcrumbs. Stir in the sugar, egg white and enough orange juice to form a soft dough. Knead on a lightly floured surface until smooth.

2 Roll out thinly and stamp out as many shapes as possible using a Christmas tree cutter. Transfer the shapes to the lined baking sheets well spaced apart. Knead the trimmings together. Using a 1 cm/½ in round cutter or the end of a plain meringue piping nozzle, stamp out and remove 6 rounds from each tree shape. Cut each sweet into 3 and place a piece in each hole. Make a small hole at the top of each tree to thread through the ribbon.

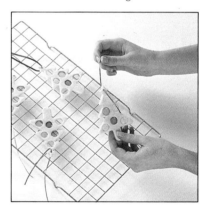

3 Bake in the oven for 15–20 minutes, until the biscuits are slightly gold in colour and the sweets have melted and filled the holes. Cool on the baking sheets. Repeat until you have used up the remaining biscuit dough and sweets. Thread short lengths of ribbon through the holes so that you can hang up the biscuits.

Mini Iced Christmas Cakes

A personal Christmas cake makes an extra special gift. Try improvising with your own designs, decorations and colour schemes.

Makes 1 large or 4 individual cakes

INGREDIENTS
350 g/12 oz/1½ cups mixed dried fruit
50 g/2 oz/¼ cup glacé cherries, sliced
50 g/2 oz/½ cup flaked almonds
grated rind of ½ lemon
15 ml/1 tbsp brandy
115 g/4 oz/1 cup plain flour
½ tsp ground mixed spice
25 g/1 oz/⅓ cup ground almonds
90 g/3½ oz/½ cup unsalted butter, softened
90 g/3½ oz/½ cup dark soft brown sugar
½ tbsp black treacle
2 eggs

ICING AND DECORATION
4 × 10 cm/4 in square cake boards
60 ml/4 tbsp Apricot Glaze
675 g/1½ lb white marzipan
900 g/2 lb ready-to-roll icing
red and green food colourings

1 Prepare a 15 cm/6 in square cake tin. Place the mixed dried fruit, cherries, flaked almonds, lemon rind and brandy into a large mixing bowl. Stir until thoroughly blended, cover with clear film and leave for 1 hour or overnight.

2 Preheat the oven to 150°C/300°F/ Gas 2. Sift the flour and mixed spice into another bowl, add the ground almonds, butter, sugar, treacle and eggs. Mix together with a wooden spoon and beat for 2–3 minutes until smooth and glossy. Alternatively use a food mixer or processor for 1 minute. Fold the fruit into the cake mixture until evenly blended. Place the mixture in the prepared tin, level the top and make a slight depression in the centre.

3 Bake the cake in the centre of the oven for 2¼–2½ hours or until a skewer inserted into the centre of the cake comes out clean. Leave the cake to cool in the tin. Spoon over a little extra brandy if desired. Remove the cake from the tin and wrap in foil until required.

lemon

glacé cherries

almonds

marzipan

4 Remove the lining paper and cut the cake into 4 square pieces. Place each cake on a small cake board and brush evenly with Apricot Glaze. Cut the marzipan into 4 pieces and roll out a piece large enough to cover one cake. Place over the cake, smooth over the top and sides and trim off the excess marzipan at the base. Repeat to cover the remaining 3 cakes.

5 Cut the ready-to-roll icing into 5 pieces, roll 4 pieces out thinly to cover each cake, smoothing the tops and sides and trimming off the excess icing at the bases. Knead the trimmings together with the remaining piece of icing and cut into 2 pieces. Colour one piece red and the other piece green using the food colourings. Roll out ½ of the red icing into a 25 × 15 cm/10 × 6 in oblong.

6 Cut the icing into 5 mm/¼ in strips and place diagonally across the cake working from corner to corner. Trim the strips at the base of the cake. Brush the ends of the strips with a little water and press onto the cake. Make a few loops of icing and place on top of the cake. Repeat to decorate the remaining cakes with green and finally red and green strips of icing. Pack into boxes when dry.

Individual Dundee Cakes

Dundee cakes are traditionally topped with almonds but also look tempting covered with glacé fruits.

Makes 3

INGREDIENTS
225 g/8 oz/1 cup raisins
225 g/8 oz/1 cup currants
225 g/8 oz/1 cup sultanas
50 g/2 oz/¼ cup glacé cherries, sliced
115 g/4 oz/¾ cup mixed peel
grated rind of 1 orange
300 g/11 oz/2¾ cups plain flour
½ tsp baking powder
5 g/1 tsp ground mixed spice
225 g/8 oz/1 cup unsalted butter, softened
225 g/8 oz/1 cup caster sugar
5 eggs

TOPPING
50 g/2 oz/½ cup whole blanched almonds
50 g/2 oz/¼ cup glacé cherries, halved
50 g/2 oz/½ cup glacé fruits, sliced
45 ml/3 tbsp Apricot Glaze

orange

glacé cherries

almonds

peel

egg

glacé fruits

1 Preheat the oven to 150°C/300°F/ Gas 2. Prepare 3 × 15 cm/5 in round cake tins. Place all the fruit and the orange rind into a large mixing bowl. Mix together until evenly blended. In another bowl sift the flour, baking powder and mixed spice. Add the butter, sugar and eggs. Mix together with a wooden spoon and beat for 2–3 minutes until smooth and glossy. Alternatively use a food mixer or processor for 1 minute.

2 Add the mixed fruit to the cake mixture and fold in using a spatula until well blended. Divide the cake mixture between the 3 tins and level the tops. Arrange the almonds in circles over the top of one cake, the glacé cherries over the second cake and the mixed glacé fruits over the last one. Bake in the oven for approximately 2–2½ hours or until a skewer inserted into the centre of the cakes comes out clean.

3 Leave the cakes in their tins until completely cold. Turn out, remove the paper and brush the tops with Apricot Glaze. Leave to set, then wrap in cellophane paper or clear film and place in pretty boxes.

Spiced Christmas Cake

This light cake mixture is flavoured with spices and fruit. It can be served with a dusting of icing sugar and decorated with holly leaves.

Makes 1

INGREDIENTS

225 g/8 oz/1 cup butter, plus extra for greasing
15 g/1 tbsp fresh white breadcrumbs
225 g/8 oz/1 cup caster sugar
50 ml/2 fl oz/¼ cup water
3 eggs, separated
225 g/8 oz/2 cups self-raising flour
7.5 g/1½ tsp ground mixed spice
25 g/1 oz/2 tbsp chopped angelica
25 g/1 oz/2 tbsp mixed peel
50 g/2 oz/¼ cup glacé cherries, chopped
50 g/2 oz/½ cup walnuts, chopped
icing sugar, to dust

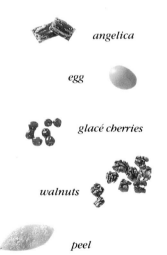

angelica

egg

glacé cherries

walnuts

peel

1 Preheat the oven to 180°C/350°F/ Gas 4. Brush a 20 cm/8 in, 1.5 litre/ 2½ pint fluted ring mould with melted butter and coat with breadcrumbs, shaking out any excess.

2 Place the butter, sugar and water into a saucepan. Heat gently, stirring occasionally, until melted. Boil for 3 minutes until syrupy, then allow to cool. Place the egg whites in a clean bowl, whisk until stiff. Sift the flour and spice into a bowl, add the angelica, mixed peel, cherries and walnuts and stir well to mix. Add the egg yolks.

3 Pour the cooled mixture into the bowl and beat together with a wooden spoon to form a soft batter. Gradually fold in the egg whites using a plastic spatula until the mixture is evenly blended. Pour into the prepared mould and bake for 50–60 minutes or until the cake springs back when pressed in the centre. Turn out and cool on a wire rack. Dust thickly with icing sugar and decorate with a sprig of holly.

PARTY FOOD & DRINK

Whether you are planning an extravagant
party for the hungry hoardes or a quiet get
together for a few close friends, these simple
snacks will ensure a relaxing and successful
time for you, and a filling and delicious
meal for your guests. Providing unusual
drinks helps make Christmas different and
special; these seven drinks ideas show you
how to create the tastes, spicy flavours
and warming atmosphere of a traditional
country festival.

Corn Muffins with Ham

These delicious little muffins are simple to make. If you like, serve them unfilled with a pot of herb butter.

Makes 24

INGREDIENTS
60 g/2 oz/scant ½ cup yellow cornmeal
70 g/2½ oz/⅔ cup plain flour
30 ml/2 tbsp sugar
7.5 ml/1½ tsp baking powder
2.5 ml/½ tsp salt
60 g/2 oz/4 tbsp butter, melted
120 ml/4 fl oz/½ cup whipping cream
1 egg, beaten
1–2 jalapeño or other medium-hot chillies, seeded and finely chopped (optional)
pinch cayenne pepper
butter, for spreading
grainy mustard or mustard with honey, for spreading
60 g/2 oz oak-smoked ham

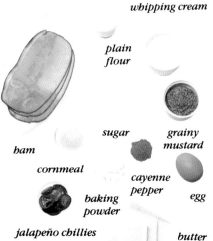

whipping cream
plain flour
sugar
grainy mustard
ham
cornmeal
cayenne pepper
egg
baking powder
jalapeño chillies
butter

COOK'S TIP
Muffins can be made in advance and stored in air-tight containers. Bring to room temperature or warm slightly before filling and serving.

1 Preheat the oven to 200°C/400°F/Gas 6 and lightly grease a mini muffin pan with 24 4 cm/1½ in cups. In a large bowl combine the cornmeal, flour, sugar, baking powder and salt. In another bowl, whisk together the melted butter, cream, beaten egg, chopped chillies, if using, and the cayenne pepper.

2 Make a well in the cornmeal mixture, pour in the egg mixture and gently stir into the dry ingredients just enough to blend (do not over-beat – the batter does not have to be smooth).

3 Drop 15 ml/1 tbsp batter into each muffin cup and bake for 12–15 minutes, until golden and just firm to the touch. Remove the tray to a wire rack to cool slightly, then turn out the muffins on to the rack, and leave to cool completely.

4 With a sharp knife, split the muffins and spread each bottom half with a little butter and mustard. Cut out small rounds of ham with a round pastry cutter or cut into small squares, and place on the buttered muffins. Sandwich together each muffin with its top and serve.

Tortelloni Kebabs

This hors d'oeuvres is easy to make, and always popular. Any favourite dipping sauce can be substituted, or just drizzle the kebabs with good virgin olive oil and sprinkle with freshly grated Parmesan.

Makes about 64

INGREDIENTS
450 g/1 lb fresh cheese-filled
    tortelloni
10 ml/2 tsp olive oil
basil leaves, to garnish

FOR THE SAUCE
1 × 450 g/16 oz jar roasted red
    peppers, drained
1 garlic clove, chopped
15 ml/1 tbsp olive oil
15 ml/1 tbsp balsamic vinegar
5 ml/1 tsp sugar
freshly ground black pepper
2–3 dashes hot pepper sauce

garlic

tortelloni

olive oil

*roasted
red pepper*

hot pepper sauce

basil

sugar

*balsamic
vinegar*

1 Put the ingredients for the sauce into the bowl of a food processor and process until smooth, scraping down the sides once or twice. Sieve into a serving bowl and cover until ready to serve.

2 Bring a large saucepan of lightly salted water to a fast boil. Add the tortelloni and cook according to the instructions on the packet, for 8–10 minutes. Drain, rinse in warm water and turn into a bowl. Toss with olive oil to prevent sticking. Cover until ready to serve.

3 Using small, 15 cm/6 in wooden skewers, thread a basil leaf and 1 tortelloni on to each skewer. Arrange on a plate and serve warm, or at room temperature with the dipping sauce.

COOK'S TIP

The sauce can be made up to a day in advance or frozen for several weeks.

Celery Sticks with Roquefort

This delicious filling can also be made with English Stilton or any other blue cheese. Diluted with a little milk or cream, it also makes a delicious dip.

Makes about 45

INGREDIENTS
7 ounces Roquefort or other blue
  cheese, softened
1¼ cups lowfat cream cheese
2 green onions, finely chopped
black pepper
1 to 2 tablespoons milk
1 celery head
chopped walnuts or hazelnuts, to
  garnish

green onions

lowfat cream cheese

Roquefort cheese

chopped walnuts

celery

1 With a fork, crumble the Roquefort in a bowl. Put in a food processor with the cream cheese, green onions, and black pepper. Process until smooth, scraping down the side of the bowl once or twice and gradually adding milk if the mixture seems too stiff.

2 If you like, peel the celery lightly to remove any heavy strings before cutting each stalk into 3- to 4-inch pieces. Using a small knife, fill each celery stick with a little cheese mixture and press on a few chopped nuts. Arrange on a serving plate and refrigerate until ready to serve.

COOK'S TIP

For a more elegant presentation, fill a pastry bag fitted with a small star tip with the cheese mixture and carefully pipe mixture into the celery sticks. Press on the nuts.

Italian-style Marinated Artichokes

Good-quality extra-virgin olive oil together with fresh herbs, turn canned or frozen artichoke hearts into a delicious snack.

Makes about 750 ml/1¼ pints/3 cups

INGREDIENTS
2 × 14-ounce cans artichoke hearts
  in salt water
¾ cup extra-virgin olive oil
1 teaspoon chopped fresh thyme, or
  ½ teaspoon dried thyme
1 teaspoon chopped fresh oregano or
  marjoram, or ½ teaspoon dried
  oregano or marjoram
½ teaspoon fennel seeds, lightly
  crushed
1 to 2 garlic cloves, finely chopped
freshly ground black pepper
grated peel and juice of ½ lemon

thyme

artichoke hearts

lemon

black pepper

oregano

lemon zest

extra-virgin olive oil

fennel seeds

1 Rinse the artichokes, then drain them on paper towels. Cut any large ones in half lengthwise.

2 Put the artichokes in a large saucepan with the next six ingredients, stir to combine, then cook, covered, over very low heat for 8 to 10 minutes until the flavors infuse. Remove from the heat and leave to cool slightly, then gently stir in the lemon peel and juice. Refrigerate. Return to room temperature before serving on toothpicks.

Mini Jacket Potatoes with Sour Cream and Chives

Jacket potatoes are always delicious, and the toppings can easily be varied – from caviar and smoked salmon to cheese and baked beans.

Makes 36

INGREDIENTS
36 potatoes, about 4 cm/1½ in
   in diameter, well scrubbed
250 ml/8 fl oz/1 cup thick sour cream
45–60 ml/3–4 tbsp snipped fresh
   chives
coarse salt, for sprinkling

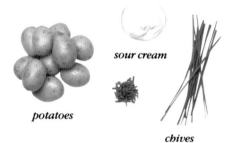

sour cream

potatoes

chives

1 Preheat the oven to 180°C/350°F/ Gas 4. Place potatoes on a baking sheet and bake for 30–35 minutes, or until tender when pierced with the tip of a knife.

2 To serve, make a cross in the top of each potato and squeeze gently to open. Using the handle of a wooden spoon, make a hole in the centre of each potato. Fill each hole with a little sour cream, then sprinkle with the salt and the chives. Serve immediately, or at room temperature.

VARIATION
If your guests are likely to be hungry, use medium size potatoes. When cooked, cut in half, scoop out the flesh, mash with the other ingredients and spoon the mixture back into the skin. Serve warm.

COOK'S TIP
The potatoes can be baked in advance, then reheated in the microwave on High (100%) for 3–4 minutes.

Savoury Cheese Balls

These colourful little cheese balls are made in four different flavours, each variety coated with a different herb or seed.

Makes about 48

INGREDIENTS

450 g/1 lb/2⅔ cups cream cheese at
   room temperature
25 g/1 oz/¼ cup grated mature
   Cheddar cheese
2.5 ml/½ tsp dry mustard powder,
   prepared
5 ml/1 tsp mango chutney, chopped
   (optional)
cayenne pepper
salt
50 g/2 oz Roquefort or Stilton cheese
15 ml/1 tbsp finely chopped spring
   onions or snipped fresh chives
5–10 ml/1–2 tsp bottled pesto sauce
15 ml/1 tbsp chopped pine nuts
1–2 garlic cloves, finely chopped
30 ml/2 tbsp chopped mixed fresh
   herbs, such as parsley, tarragon,
   chives, dill or coriander

TO COAT

30 ml/2 tbsp paprika
30 ml/2 tbsp finely chopped fresh
   parsley
30 ml/2 tbsp toasted sesame seeds
coarsely ground black pepper mixed
   with poppy seeds

1 Divide the cream cheese equally among four small bowls. Into one mix the Cheddar cheese, mustard and mango chutney if using. Season with cayenne pepper and a little salt. Into the second bowl, mix the Roquefort or Stilton cheese and spring onions or chives and season with a little cayenne.

2 Mix the pesto sauce and pine nuts into the third bowl and season with a little cayenne. Mix the chopped garlic and mixed fresh herbs into the last bowl of cream cheese. Cover and refrigerate all four bowls for about 30 minutes, until the cheese is firm enough to handle. Roll each of the different cheese mixtures into small balls, keeping them separate.

3 Lightly dust the Cheddar flavoured balls with paprika, rolling to cover completely. Roll the pesto balls in chopped parsley and the Roquefort balls in sesame seeds. Roll the garlic-herb cheese balls in coarsely ground black pepper and poppy seeds. Arrange the balls on leaves, a plate or in a lined basket and serve with cocktail sticks.

spring onions

sesame seeds

garlic

parsley

Cheddar cheese

poppy seeds

cream cheese

black pepper

dry mustard

pesto sauce

Roquefort cheese

paprika

cayenne pepper

chopped pine nuts

mango chutney

Nutty Cheese Balls

These tasty morsels are perfect for nibbling with drinks.

Makes 32

INGREDIENTS
115 g/4 oz cream cheese
115 g/4 oz Roquefort cheese
115 g/4 oz/1 cup chopped walnuts
chopped fresh parsley, to coat
paprika, to coat
salt and freshly ground black pepper

1 Beat the two cheeses together until smooth using an electric beater.

2 Stir in the chopped walnuts and season with salt and pepper.

3 Shape into small balls (about a rounded teaspoonful each). Chill on a baking sheet until firm.

4 Roll half the balls in the chopped parsley and half in the paprika. Serve on cocktail sticks.

Salami and Olive Cheese Wedges

Use good quality salami for best results.

Makes 24

INGREDIENTS
225 g/8 oz cream cheese
5 ml/1 tsp paprika
2.5 ml/½ tsp English mustard powder
50 g/2 oz/2 tbsp stuffed green olives, chopped
225 g/8 oz sliced salami
sliced olives, to garnish

2 Spread the salami slices with the olive mixture and stack five slices on top of each other. Wrap in clear film and chill until firm. With a sharp knife, cut each stack into four wedges. Garnish with additional sliced olives and serve with a cocktail stick through each wedge, to hold the slices together.

1 Beat the cream cheese with the paprika and mustard and mix well. Stir in the chopped olives.

Spiced Mixed Nuts

Spices are a delicious addition to mixed roasted nuts.

Makes 350 g/12 oz/2 cups

INGREDIENTS
115 g/4 oz/²⁄₃ cup brazil nuts
115 g/4 oz/²⁄₃ cup cashew nuts
115 g/4 oz/²⁄₃ cup almonds
2.5 ml/½ tsp mild chilli powder
2.5 ml/½ tsp ground coriander
2.5 ml/½ tsp salt
25 g/1 oz/2 tbsp butter, melted

1 Preheat the oven to 180°C/350°F/ Gas 4. Put all the nuts and spices and the salt on to a baking tray and mix well.

2 Pour over the melted butter and bake for 10–15 minutes, stirring until golden brown.

3 Drain on kitchen paper and allow to cool before serving.

Herby Cheese Biscuits

Use a selection of festive shapes for cutting out these biscuits.

Makes 32

INGREDIENTS
350 g/12 oz/3 cups plain flour
2.5 ml/½ tsp cayenne pepper
5 ml/1 tsp English mustard powder
175 g/6 oz/¾ cup butter
175 g/6 oz strong Cheddar cheese, grated finely
15 ml/1 tbsp mixed dried herbs
1 egg, beaten
salt and freshly ground black pepper

2 Rub the butter into the flour and add the cheese, herbs and seasoning. Stir in the beaten egg to bind, and knead to a smooth dough.

1 Preheat the oven to 200°C/400°F/ Gas 6. Sift the flour, cayenne pepper and mustard powder together into a bowl or food processor.

3 On a lightly floured work surface, roll the dough out thinly. Stamp it into small biscuits with cutters. Bake for 10–15 minutes, or until golden. Cool on a wire rack. Store in an airtight container.

Bombay Prawns

These larger prawns are expensive, so save this dish for a special occasion.

Makes 24

INGREDIENTS

175 ml/6 fl oz/¾ cup olive oil
5 ml/1 tsp ground turmeric (or to taste)
5 ml/1 tsp ground cumin
5 ml/1 tsp garam masala or curry powder
2.5 ml/½ tsp salt
2.5 ml/½ tsp cayenne pepper (or to taste)
juice of 2 limes
24 large uncooked Madagascar or tiger prawns, shelled and deveined, tails attached
coriander leaves, to garnish

limes

shelled prawns

olive oil

turmeric *cumin*

garam masala

coriander

cayenne pepper

1 In a medium-sized bowl, whisk together well the oil, turmeric, cumin, garam masala, salt, cayenne pepper and lime juice.

2 With a small sharp knife, slit three-quarters of the way through each prawn, cutting down the centre back (be careful not to cut right through). Add the prawns to the marinade and allow to stand in a cool place for 40 minutes.

3 Preheat the grill. Arrange the prawns on a foil-lined grill pan in a single layer. Drizzle over a little of the marinade. Grill for about 2 to 3 minutes, until the prawns are glazed and curled. Serve immediately, on cocktail sticks if you like, garnished with coriander leaves.

COOK'S TIP

Wrap the prawn tails in small pieces of foil to prevent them catching and burning under the grill, then remove halfway through cooking. Make sure the prawns are cooked through and test one by cutting in half.

Thai-fried Vegetables in Wonton Cups

These crispy cups are an ideal way to serve stir-fried vegetables; use your imagination to vary the fillings.

Makes 24

INGREDIENTS

30 ml/2 tbsp vegetable oil, plus extra
   for greasing
24 small wonton wrappers
120 ml/4 fl oz/½ cup Hoi Sin sauce or
   plum sauce (optional)
5 ml/1 tsp sesame oil
1 garlic clove, finely chopped
1 cm/½ in piece fresh root ginger,
   finely chopped
5 cm/2 in piece of lemon grass,
   crushed
6–8 asparagus spears, cut into 3 cm/
   1¼ in pieces
8–10 baby sweetcorn, cut in half
   lengthways
1 small red pepper, seeded and cut
   into short slivers
15–30 ml/1–2 tbsp sugar
30 ml/2 tbsp soy sauce
juice of 1 lime
5–10 ml/1–2 tsp Chinese-style chilli
   sauce (or to taste)
1 tsp *huac nam* or Thai or other fish
   sauce

1 Preheat the oven to 180°C/350°F/ Gas 4. Lightly grease 24 4 cm/1 ½ in bun tins. Press 1 wonton wrapper into each cup, turning the edges up to form a cup shape. Bake for 8–10 minutes, until crisp and golden. Carefully remove to a wire rack to cool. If you like, brush each cup with a little Hoi Sin or plum sauce (this will help keep the cups crisp if preparing them in advance).

2 In a wok or large frying pan, heat 30 ml/2 tbsp vegetable oil and the sesame oil until very hot. Add the garlic, ginger and lemon grass and stir-fry for 15 seconds until fragrant. Add the asparagus, sweetcorn and red pepper pieces and stir-fry for 2 minutes until tender crisp.

3 Add the sugar, soy sauce, lime juice, chilli sauce and fish sauce and toss well to coat. Stir-fry for 30 seconds longer.

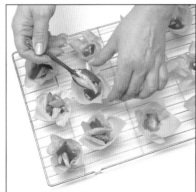

4 Spoon an equal amount of vegetable mixture into each of the prepared wonton cups and serve hot.

lemon grass

Hoi Sin sauce

red pepper

wonton wrappers

vegetable oil

baby sweetcorn

asparagus

sesame oil

soy sauce

garlic

lime

Tequila Sunset

A variation on the popular party drink which can be mixed and chilled in a jug, ready to pour into glasses, and finished off at the last minute with the addition of crème de cassis and honey.

Serves 1

INGREDIENTS
1 measure/22.5 ml/1½ tbsp clear or golden tequila
5 measures/120 ml/4 fl oz lemon juice, chilled
1 measure/22.5 ml/1½ tbsp orange juice, chilled
10–30 ml/1–2 tbsp clear honey
⅔ measure/15 ml/1 tbsp crème de cassis

crème de cassis

lemon juice

tequila

clear honey

orange juice

1 Pour the tequila and then the lemon and orange juices straight into a well-chilled cocktail glass.

2 Using a swizzle stick, mix the ingredients by twisting the stick between the palms of your hands.

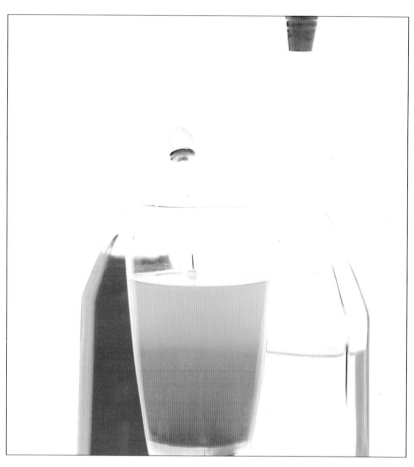

3 Drizzle the honey into the centre of the cocktail and it will fall and create a layer at the bottom of the glass.

4 Add the crème de cassis, but do not stir. It will create a glowing layer above the honey at the bottom of the glass.

VARIATION

To make a Tequila Sunrise, mix 2 parts tequila with 6 parts orange juice and 2 parts grenadine and stir gently together.

Brandy Alexander

A warming digestif, made from a blend of crème de cacao, brandy and double cream, that can be served at the end of the meal with coffee.

Serves 1

INGREDIENTS
1 measure/22.5 ml/1¹⁄₂ tbsp
   brandy
1 measure/22.5 ml/1¹⁄₂ tbsp
   crème de cacao
1 measure/22.5 ml/1¹⁄₂ tbsp
   double cream
whole nutmeg, grated,
   to decorate

crème de cacao

nutmeg

double cream

brandy

1 Half-fill the cocktail shaker with ice and pour in the brandy, crème de cacao and, finally, the cream.

2 Shake for about 20 seconds, to mix together well.

3 Strain the chilled cocktail into a small wine glass.

4 Finely grate a little nutmeg over the top of the cocktail.

VARIATION
Warm the brandy and the double cream gently and add to a blender with the crème de cacao. Whizz until frothy. Serve with a cinnamon stick.

Festive Liqueurs

These are easier to make than wines and may be made with a variety of flavours and spirits. All these liqueurs should be allowed to mature for 3 months before drinking.

Makes 850 ml/1½ pints/ 3¾ cups of each liqueur

PLUM BRANDY
450 g/1 lb plums
225 g/8 oz/1 cup demerara sugar
575 ml/1 pint/2½ cups brandy

FRUIT GIN
450 g/1 lb/3 cups raspberries,
   blackcurrants or sloes
350 g/12 oz/1½ cups granulated sugar
700 ml/1¼ pints/3 cups gin

CITRUS WHISKY
1 large orange
1 small lemon
1 lime
225 g/8 oz/1 cup granulated sugar
575 ml/1 pint/2½ cups whisky

orange

peaches

lemon

lime

blackcurrants

1 Sterilize 3 jars and lids. Wash and halve the plums, remove the stones and finely slice. Place the plums in the sterilized jar with the sugar and brandy. Crack 3 stones, remove the kernels and chop. Add to the jar and stir until well blended.

2 Place the raspberries, blackcurrants or sloes into the prepared jar. If using sloes, prick the surface of the berries using a stainless steel pin to extract the flavour. Add the sugar and gin and stir until well blended.

3 To make the Citrus Whisky, first scrub the fruit. Using a sharp knife or potato peeler pare the rind from the fruit, taking care not to include the white pith. Squeeze out all the juice and place in the jar with the fruit rinds. Add the sugar and whisky, stir until well blended.

4 Cover the jars with lids or double thickness plastic tied well down. Store the jars in a cool place for 3 months.

5 Shake the Fruit Gin every day for 1 month, and then occasionally. Shake the Plum Brandy and Citrus Whisky every day for 2 weeks, then occasionally. Sterilize the chosen bottles and corks or stoppers for each liqueur.

6 When each liqueur is ready to be bottled, strain, then pour into the bottles through a funnel fitted with a filter paper. Fit the corks or stoppers and label with a festive label.

Mulled Red Wine

Excellent to serve on a cold winter's evening; it will really get the party started.

Makes 900 ml/1½ pints/2½ cups

INGREDIENTS
1 bottle red wine
75 g/3 oz/6 tbsp soft light brown sugar
2 cinnamon sticks
1 lemon, sliced
4 whole cloves
150 ml/¼ pint/⅔ cup brandy or port
lemon slices, to serve

1 Put all the ingredients, except the brandy or port, into a large pan. Bring the wine to the boil to dissolve the sugar. Remove, cover the pan and leave it to stand for 5 minutes, to allow the flavours to infuse.

2 Strain to remove the spices and lemon slices.

3 Add the brandy and serve warm, with a fresh slice of lemon.

Sparkling Cider Cup

This is a very refreshing, sparkling drink, best served as cold as possible.

Makes 2.6 litres/4½ pints/10½ cups

INGREDIENTS
1 orange
1 lemon
1 apple
1 litre/1¾ pints/4 cups sparkling cider, chilled
1 litre/1¾ pints/4 cups lemonade, chilled
600 ml/1 pint/2½ cups apple juice, chilled
fresh mint sprigs, to serve

2 Add the cider, lemonade and apple juice. Serve cold with sprigs of fresh mint.

1 Slice all the fruit into a large bowl.

Spiced Fruit Cocktail

This non-alcoholic fruit drink is a real treat.

Makes 2 litres/3½ pints/8¾ cups

INGREDIENTS
600 ml/1 pint/2½ cups orange juice, chilled
300 ml/½ pint/1¼ cups pineapple juice, chilled
pared rind and juice of 1 lemon
4 whole cloves
1 cinnamon stick, broken into pieces
50 g/2 oz/4 tbsp caster sugar
orange slices
ice cubes
600 ml/1 pint/2½ cups sparkling mineral water, chilled
600 ml/1 pint/2½ cups ginger ale, chilled

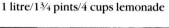

1 Mix the orange and pineapple juices together in a large bowl. Add the lemon rind and juice, spices and sugar. Chill.

2 Put the orange slices and ice cubes in a serving bowl. Strain the fruit juice mixture into the bowl. Add the mineral water and ginger ale.

Fruit Punch

This is a quick punch to assemble. Make sure that all the ingredients are well chilled.

Makes 2.5 litres/4¼ pints/10¼ cups

INGREDIENTS
1 bottle white wine, chilled
1 bottle red wine, chilled
45 ml/3 tbsp orange-flavoured liqueur
1 orange, cut in quarters and sliced
seedless grapes
ice cubes
1 litre/1¾ pints/4 cups lemonade

2 Add the orange pieces, grapes and ice, and finally the lemonade.

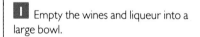

1 Empty the wines and liqueur into a large bowl.

Gifts & Giving

COUNTRY GIFTS

These practical presents take themes
from nature or use natural products in
the making – perfect ideas for country
visits, hostess gifts or even to keep at
home for decoration.

Needlepoint Cushion

This cushion won't take long to stitch and makes a lovely gift for a fellow needlework enthusiast. The starry theme and trimming of glossy cord give it a Christmassy feel, but its subtle shading will make it a joy to use all year round.

YOU WILL NEED

23 cm (9 in) square of white needlepoint canvas with 24 holes per 5 cm/12 holes per in
ruler
permanent marker pen
masking tape
small lengths of tapestry wool in 12 shades
scissors
tapestry needle
co-ordinating furnishing fabric for backing
matching thread
needle
polyester wadding
70 cm (¾ yd) decorative cord

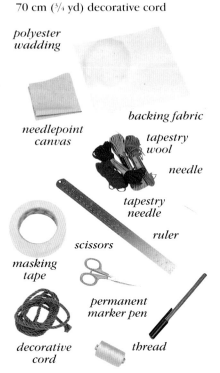

polyester wadding

needlepoint canvas

backing fabric

tapestry wool

needle

tapestry needle

ruler

scissors

masking tape

permanent marker pen

decorative cord

thread

1 To prepare the canvas, draw a vertical line down the centre and a horizontal line across the centre with a permanent marker pen.

2 Bind the edges of the canvas with masking tape to prevent the yarn from catching as you work. Select three colours for each corner star.

3 Work the design from the chart at the back of the book in tent stitch, beginning in the centre and counting each square as one intersection of canvas threads. Complete all four squares. Remove the masking tape. Press with a steam iron, pulling the canvas gently back into a square. Dry quickly so that the canvas does not distort.

4 Cut a square of backing fabric and pin it to the canvas, right sides together. Machine or hand-stitch around the edges, leaving a gap on one side. Trim the seams and corners and turn to the right side. Stuff with polyester wadding to make a nice plump shape.

5 Beginning near the opening, hand-stitch the cord around the edges of the cushion. Make a knot in the cord as you reach each corner. Push both ends of the cord into the opening and sew it up neatly, securing the cord as you stitch.

CRAFT TIP

This pincushion is ideal for using up small quantities of tapestry wool left over from other projects, but if you do use scraps make sure you will have enough to complete the design.

Appliqué Christmas Tree

A charmingly simple little picture which you can frame or mount on card as a seasonal greeting for a special person. Contrasting textures in the homespun fabrics and simple, childlike stitches give it a naïve appeal.

YOU WILL NEED
scraps of homespun fabrics in
    greens, red and orange
scissors
matching thread
needle
coarse off-white cotton
pins
stranded embroidery thread
gold embroidery thread
iron
picture frame

gold embroidery thread

embroidery thread

thread

scissors

coarse off-white cotton

scraps of homespun fabrics

needle

pins

1 Following the template at the back of the book, cut out the pieces for the Christmas tree from three different shades and textures of green fabric. Cut out a red rectangle for the background and an orange stem. Join the three sections of the tree with running stitches.

2 Pin all the pieces to a backing of off-white cotton, large enough to fill your picture frame.

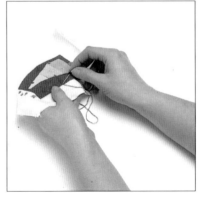

3 Sew the pieces together invisibly in slip-stitch, tucking the edges under with your needle as you sew. Aim for a slightly uneven, naïve appearance. Add gold stars and coloured stitch details using three strands of embroidery thread. Press gently before framing.

Tin Gift Box

Embossed aluminium foil combines festive glitter with the gentle, naïve appeal of tinware, and it's a perfect match for the simplicity of this Shaker box. The embossing is easy to do – simple designs really are the most successful.

YOU WILL NEED
tracing paper
heavy-gauge aluminium foil
masking tape
dried-out ballpoint pen
scissors
gift box
glue-stick

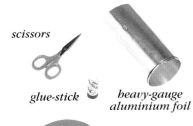

scissors

glue-stick *heavy-gauge aluminium foil*

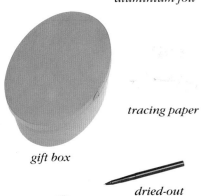

tracing paper

gift box

dried-out ballpoint pen

masking tape

1 Trace the reindeer and stars motifs from the back of the book. Attach the tracings to the foil with masking tape and draw over the outlines with an old ballpoint pen.

2 Remove the tracing paper and go over the embossing again if necessary. Cut out the motifs with scissors, leaving a narrow border of about 2 mm (¹⁄₁₆ in) around the edge – don't cut into the embossing.

3 Add more embossed details to the motifs if you wish.

4 Turn the motifs over and arrange them on the box lid and sides. Attach them using a glue-stick applied liberally.

Fragrant Herb Pillow

This lovely scented sachet looks as if it has been thickly encrusted with gold. It's made using a cutwork technique in which the different fabrics are revealed as if by magic. It's enjoyable to make and a wonderful gift to receive. Choose fabrics of similar weights but different textures and shades of gold, such as taffeta and lamé.

YOU WILL NEED
four 17 cm (6½ in) squares of
  different gold fabrics
pins
matching thread
sewing machine
sharp-pointed scissors
two 25 cm (10 in) squares of gold
  fabric chosen from the selection
  above
gold braid
needle
fragrant herbs or pot-pourri to fill

fragrant herbs and pot-pourri

gold braid

needle

pins

thread

sharp-pointed scissors

selection of gold fabrics

1 Pin the four 17 cm (6½ in) squares of different gold fabric together.

2 Sewing through all four layers, machine-stitch across the middle of the square in both directions, then stitch a simple star motif in each quarter. Don't worry if the four stars don't match each other exactly – you are aiming for a freehand effect.

3 With the point of the scissors, pierce the top layer of fabric, then cut out a section of a star. Work around each star, cutting through different areas and layers to reveal the one below, until you are pleased with the effect.

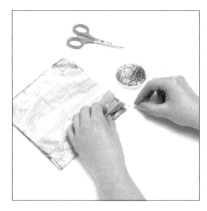

4 Pin the appliqué square in the centre of the right side of one of the large squares and machine-stitch all around the edge. Hand-stitch a length of gold braid over the seam to hide the raw edges.

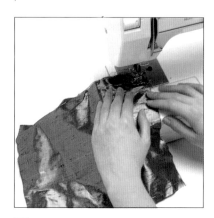

5 Pin the other gold square to the front of the cushion, right sides together, and machine around the edge with a 1 cm (½ in) seam allowance, leaving an opening down one side.

CRAFT TIP

It is essential to use really sharp, pointed small scissors for this type of appliqué, as you will be cutting through small areas, some of which may be quite delicate and difficult to manoeuvre around.

6 Turn the work right side out, fill loosely with fragrant herbs or pot-pourri and slip-stitch the opening closed.

Yuletide Pot-pourri

Scour ethnic food shops for large bags of bay leaves, cardamom and other exotic ingredients for pot-pourri. Try to include dried flowers (I used hibiscus flowers) for colour and texture.

YOU WILL NEED
oranges
paring knife
large bowl
selection of dried herbs, flowers
    and barks
orris root powder
essential oils
decorative box
cellophane
ribbon

large bowl
cellophane

orris root
powder
essential oils
ribbon
oranges
paring
knife
decorative
box
dried herbs,
flowers and barks

1 Pare the rind from several oranges, keeping the strips as long as possible. Dry them in the lowest shelf of a very low oven and store in a dry place until you are ready to use them. Slices of orange can be dried in the same way and are very decorative in pot-pourri.

2 Mix all the ingredients for the pot-pourri in a large bowl. Do not be tempted to use too many different ingredients or the result will be an untidy-looking mixture.

3 Add the orris root powder, which is used as a fixative for the fragrance, sparingly at first –: you do not want to see any residue in the finished mixture. Toss the mixture. Sprinkle with your chosen essential oils.

4 Line a decorative box with a large piece of cellophane and fill generously with the pot-pourri. Gather up the edges and secure with a ribbon.

Fun Wreath

Although every house deserves an elegant fresh Christmas wreath on the front door, all the family can have plenty of fun making this rather alternative wreath. Think of it as a seasonal joke and load it with all the ephemera of Christmas past and present.

YOU WILL NEED
newspaper
adhesive tape
string
scissors
gold spray paint
hot glue gun
assortment of novelties, sweets and
  decorations

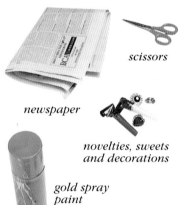

newspaper

scissors

novelties, sweets and decorations

gold spray paint

adhesive tape

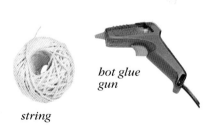

string

hot glue gun

1 Join two sheets of newspaper together down their short sides with adhesive tape. Scrunch up the paper along its length, squeezing it together while gently twisting it to make a paper rope. When it is quite tightly twisted, join the ends with tape to make a ring.

2 Make a second ring in the same way, cutting it a little shorter so that it will fit inside the first ring. Bind the two rings together with string.

3 Spray the ring on both sides with gold paint and leave to dry.

4 Using a hot glue gun, cover the ring completely with an assortment of Christmas ephemera, such as old decorations, cracker novelties, sweets, decorated pine cones, and bows from gift wrappings.

CHRISTMAS CRAFTS

Nothing is more satisfying than making
Christmas essentials and accessories
yourself – in your own style, and to tone in
with your home decorations and family
traditions. Here are ideas for a toy sack
and stocking, an advent calendar, crackers,
and country-style napkin rings, a table
decoration and a tablecloth for
the main event.

White Christmas Tree

Stand this abstract, modern interpretation of the traditional star-topped Christmas tree on a side table or the mantelpiece. It looks best as part of a cool, monochrome arrangement in white or gold.

YOU WILL NEED
hot glue gun
coarse sisal string
large polystyrene cone
scissors
small polystyrene star
white emulsion paint
paintbrush
gold paint

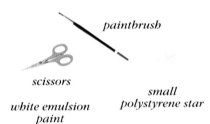

paintbrush

scissors

white emulsion paint

small polystyrene star

gold paint

large polystyrene cone

coarse sisal string

hot glue gun

2 Wind a short length of string in a coil and glue it to the top of the cone for the star to sit on.

1 With a hot glue gun, attach the end of the string to the base of the cone. Wind the string up the cone towards the point, then down to the base again, gluing it as you work and securing it where it crosses. Each time you reach the base, cut the string and start again from another point, so that the cone is evenly covered.

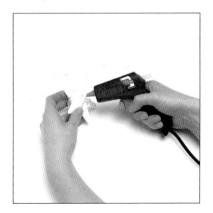

CRAFT TIP
Make sure the ends of the string are evenly spaced around the base of the cone so that it stands upright.

3 Wind and glue string around the star in the same way. Hide the raw ends under the string. Glue the star to the top of the cone.

4 Paint the cone and star with several coats of white emulsion paint, covering the string and filling in any unsightly dents in the polystyrene.

5 Finish by brushing roughly over the string with gold paint.

Gold Crown Tablecloth

Set the festive tone with this lovely white and gold tablecloth. The stencilling is easy and enjoyable to do, but it's important to plan your design carefully before you start work with the paint, so that the motifs are evenly spaced.

YOU WILL NEED
white cotton fabric 135 cm
    (54 in) square
iron
pins
stencil card
craft knife
masking tape
gold stencil paint
stencil brush
fine paintbrush
sewing machine
white thread

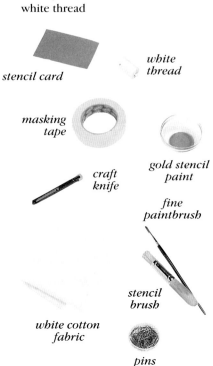

stencil card

white thread

masking tape

craft knife

gold stencil paint

fine paintbrush

stencil brush

white cotton fabric

pins

1 Iron the fabric to remove creases, then fold in quarters and press the folds. Fold each quarter to find the centre point, press and mark with pins. Copy the crown and shooting star templates from the back of the book, transfer onto stencil card and cut out with a craft knife. Stencil the crowns in the corners, then the edges and finally the centre.

2 Stencil the shooting stars between the crowns, all pointing in the same direction around the edge of the cloth.

3 Complete the stars by touching up the gaps left by the stencil with a fine brush and gold stencil paint.

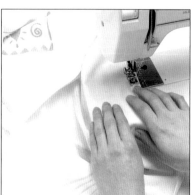

4 Press on the wrong side of the fabric to fix the paint. Hem the fabric all around the edge on a sewing machine.

CRAFT TIP
Don't overload your brush, as too much paint may bleed underneath the edges of the stencil.

Sparkling Flowerpot

This shiny flowerpot is covered with the foil wrappings from chocolates and sweets. You'll need to prepare in advance by eating plenty of foil-wrapped chocolates. Choose the colours carefully, and don't forget to save the wrappers! Fill the pot with baubles for a table decoration.

YOU WILL NEED
coloured foil sweet wrappers
terracotta flowerpot
PVA glue
paintbrush

paintbrush

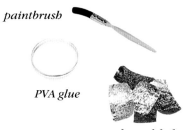

PVA glue

*coloured foil
sweet wrappers*

*terracotta
flowerpot*

1 Smooth out the coloured foil wrappers and select as many rectangular shapes as possible. If any wrappers have tears, you may be able to hide these by overlapping them with perfect pieces.

2 Paint the flowerpot all over with PVA glue to seal the surface.

CRAFT TIP

Although you can arrange the foils in a haphazard manner for a crazy patchwork effect, this project looks best if you keep to a more regular design by placing the foil pieces horizontally and vertically.

3 Paint the back of a piece of foil with PVA glue and apply it to the pot, smoothing it with the paintbrush and brushing on more glue to secure it. Continue adding the foil wrappers in an attractive pattern. When the pot is completely covered, seal it inside and out with another coat of glue.

Willow Twig Napkin Rings

You can decorate with natural, homespun materials but still achieve a sparkling effect if you choose bright, glowing colours. Using glue to assemble these rings reinforces the fabric and is a welcome shortcut if making a large quantity.

YOU WILL NEED
willow twigs
secateurs
11 x 22 cm (4½ x 9 in) coarsely
    woven cotton fabric per ring
fabric glue
paintbrush
stranded embroidery thread
needle
scissors
pins
matching thread

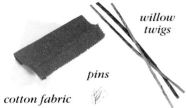

cotton fabric *pins* *willow twigs*

needle *thread* *stranded embroidery thread*

scissors *paintbrush*

fabric glue *secateurs*

1 Cut four pieces of twig, each 9 cm (3½ in) long.

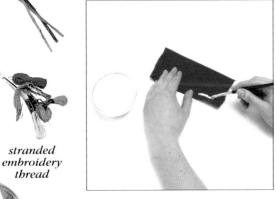

2 Make a 1 cm (½ in) hem along one short end of the fabric and glue it down. Fold the long sides of the fabric rectangle to the centre and glue.

3 Position the twigs evenly across the centre of the right side of the fabric. Using three strands of embroidery thread oversew the twigs on to the napkin ring.

4 Pin the ends of the ring together, tucking the raw edge into the folded edge. Slip-stitch together.

Holly Leaf Napkin

The Christmas table deserves something more distinctive than paper napkins, and your guests will love these specially embroidered cotton ones in festive but definitely non-traditional colours. The holly leaf motif is quick and easy to work in stem stitch.

YOU WILL NEED
paper for template
scissors
50 cm (20 in) square of washable cotton fabric in hot pink for each napkin
pins
tailor's chalk
stranded embroidery thread in acid green, acid yellow and bright orange
needle

cotton fabric   *paper*

tailor's chalk   *pins*

stranded embroidery thread

scissors

needle

1 Trace the holly leaf motif from the back of the book and use it to make a paper template. Pin it to one corner of the fabric, allowing room for a hem, and draw round it with tailor's chalk.

2 Using three strands of embroidery thread and working in stem stitch, embroider the outline of the holly leaf in acid green and the veins in acid yellow.

3 Fold under and pin a 5 mm (¼ in) double hem all around the napkin.

4 Using three strands of bright orange embroidery thread, work a neat running stitch evenly around the hem.

Christmas Crackers

Making your own Christmas crackers is really rewarding and it's great fun watching friends and family pull them open to discover the treats inside. Make exactly the number you need for your party and collect small gifts to put in them.

YOU WILL NEED
double-sided crêpe paper in
    bright colours
craft knife
metal ruler
cutting mat
thin card in black and white
double-sided adhesive tape
cracker snaps
paper hats, jokes and gifts to
    go in the crackers
narrow black ribbon
gold paper-backed foil
corrugated cardboard
gold crêpe paper
fine gold cord

metal ruler

craft knife

cracker snaps

gold crêpe paper

double-sided crêpe paper

fine gold cord

narrow black ribbon

thin card

gold paper-backed foil

double-sided adhesive tape

paper hats, jokes and gifts

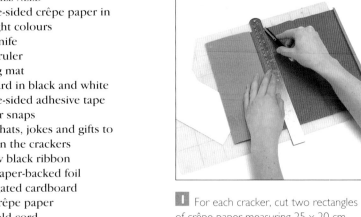

1 For each cracker, cut two rectangles of crêpe paper measuring 25 × 20 cm (10 × 8 in). Join them together, overlapping the ends, to make a rectangle 45 × 20 cm (18 × 8 in).

2 Cut three pieces of thin white card 22 × 10 cm (9 × 4 in). Roll each into a cylinder, overlapping the short ends by 3.5 cm (1¼ in). Lay strips of double-sided adhesive tape across the crêpe paper with which to attach the card cylinders: one in the centre and the other two about 4 cm (1½ in) in from each end of the rectangle. Roll up and secure the edge with double-sided tape.

3 Decorate the cracker with strips of the gold papers. To make the corrugated paper, lay a strip of paper-backed foil over a piece of corrugated cardboard and ease the foil into the ridges with your thumb. Cut a simple star shape from thin black card, wrap some fine gold cord around it and stick it on top of the gold decorations (use one of the star templates at the back of the book or draw your own).

4 Insert the snap and place the novelties and a paper hat in the central section of the cracker.

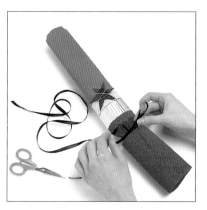

5 Tie up the ends with narrow black ribbon, easing the crêpe paper gently, so that you can tie the knots very tightly.

6 Complete the cracker by folding the edges of the crêpe paper over the ends of the card cylinders.

Santa's Toy Sack

Leave this gorgeous sack by the fireplace on Christmas Eve and Santa's guaranteed to fill it. Alternatively, it would be a wonderful way to deliver all your gifts if you're visiting friends. The contrast in texture between the luxurious satin ribbons and the coarse weave of the sack is novel and effective.

YOU WILL NEED

1.6 x 1.1 m (1 ¾ x 1¼ yd) hessian, washed
tape measure
scissors
pins
sewing machine
selection of contrasting satin ribbons, 3.5 – 4.5 cm (1¼–1¾ in) wide
matching thread
needle

bodkin

needle

scissors

thread

hessian

pins

tape measure

satin ribbons

1 Trim the washed hessian so that it measures 1 x 1.5 m (39 x 55 in). Fold it in half, right sides together, bringing the shorter sides together, and pin across the bottom and up the side, making a seam allowance of approximately 4 cm (1½ in).

2 Machine-stitch the bottom and one side of the sack.

4 With a bodkin, or safety pin, thread a length of contrasting ribbon through the channel you have created. Make sure it is long enough to make a generous bow when the top of the sack is gathered up. Turn the sack the right side out.

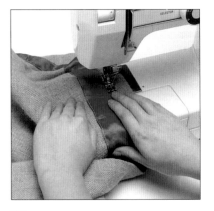

3 Still working on the wrong side, turn down the top edge by approximately 7 cm (3 in). Pin, then cover the raw edge with a length of satin ribbon. Fold under the raw ends of the ribbon to leave an opening. Machine-stitch close to the top and bottom edges of the ribbon.

5 Using a double thread, stitch along one edge of a length of ribbon in running stitch. Draw the ribbon up into tight gathers and measure how much you need to make a rosette, allowing for joining the ends. You can then cut all the ribbons to this length. Gather again and secure tightly, joining the raw edges invisibly from the wrong side.

6 Make enough rosettes in assorted colours to make a pleasing arrangement on the front of the sack. Stitch on the rosettes by hand.

CRAFT TIP

Hessian is not pre-shrunk, so wash the fabric before you begin to make the sack. Use your machine's hottest setting, then press with a steam iron or damp cloth to remove all the creases.

Velvet Stocking

This rather grown-up stocking is so grand that it's just asking to be filled with exquisite treats and presents. Make it in rich, dark colours for a really Christmassy look.

YOU WILL NEED
paper for templates
dress-weight velvet in three
    toning colours
scissors
pins
tailor's chalk
sewing machine
matching thread
decorative braid
sequin ribbon
gold satin fabric
sewing needle
gold buttons

gold satin fabric

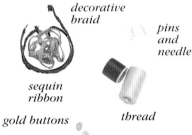
dress-weight velvet

scissors

decorative braid

sequin ribbon

pins and needle

thread

gold buttons

tailor's chalk

paper

1 Copy the templates from the back of the book on to paper and increase to the size required. Place the template for each section on a double thickness of each colour velvet. Pin and draw around each pattern piece with tailor's chalk. Cut out, leaving a narrow seam allowance.

2 Pin together the three sections of each side of the stocking and then machine-stitch.

3 On the right side of each piece, pin a strip of decorative braid and a row of sequins. Sew these on invisibly by hand.

4 With right sides together, machine the two sides of the stocking together. Turn through to the right side.

5 Cut out the satin stocking top and machine-stitch the ends together to form a tube. Pin to the top of the stocking, right sides together. Machine-stitch and turn through, leaving a cuff of satin folded over the top of the stocking. Turn in the raw edge on the inside and catch it to the seams of the velvet stocking.

6 Trim the satin cuff with a few gold buttons and attach a loop of decorative braid for hanging.

Christmas Countdown

Christmas is coming! Excitement builds as the windows of an Advent calendar are opened day by day. Paint the façade of this three-dimensional house in hot, bright colours with lots of gilding.

YOU WILL NEED
tracing paper
pencil
thin white card
craft knife
metal ruler
cutting mat
gouache paints
paintbrush
white cartridge paper
watercolour inks
gold marker pen
glue-stick
white polystyrene-filled
  mounting board
multi-cup sequins

mounting board

watercolour ink

gouache paint

glue-stick

craft knife

metal ruler

multi-cup sequins

pencil

gold marker pen

white cartridge paper

tracing paper

paintbrush

1 Enlarge and trace the template for the front of the Advent calendar and transfer it on to a sheet of white card. Cut around three sides of each window with a craft knife.

2 Turn over the sheet and paint the backs of the windows and a little of the area around them with gouache paint, so that they will look neat when the windows are opened.

3 Using the front tracing again, mark the window frames on cartridge paper and draw on the inside motifs. Paint with watercolour inks and draw in details with a gold marker pen. Cut out and attach with a glue-stick.

4 Cut the work into three sections, as shown on the template. Cut three pieces of mounting board, making the largest the size and shape of the whole calendar with two more graded steps to go in front. Mount the pieces of card on the boards, gluing the edges, and glue the sections together.

5 Paint the front of the calendar, carefully avoiding getting any paint inside the windows. Add details and number the windows with a gold marker pen. Don't forget to paint the edges of the mounting boards.

6 Finish the calendar with shiny multi-cup sequins. Using a glue-stick, attach them all around the edges of the Advent calendar.

GIFT-WRAPPING

Everybody likes receiving gifts, and when
they have been wrapped and dressed with
loving care and attention it adds even more
pleasure and satisfaction to the occasion.

Classy Golden Gift Wrap

For a special present, or just to make yours the gift everyone notices under the tree, nothing beats a beautiful golden package. When you are wrapping with gold, make it bold! There are different kinds of gold paper; the brightest is cellophane with a metallic coating on both sides. Matt antique gold paper has a dull gold sheen and is more muted in appearance.

YOU WILL NEED
sheet of gold wrapping paper,
  depending on size of gift
scissors
double-sided adhesive tape
broad gold ribbon
florist's wire
plastic pear and grapes
antique gold spray paint

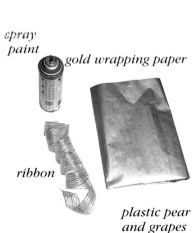

spray paint

gold wrapping paper

ribbon

plastic pear and grapes

scissors

florist's wire

double-sided adhesive tape

1 If your gift is not already boxed, find a box of a suitable size. Using the side of the box as a measuring guide, trim the paper to fit. You need no more than a 7.5 cm (3 in) overlap, and the ends should fold into neat triangles, with no bulky seams.

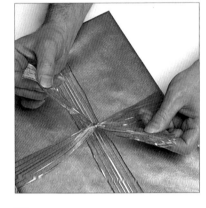

3 Cut a long length of ribbon and tie it around the box, crossing over underneath and tying firmly on the top. Trim off the ends.

CRAFT TIP
Try to find gold ribbon in a slightly deeper shade than the paper and choose trimmings that co-ordinate well. You can either spray the plastic fruit with antique gold aerosol, or use gilt cream, that is simply rubbed on to the surface and buffed when dry.

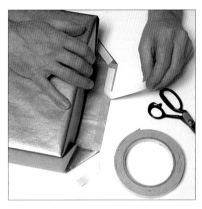

2 Use double-sided adhesive tape inside the top seam and at the centre points of the ends, to secure the paper invisibly.

4 Make a large bow, securing the loops of ribbon in the centre with a binding of florist's wire, then cover the wire with a double thickness of ribbon, tying it loosely and tucking the ends under the bow, and using them to tie it to the box ribbons.

5 Apply the gold spray to the fruit and, when dry, make up a bunch of the grapes and the pear.

6 Attach the fruit to the top of the box by twisting florist's wire around the ribbon.

Rubber Bands and Sealing Wax

Children love doing up parcels but their enthusiasm for the roll of adhesive tape may leave you feeling exasperated! Rubber bands are the perfect alternative to tape!

Sealing wax recalls the days when all parcel post had to have string and labels, and be sealed with irregular shapes of hard red wax.

FOR RUBBER BANDS YOU WILL NEED
parcel-wrap
scissors
pack of coloured rubber bands
small folded card

FOR SEALING WAX YOU WILL NEED
checked paper
scissors
double-sided adhesive tape
coarse, thick string
sealing wax stick
cigarette lighter
gift tag

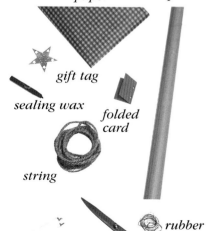

paper
parcel-wrap
gift tag
sealing wax
folded card
string
cigarette lighter
rubber bands
scissors

1 For the rubber bands, wrap the parcel, then stretch the bands length-ways and crossways to secure the flaps.

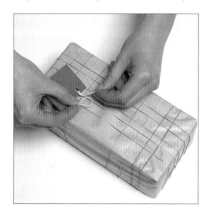

2 Add a criss-cross pattern in a sequence of colours. Loop a rubber band through the holes punched in the card, and tie it on to the gift.

3 For the sealing wax, wrap the gift with tape. Wind a long length of the string around the parcel three times. Loop the string around the three strands, knot it, then take it along the top of the parcel. Hold it in place, wrap the remaining string round three times, bringing the end up to loop around the crosspiece. Tie a knot.

4 Light the sealing wax wick and let the hot wax drip on to all the knots, then dip all the loose string ends in sealing wax. The hardened wax will hold the knots in place. Attach a gift tag to the string if you wish.

Bold Red and Gold

There is something sumptuous about red tissue paper – the rustling noise and smooth texture seem to impart a sense of luxury, and the colour deepens with layering. Stamp the paper with large gold stars and you will have one of the most stunning gift-wraps around.

YOU WILL NEED
pack of red tissue paper
big star rubber stamp
gold ink
saucer
adhesive tape
scissors
gold ribbon, cord or tinsel

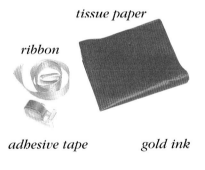

tissue paper

ribbon

adhesive tape　　*gold ink*

scissors

rubber stamp

1 Lay a sheet of tissue paper on to scrap paper and, beginning in one corner, work diagonally across the sheet, stamping stars about 5 cm (2 in) apart. Leave to dry.

2 Wrap the gift using a lining of one or two sheets of plain red tissue paper under the stamped sheet. Use adhesive tape to secure the ends. (If desired, you could use double-sided adhesive tape for invisible joins.)

3 Trim the gift with a gold ribbon tied on top with a single bow.

4 Swallowtail the ribbon ends for a professional finish.

Season's Greetings – the Natural Look

This project will appeal to those who feel a sense of visual indigestion when faced with all the glitz of Christmas.

A sheet of plain brown parcel-wrap is folded around the gift, then a light, airy collage of festive tissue paper shapes is applied. The gift is tied up with coarse brown string and decorated with cones and pods.

YOU WILL NEED
parcel-wrap
scissors
double-sided adhesive tape
pencil
tracing paper
white chalk
dark blue and orange tissue
  paper
PVA glue
thick, coarse string
selection of dried cones and
  pods
hot glue gun

tracing paper
hot glue gun
cones and pods
PVA glue
scissors
coarse string
double-sided adhesive tape
parcel-wrap
tissue paper

1 Use the box as a measuring guide and cut the parcel-wrap to size.

2 Wrap the box using double-sided adhesive tape.

3 Trace the shapes from the back of the book and cut them out of blue and orange tissue paper. Use chalk to transfer the shapes on to the darker paper. The number you will need depends upon the size of your gift.

4 Experiment with the positioning of the shapes until you are happy with the arrangement, then apply a thin layer of glue, spread with your finger, directly on to the paper. Quickly smooth the tissue shapes on to the glue.

5 Tie coarse string around the gift, crossing it over underneath and knotting it on top. Untwist the string ends and fluff them out, then trim neatly.

6 Use the glue gun to stick a small arrangement of miniature cones and pods to the knotted string.

The Ice Box

A great big box under the Christmas tree always attracts attention, but this stunning present is in danger of upstaging the Christmas tree itself!

The blue paper is stencilled with snowflakes, then the whole gift is bunched up in clear icy cellophane. Foil ribbons and Christmas tree ornaments complete the effect.

YOU WILL NEED
tracing paper
pencil
cardboard or mylar
craft knife
bright blue paper
small sponge
bowl of water
white watercolour paint
saucer
adhesive tape
scissors
roll of clear, wide cellophane
silver foil ribbon
selection of Christmas tree
  ornaments

paper

tracing paper

paint   *foil ribbon*

ornaments   *pencil*   *adhesive tape*

craft knife   *scissors*

cellophane   *sponge*

mylar

1 Trace and cut out the stencil at the back of the book. You can use cereal box cardboard or special stencil plastic called mylar. Take care when using the craft knife.

2 Place scrap paper on your work surface and use a small sponge to apply the white paint. Dip the sponge in the bowl of water then squeeze it out thoroughly. Stencil paints should always be on the dry side to prevent any from seeping under the stencil. Apply the snowflakes randomly all over the blue paper and right over the edges. Allow to dry thoroughly.

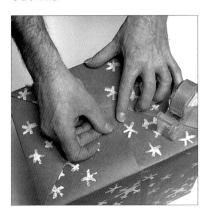

3 If one sheet of paper is not big enough to cover the box, lay two sheets side by side and run a length of adhesive tape along the join. Repeat with other sheets until you have a single sheet large enough for the box. Wrap up the box, using adhesive tape to hold the wrapping securely in place.

4 Unroll a length of cellophane on your work surface long enough to pass under the box, up the sides and allowing at least 30 cm (12 in) extra on both ends. Do the same in the other direction, to cross over the first sheet under the box.

CRAFT TIP

This gift-wrap really works best on a large scale, so if you have a boxed toy, stereo or television to wrap, look no further.

5 Gather up the cellophane on top of the box, making sure that the sides of the box are completely covered, then tape around the bunch, close to the box top.

6 Cover the adhesive tape with silver foil ribbon and attach the Christmas tree decorations.

Collage Gift-wrap

Look along the racks on the newspaper stand for interesting foreign scripts to incorporate in this fascinating gift-wrap. The newspaper is painted with translucent watercolour inks so that the print shows through.

YOU WILL NEED
foreign language newspaper
watercolour inks
paintbrush
white cartridge paper
coloured card
stencil card
craft knife
gold and black stencil paint
kitchen sponge
scissors
corrugated card
plain gold gift-wrap
glue-stick

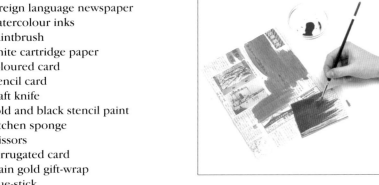

watercolour ink

stencil paint
stencil card and white card
coloured card

stencil brush

foreign language newspaper

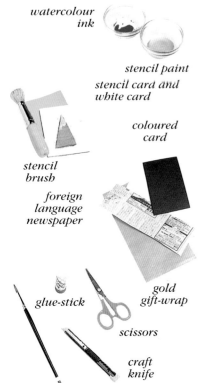

gold gift-wrap
glue-stick
scissors
craft knife
paintbrush

1 Paint sections of the newspaper in bright watercolour inks.

2 Transfer the Christmas tree template at the back of the book to a piece of stencil card and cut out. Paint plain white cartridge paper in different coloured inks or use coloured card. Stencil the paper in black and gold.

3 Cut a triangular Christmas tree shape out of kitchen sponge and stick it to a piece of corrugated card. Stamp some of the coloured newsprint with gold trees.

4 Tear strips, rectangles and simple tree shapes from the coloured newsprint. Tear around the stamped and stencilled motifs, and cut some out with scissors to give a different texture.

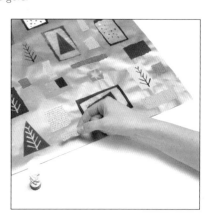

5 Arrange the motifs on the gold gift-wrap and attach them down using a glue-stick.

Wrapping Unusual Shapes

Not all gifts come in convenient shapes and sizes for wrapping. While a stock of tubes and boxes may help wrap an awkwardly shaped gift, you may not always have a suitable container to hand.

1 Decide on a surface that is going to be the base; in this case the teddy is able to sit up. Cut out a regular shape, either square, rectangular or round, from thick cardboard. Cover with a piece of your gift-wrap.

3 Pull up the paper from opposite sides and bunch it up on top of the gift. Tissue paper works well for this, because it creases in an attractive way. If you are using thicker paper, gather and pleat it as you make the bunch.

2 Place the cardboard in the middle of a large sheet of paper, or cross two lengths over for a larger gift.

4 Tie a ribbon or cord firmly around the bunch, then arrange the paper into a balanced decorative shape. An ornament hanging down from the ribbon will help to draw attention back down to the gift.

Trimmings

The finishing touches to your present are all-important. The simple tying of an attractive bow can transform a gift. Here are just a few suggestions for completing your gift-wrap.

TYING A BASIC BOW

1 Pass the ribbon under the gift so that you have two ends of equal length. Tie the two together at the top.

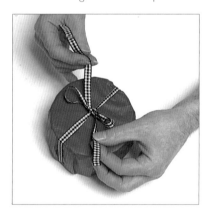

3 Form two loops and tie together to make a simple bow.

2 Knot the tied ends so that both your hands are freed for tying the bow.

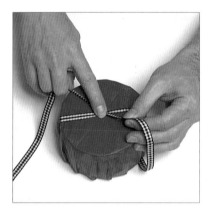

4 Finish off the bow by cutting the ribbon ends into swallowtails. Fold the ribbon down the middle then cut from the fold towards the open edges at a slant. Make the cut towards the ends of the ribbon.

Different Ways of Fastening Gifts

STRING AND RIBBON

1 Wrap your gift in tissue paper, then wind coarse string around the box at least four times in each direction.

2 Take a short, narrow red ribbon and use it to gather all the string together at the centre point. Tie a simple bow in the red ribbon and separate the strands of string out towards the edges of the box.

PINK AND GREY GIFT

1 Use a broad, fancy ribbon on a plain background. Cross the ribbon over on top of the box, then take the ends around underneath it.

2 Instead of tying the ribbon in a bow or knot, use double-sided adhesive tape to join it and give a taut, flat finish. The ribbon is shown off without the need for additional decoration.

PURPLE AND GOLD GIFT

1 Wrap a gift box in several layers of deep purple tissue paper, then surround it with a rope of gold.

2 Tie a double knot and let the tasselled ends fall across the gift as a decoration. Experiment with scarves, tie-backs and even pyjama cords!

PINK ON PINK GIFT

1 Wrap the gift in pink tissue paper and tie it up with a pink spotted ribbon.

2 Thread a biscuit cutter (this one is in the shape of a Christmas tree) on to the ribbon and tie a small bow. Christmas biscuit cutters make great decorative tags, and with luck you may even get some biscuits baked for you!

CARDS & TAGS

Here are lively ideas for making cards and
labels to complete your parcels – from
edible tags to shaker-style patterns and
cards made in natural and recycled
materials.

Recycled Look

There is a huge variety of rough-textured, hand-made papers and card around, many imported from the East and made from unusual exotic plants. Some have visible fibres, flowers or leaves and others are finer, with embossed textures applied to them.

YOU WILL NEED
black corrugated card
scissors
eyelets and punch
3 contrasting sheets of hand-
 made textured paper
PVA glue
raffia
selection of tissue paper scraps
hole punch
coarse string

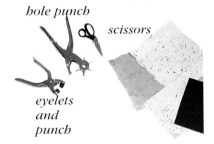

card and paper

hole punch

scissors

eyelets and punch

PVA glue

raffia

string

1 For a star tag, draw a star and cut the shape from tissue paper. Cut a disc from handmade paper, spread it lightly with PVA glue and press the star on to it.

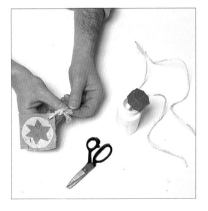

2 Cut a square to give a 1 cm (½ in) border to the disc, from contrasting handmade paper. Punch a hole in one corner and thread it with coarse string. Tie a knot and untwist the end to make a tassel.

3 To make a heart and bow, cut a rectangle from the black corrugated card and fix an eyelet in the centre at one end.

4 Cut a heart from textured paper, and glue it, point down, at the other end of the rectangle. Thread some raffia through the eyelet and tie a bow that rests above the heart.

Pierced Patterns

These folk-art-influenced labels have patterns pricked through, like the old tinware used in lamps and kitchen cupboards. A simple motif can be depicted on a piece of metallic or plain card by pricking out holes at regular distances apart, then the shape can be made ornate by the addition of holes of different sizes.

YOU WILL NEED
scissors
metallic card
pair of compasses
dressmaker's pattern wheel,
  or selection of pins, needles
  and nails
hole punch
ribbon

hole punch

compasses

ribbons

scissors

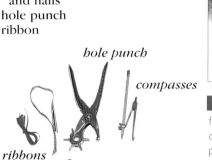

metallic card

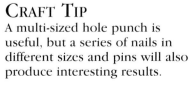

dressmaker's pattern wheel

CRAFT TIP

A multi-sized hole punch is useful, but a series of nails in different sizes and pins will also produce interesting results.

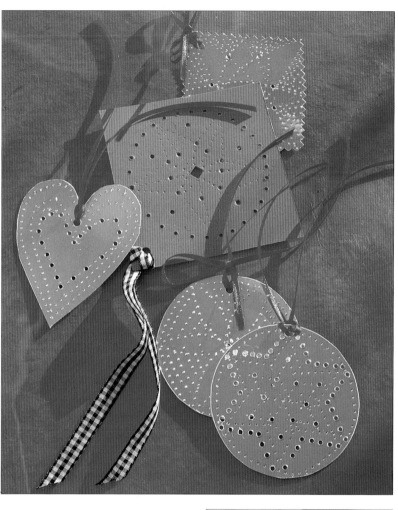

1 Cut out several different shapes from the metallic card. Use a pair of compasses to draw the pinwheel pattern on the back of the card.

2 Practise to get the feel of the pattern wheel, then, pressing evenly and firmly, use it to go over the pattern. Draw the other patterns in the same way.

3 Add a few strategically placed larger holes with the punch or a nail, then make a hole and thread with ribbon to complete the gift tag.

Edible Labels

These spice-biscuit labels have the great advantage of wafting delicious smells around the house while they bake. A word of warning – tie them to the gifts at the last moment, lest the temptation to nibble is too great and the result is a pile of unnamed presents!

YOU WILL NEED
ready-mixed biscuit dough
rolling pin
board
biscuit cutters
ready-mixed icing
ribbon

biscuit cutters

*ready-mixed
icing*

ribbon

*biscuit dough mixture
rolling pin
board*

COOK'S TIP
Remember to make a hole in your biscuit labels before you bake them.

1 Roll out the dough to 1 cm (½ in) thick and cut out the biscuits using different shaped cutters. Make holes for the ribbon (using a skewer is easiest). Bake in the oven at 180°C/350°F/Gas 4 for 10–12 minutes. Transfer to a wire rack to cool.

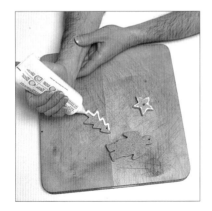

2 Decorate the biscuits by piping on ready-mixed icing.

3 Thread the biscuit labels with thin ribbon.

4 Tie red ribbon around the gift and secure the edible label, so that it lies flat on top of the parcel.

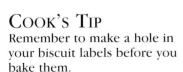

Elegant Embossed Cards

Embossed paper has a very subtle, expensive look about it, but is in fact not at all difficult to make. There are several different methods, but for a unique card or label the simplest way to do it is to place the paper over a stencil on a flat surface, and simply rub the back of the paper.

YOU WILL NEED
ready-cut stencil or card cut-out
coloured paper, card and envelopes
embossing tool – blunt, smooth-ended plastic
scissors
PVA glue

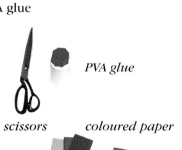
PVA glue

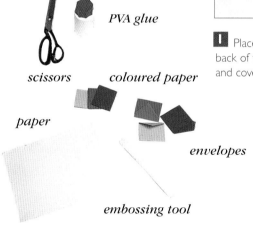
scissors   *coloured paper*

paper

envelopes

embossing tool

stencil

CRAFT TIP
You can cut a shape for embossing from thin card. Experiment with different papers too; they all give different results. Remember that if it is too thin it will tear easily, so thicker paper is best.

1 Place the heart stencil from the back of the book on a flat work surface and cover it with the paper.

2 Holding down firmly, begin rubbing the paper gently over the cut-out area to define the shape. Increase the pressure until the shape shows up as a clear indentation. Turn the paper over to reveal the embossed shape.

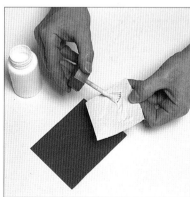

3 Trim the paper to shape and stick it on to a red card background. Pair it up with a contrasting envelope or punch a hole in it, thread with ribbon and use it as a gift tag, if you wish.

EDIBLE GIFTS

Home-made edible gifts are a true
expression of the country festival spirit,
and the perfect way to spread an
atmosphere of goodwill amongst friends
and guests throughout the holidays.

Marzipan Fruits

These eye-catching and realistic fruits will make a perfect gift for lovers of marzipan.

Makes 450 g/1 lb

INGREDIENTS
450 g/1 lb white marzipan
yellow, green, red, orange and
 burgundy food colouring dusts
30 g/2 tbsp whole cloves

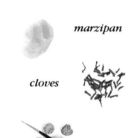

marzipan

cloves

food colouring dusts

1 Cover a baking sheet with non-stick baking paper. Cut the marzipan into quarters. Take 1 piece and cut it into 10 even-sized pieces. Place a little of each of the food colouring dusts into a palette, or place small amounts spaced apart on a plate. Cut ⅔ of the cloves into 2 pieces, making a stem and core end.

2 Taking the 10 pieces, shape each one into a neat ball. Dip 1 ball into the yellow food colouring dust and roll between the palms of the hands to colour. Re-dip into the green colouring and re-roll to tint a greeny-yellow colour. Using your forefinger, roll one end of the ball to make a pear shape. Press a clove stem into the top and a core end into the base. Repeat with the remaining 9 balls of marzipan. Place on the baking sheet.

3 Cut another piece of the marzipan into 10 pieces and shape into balls. Dip each piece into green food colouring dust and roll in the palms to colour evenly. Add a spot of red colouring dust and roll to blend the colour. Using a ball tool or the end of a paintbrush, indent the top and base to make an apple shape. Insert a stem and core.

4 Repeat as above using another piece of the marzipan to make 10 orange coloured balls. Roll each over the surface of a fine grater to give the texture of an orange skin. Press a clove core into the base of each.

5 Take the remaining piece of marzipan, reserve a small piece, and mould the rest into lots of tiny marzipan beads. Colour them burgundy with the food colouring dust. Place a whole clove on the baking sheet. Arrange a cluster of burgundy beads in the shape of a bunch of grapes. Repeat with the remaining burgundy beads of marzipan to make another 3 bunches of grapes.

6 Roll out the remaining tiny piece of marzipan thinly and brush with green food colouring dust. Using a small vine leaf cutter, cut out 8 leaves, mark the veins with a knife and place 2 on each bunch of grapes, bending to give a realistic appearance. When all the marzipan fruits are dry, pack into gift boxes.

Turkish Delight

Turkish Delight is always a favourite at Christmas, and this versatile recipe can be made in minutes. Try different flavours such as lemon, crème de menthe and orange and vary the colours accordingly.

Makes 450 g/1 lb

INGREDIENTS
450 g/1 lb/2 cups granulated sugar
300 ml/½ pint/1¼ cups water
25 g/1 oz powdered gelatine
½ tsp tartaric acid
30 ml/2 tbsp rose-water
pink food colouring
25 g/1 oz/3 tbsp icing sugar, sifted
15 g/1 tbsp cornflour

tartaric acid

gelatine

rose-water

sugar

food colourings

1 Wet the insides of 2 × 18 cm/7 in shallow square tins with water. Place the sugar and all but 60 ml/4 tbsp of water into a heavy-based saucepan. Heat gently, stirring occasionally, until the sugar has dissolved.

2 Blend the gelatine and remaining water in a small bowl and place over a saucepan of hot water. Stir occasionally until dissolved. Bring the sugar syrup to the boil and boil steadily for about 8 minutes or until the syrup registers 127°C/260°F on a sugar thermometer. Stir the tartaric acid into the gelatine, then pour into the boiling syrup and stir until well blended. Remove from the heat.

3 Add the rose-water and a few drops of pink food colouring to tint the mixture pale pink. Pour the mixture into the tins and allow to set for several hours or overnight. Dust a sheet of greaseproof paper with some of the icing sugar and cornflour. Dip the base of the tin in hot water. Invert onto the paper. Cut into 2.5 cm/1 in squares using an oiled knife. Toss in icing sugar to coat evenly.

Truffle Christmas Puddings

Truffles disguised as Christmas puddings are great fun to make and receive. Make any flavoured truffle, and decorate them as you like.

Makes 20

INGREDIENTS
20 plain chocolate truffles
15 g/1 tbsp cocoa
15 g/1 tbsp icing sugar
225 g/8 oz/1 cup white chocolate
    dots, melted
50 g/2 oz white marzipan
green and red food colourings
yellow food colouring dust

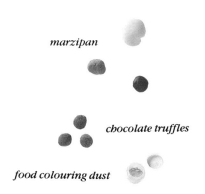
marzipan

chocolate truffles

food colouring dust

white chocolate dots

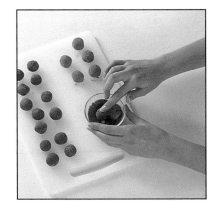

1 Sift the cocoa and icing sugar together and coat the truffles.

2 Spread ⅔ of the melted white chocolate over a piece of non-stick baking paper. Pick up the corners and shake to level the surface. Using a 2.5 cm/1 in daisy cutter, stamp out 20 rounds when the chocolate has just set. Place a truffle on the centre of each daisy shape, secured with a little of the reserved melted chocolate. Leave to set.

3 Colour ⅔ of the marzipan green and ⅓ red using the food colourings. Roll out the green thinly and stamp out 40 leaves using a tiny holly leaf cutter. Mark the veins with a knife. Mould lots of tiny red beads. Colour the remaining white chocolate with yellow food colouring dust and place in a greaseproof paper piping bag. Fold down the top, cut off the point and pipe over the top of each truffle to resemble custard. Arrange the holly leaves and berries on the top. When set, arrange in gift boxes and tie with ribbon.

Glacé Fruits

These luxury sweetmeats are very popular at Christmas and they cost a fraction of the shop price if made at home. The whole process takes about 4 weeks, but the result is well worth the effort. Choose one type of fruit, or select a variety of fruits such as cherries, plums, peaches, apricots, starfruit, pineapple, apples, oranges, lemons, limes and clementines.

Makes 24 pieces

INGREDIENTS
450 g/1 lb fruit
1 kg/2¼ lb/4½ cups granulated sugar
115 g/4 oz/1 cup powdered glucose

cherries

oranges

lemons

clementines

starfruit

apricots

1 Remove the stones from cherries, plums, peaches and apricots. Peel and core pineapple and cut into cubes or rings. Peel, core and quarter apples and thinly slice citrus fruits. Prick the skins of cherries with a stainless steel needle so the syrup can penetrate the skin.

2 Place enough of the prepared fruit in a saucepan to cover the base, keeping individual fruit types together. Add enough water to cover the fruit and simmer very gently, to avoid breaking it, until almost tender. Use a slotted spoon to lift the fruit and place in a shallow dish, removing any skins if necessary. Repeat as above until all the fruit has been cooked.

3 Measure 300 ml/½ pint/1¼ cups of the liquid, or make up this quantity with water if necessary. Pour into the saucepan and add 50 g/2 oz/4 tbsp sugar and the glucose. Heat gently, stirring occasionally, until dissolved. Bring to the boil and pour over the fruit in the dish, completely immersing it, and leave overnight.

4 DAY 2. Drain the syrup from the fruit into the saucepan and add 50 g/2 oz/ 4 tbsp sugar. Heat gently to dissolve the syrup and bring to the boil. Pour over the fruit and leave overnight. Repeat this process each day, draining off the syrup, dissolving 50 g/2 oz/4 tbsp sugar, boiling the syrup and immersing the fruit and leaving overnight on Days 3, 4, 5, 6 and 7.

5 DAY 8. Drain the fruit, dissolve 75 g/ 3 oz/½ cup sugar in the syrup and bring to the boil. Add the fruit and cook gently for 3 minutes. Return to the dish and leave for 2 days. DAY 10. Repeat as above for Day 8; at this stage the syrup should look like clear honey. Leave in the dish for at least a further 10 days, or up to 3 weeks.

6 Place a wire rack over a tray and remove each piece of fruit with a slotted spoon. Arrange on the rack. Dry the fruit in a warm dry place or in the oven at the lowest setting until the surface no longer feels sticky. To coat in sugar, spear each piece of fruit and plunge into boiling water, then roll in granulated sugar. To dip into syrup, place the remaining sugar and 175 ml/6 fl oz/¾ cup of water in a saucepan. Heat gently until the sugar has dissolved, then boil for 1 minute. Dip each piece of fruit into boiling water, then quickly into the syrup. Place on the wire rack and leave in a warm place until dry. Place the fruits in paper sweet cases and pack into boxes.

Smokie Spread

This wonderful spread will be a welcome change of flavour at Christmas. Spread it on hot toast for an instant snack.

Makes enough to fill 4 small ramekin dishes

INGREDIENTS
115 g/4 oz/½ cup unsalted butter
350 g/12 oz smokie or kipper fillets, cooked
grated rind and juice of 1 lime
10 ml/2 tsp tomato purée
30 ml/2 tbsp whisky
50 g/2 oz/1 cup wholemeal breadcrumbs
½ tsp freshly ground black pepper

TO GARNISH
4 bay leaves
4 black olives, halved

black olives

bay leaves

lime

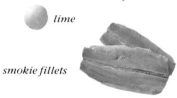

smokie fillets

tomato purée

1 Melt 75 g/3 oz of the butter and place with the smokies into a food processor. Process until smooth. Add the lime rind and juice, tomato purée, whisky, breadcrumbs and pepper. Process again, until smooth.

2 Fill 4 individual ramekins with the smokie spread and press down well leaving a 1 cm/½ in space at the top. Cover and chill.

3 Melt the remaining butter and cool. Pour over each pot to fill to the top. Garnish with bay and olives. Chill until set, then cover with clear film.

128

Potted Cheese Rarebit

An instant 'cheese on toast' in a pot. Try using Gruyère cheese instead of the Cheddar as a variation. You may wish to serve it with a sprinkling of Worcestershire sauce or anchovy essence.

Makes 775 g/1 ¹/₂ lb

INGREDIENTS
50 g/2 oz/4 tbsp butter
15 ml/1 tbsp herbed French mustard
¹/₂ tsp freshly ground black pepper
100 ml/4 fl oz/¹/₂ cup ale or cider
450 g/1 lb mature Cheddar, grated

Cheddar

black pepper

French mustard

1 Place the butter, mustard, pepper and ale or cider into a saucepan. Heat gently, stirring occasionally, until boiling.

2 Add the cheese, take off the heat and stir until the cheese has melted and the mixture is creamy.

3 Pour the mixture into sterilized pots, cover and leave until cold. Chill to set, then label.

Farmhouse Pâté

This pâté is full of flavour and can be cut into slices for easy serving. You can make the pâté in 4 individual dishes, or make 1 pâté in a 450 g/1 lb container.

Makes 450 g/1 lb

INGREDIENTS
8 slices rindless streaky bacon
175 g/6 oz/2 chicken breasts
225 g/8 oz chicken livers
1 onion, chopped
1 garlic clove, crushed
½ tsp salt
½ tsp freshly ground black pepper
5 ml/1 tsp anchovy essence
5 g/1 tsp ground mace
15 g/1 tbsp chopped fresh oregano
75 g/3 oz/1 cup fresh white
    breadcrumbs
1 egg
30 ml/2 tbsp brandy
150 ml/¼ pt/⅔ cup chicken stock
10 ml/2 tsp gelatine

TO GARNISH
strips of pimento and black olives

onion

egg

chicken breast

chicken livers

streaky bacon

1 Preheat the oven to 160°C/325°F/ Gas 3. Press the bacon slices flat with a knife to stretch them. Line the base and sides of each dish with bacon and neatly trim the edges.

2 Place the chicken breasts and livers, onion and garlic into a food processor. Process until smooth. Add the salt, pepper, anchovy essence, mace, oregano, breadcrumbs, egg and brandy. Process until smooth.

3 Divide the mixture between the dishes and fill to the top. Cover each with double thickness foil and stand the dishes in a roasting tin. Add enough hot water to come halfway up the side of the dishes.

4 Bake in the centre of the oven for 1 hour or until firm to touch. Release the foil to allow the steam to escape. Place a weight on the top of each dish to flatten the surface until cool.

5 Pour the juices from each dish into a measuring jug and make up to 150 ml/ ¼ pint/⅔ cup with chicken stock. Heat in a small saucepan until boiling. Blend the gelatine with 2 tbsp water and pour into the hot stock, stir until dissolved. Allow to cool thoroughly.

6 When the pâté is cold, arrange strips of pimento and black olives on the top of each. Spoon the cold gelatine mixture over the top of each and chill until set. Cover each with clear film. Store in the fridge until required.

Fresh Fruit Preserve

The wonderfully fresh flavour of this fruit spread makes it a welcome gift. To vary the recipe, use a mixture of soft fruits, or other individual fruits such as strawberries or blackberries.

Makes 900 g/2 lb

INGREDIENTS
675 g/1½ lb/3½ cups raspberries
900 g/2 lb/4 cups caster sugar
30 ml/2 tbsp lemon juice
100 ml/4 fl oz/½ cup liquid pectin

raspberries

lemon

1 Place the raspberries in a large bowl and lightly crush with a wooden spoon. Stir in the caster sugar. Leave for 1 hour at room temperature, giving the mixture an occasional stir to dissolve the sugar.

2 Sterilize several small jars or containers, and their lids if being used. Add the lemon juice and liquid pectin to the raspberries and stir until thoroughly blended.

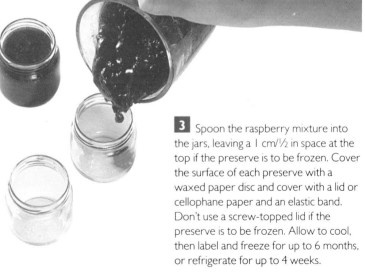

3 Spoon the raspberry mixture into the jars, leaving a 1 cm/½ in space at the top if the preserve is to be frozen. Cover the surface of each preserve with a waxed paper disc and cover with a lid or cellophane paper and an elastic band. Don't use a screw-topped lid if the preserve is to be frozen. Allow to cool, then label and freeze for up to 6 months, or refrigerate for up to 4 weeks.

Flavoured Oils

Any good quality oils may be flavoured with herbs, spices, peppers, olives or anchovies. They look attractive in the kitchen, as well as being ready flavoured for use in cooking or salad dressings.

Makes 300 ml/¹/₂ pint/1¹/₄ cups of each flavour

INGREDIENTS
olive, grapeseed or almond oil

HERB OIL
sage, thyme, oregano, tarragon and
    rosemary sprigs
1 bay leaf sprig

SPICED OIL
30 g/2 tbsp whole cloves
3 mace blades
15 g/1 tbsp cardamom pods
15 g/1 tbsp coriander seeds
3 dried chillies
1 bay leaf sprig
2 lime slices
2 cinnamon sticks

MEDITERRANEAN OIL
2 mini red peppers
3 black olives
3 green olives
3 anchovy fillets
1 bay leaf sprig
strip of lemon rind

1 Have ready 3 bottles and corks which have been sterilized and are completely dry inside. Place all the fresh herb sprigs together and trim to fit inside the first bottle. Insert the short lengths first and arrange them using a long skewer, adding them stem by stem.

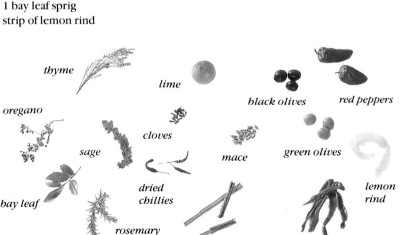

thyme
lime
black olives
red peppers
oregano
cloves
sage
mace
green olives
bay leaf
dried chillies
lemon rind
rosemary
cinnamon
anchovy fillets

2 Add the cloves, mace, cardamom pods, coriander seeds and chillies to the second bottle. Insert the sprig of bay leaves, lime slices and cinnamon sticks.

3 Grill the mini red peppers until they are tender, turning once. Add the olives, anchovies and peppers to the last bottle. Insert the bay leaf sprig and strip of lemon rind. Fill each bottle with the chosen oil and cork or cap. Label clearly and keep cool until required.

Christmas Decorating

THE CHRISTMAS HOME

These delightful suggestions for decorating
with natural materials or in country
themes will help to add the finishing touch
to any Christmas at home.

Velvet Fruits

A lavish bowl full of sumptuous apples and pears in rich, fruity-coloured velvets will look like a still-life painting. You may not be able to eat them, but these fruits feel delicious!

YOU WILL NEED
paper for templates
small amounts of dress-weight velvet
    in red, plum and green
pins
scissors
sewing machine
matching thread
polyester wadding
needle

thread

dress-weight velvet

needle

pins

polyester wadding

scissors

paper

1 Trace the pear, apple and leaf templates from the back of the book and enlarge as required. Transfer to paper and cut out the templates. Pin to the velvet and cut out, adding a 5 mm (¹/₄ in) seam allowance all round. You will need four sections for the pear and three for the apple.

CRAFT TIP
You could also use this idea to create other velvet objects on a festive theme. Why not try making some stars or holly leaves following the other templates at the back of the book?

2 With right sides together, pin together the side seams and machine-stitch, leaving the top of the fruits open. Turn to the right side.

3 Cut two pieces of green velvet for each leaf. Machine-stitch together, leaving the end open, and turn to the right side. Gather the end with a needle and thread to give a realistic leaf shape.

4 Stuff each fruit with polyester wadding. Sew up the opening at the top with a needle and thread, catching in the leaf as you sew.

The Christmas Mantelpiece

In restrained tones of cream and green, this elegant arrangement concentrates on contrasting shapes and textures. Placing it in front of a mirror makes it doubly effective. The key to success is scale: use the largest-leaved ivy and the thickest candles you can find to make a really stylish design statement.

YOU WILL NEED
polystyrene balls
double-sided adhesive tape
scissors
reindeer moss
ivory candles of various heights
    and widths
foil dishes (for baking or
    take-away food)
plastic adhesive
stems of ivy
florist's wire

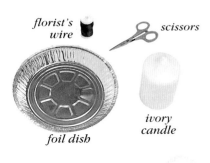

florist's wire

scissors

foil dish

ivory candle

plastic adhesive

polystyrene ball

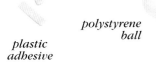

ivy

reindeer moss

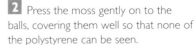

double-sided adhesive tape

1 To make the moss balls, cover the polystyrene shapes all over with double-sided adhesive tape.

2 Press the moss gently on to the balls, covering them well so that none of the polystyrene can be seen.

3 Arrange the candles on foil dishes to protect the mantelpiece from hot, dripping wax. Secure the candles in the dishes with pieces of plastic adhesive.

4 Wire together small bunches of ivy and attach them to a longer main stem to make a lush garland. Arrange the candles on the mantelpiece and drape the garlands in front of them. Position the moss balls around the candles.

SAFETY TIP
Never leave burning candles unattended and do not allow them to burn down to within 5 cm (2 in) of the foliage or other decoration.

Citrus Centrepiece

Perhaps because they're at their best at this time of year, oranges feature in many traditional Christmas recipes and their warm spicy smell readily evokes the festive season. A sparkling glass bowl of citrus fruits brings a flash of sunshine into the house in the depths of winter and makes a glowing, fragrant centrepiece.

CRAFT TIP

If you are using a lino-cutting tool for this project, paint the blade with a coat of clear nail varnish to prevent it discolouring the fruit.

YOU WILL NEED
oranges, lemons and limes
V-shaped lino-cutting tool or
    canelle knife
sharp knife
wire-edged ribbon
scissors
florist's stub wire
glass dish or bowl
sprigs of fresh bay leaves
secateurs

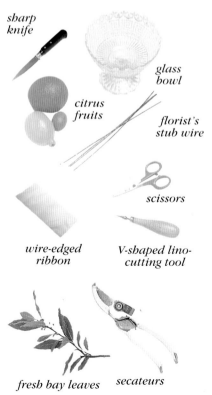

sharp knife

glass bowl

citrus fruits

florist's stub wire

scissors

wire-edged ribbon

V-shaped lino-cutting tool

fresh bay leaves   *secateurs*

1 Use the lino-cutting tool or canelle knife to cut grooves in the peel of the fruits and reveal the white pith beneath. Follow the contours of the fruit in a spiral or make straight cuts.

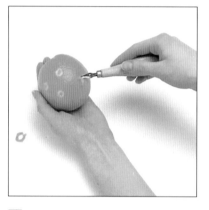

2 On other fruits, try making an overall pattern of small circles. Practise the patterns on spare fruits you intend to cook with or eat.

3 With a very sharp knife, cut thin spirals of orange peel as long as possible to drape over the arrangement.

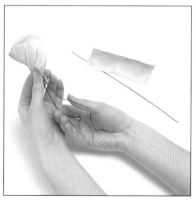

4 Cut short lengths of wire-edged ribbon, fold into loops and secure the ends with florist's stub wire.

5 Arrange the fruits in your chosen container, tucking in the ribbon loops and adding a few sprigs of fresh green bay leaves.

Festive Wine Glasses

With the same gold glass outliner used to decorate glass ornaments, you can also transform plain, everyday wine glasses. Add clear, stained-glass colours for a jewelled effect, to give your Christmas dinner the air of a medieval feast.

YOU WILL NEED
plain wine glasses
white spirit
gold glass outliner
oil-based glass paints
fine paintbrush
old glass or jar
paper towel

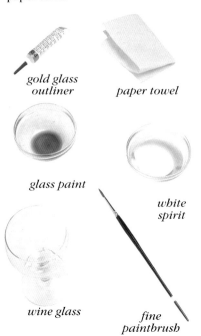

gold glass outliner

paper towel

glass paint

white spirit

wine glass

fine paintbrush

1 Wash the glasses with detergent and wipe over with white spirit to remove all traces of grease.

2 Pipe your design directly on to the glass with the gold outliner. Leave to dry thoroughly for at least 24 hours.

CRAFT TIP

When planning your design, it's best to avoid the rim of the glass as the relief outliner will feel bumpy against the drinker's lips. The paint colours can be mixed if you wish.

3 Check the colour and get the feel of the rather viscous glass paint by practising on an old glass or jar first. Use a fine paintbrush to colour in your design, and be careful not to get paint on the gold relief. Try to finish with each colour before changing to the next one. Clean the brush with white spirit between each colour.

Heavenly Gold Star

Collect as many different kinds of gold paper as you can find to cover this sparkling star with its subtle variations of texture. It makes a lovely wall or mantelpiece decoration, and would look equally splendid at the top of the tree.

YOU WILL NEED
assorted gold paper: sweet
    wrappers, metallic crêpe paper,
    gift-wrap, etc
polystyrene star
fine wire
scissors
masking tape
PVA glue
paintbrush
gold glitter paint

paintbrush   *masking tape*

PVA glue

polystyrene star

gold glitter paint   *scissors*

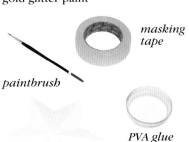

fine wire   *assorted gold paper*

1 Tear the various gold papers into odd shapes of slightly different sizes.

2 Dilute the PVA glue with a little water. Paint it on to the back of a piece of gold paper and stick on to the polystyrene star. Paint more glue over the piece to secure it. Work all over the front of the star, using different papers to vary the texture and colour.

3 Make a loop of wire and stick the ends into the back of the star for hanging. Secure with masking tape. Cover the back with gold paper in the same way as the front.

4 Leave to dry, then cover with a coat of gold glitter paint.

THE CHRISTMAS TREE

Inevitably the visual focus of any
Christmas event, the tree can be
transformed into something quite
magical with just a few simple touches
and flourishes and a hint of
imagination and flair.

Cookies for the Tree

Use your favourite gingerbread biscuit recipe to make some delicious edible decorations. If you'd rather they didn't all disappear from the tree before Christmas has even begun, you can dry them out completely in the oven. Either way, don't forget to make a small hole at the top of each biscuit while they're still warm so that you can hang them up.

YOU WILL NEED
rolling pin
gingerbread biscuit dough
a festive assortment of biscuit
    cutters
skewer
garden twine
scraps of homespun checked fabric

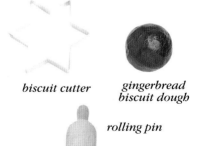

skewer

checked fabric

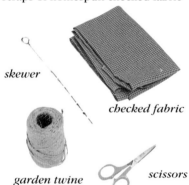

garden twine   *scissors*

biscuit cutter   *gingerbread biscuit dough*

rolling pin

1 Roll out the gingerbread dough to a thickness of about 1 cm (½ in).

2 Gently cut out your chosen shapes with biscuit cutters. Bake the biscuits in batches according to the recipe.

3 While the biscuits are still warm from the oven, carefully pierce a small hole in the top of each one with a skewer. If the biscuits are not intended for eating, return them to the lowest shelf of a very low oven to allow them to dry out thoroughly.

4 Thread a loop of garden twine through each hole. Cut a small strip of homespun fabric and tie this around the loop of twine to finish the decoration.

Victorian Boots

Use the richest fabrics you can find to make these delicate boots: fine raw silks and taffetas in glowing colours are perfect. The two sides of the decoration should harmonize well.

YOU WILL NEED
thin white card
pencil
stapler
scissors
scraps of fabric
fabric glue
paintbrush
fine gold cord

scraps of fabric

fine gold cord

scissors

pencil

thin white card

fabric glue

paintbrush

stapler

1 Trace the boot template from the back of the book and transfer it on to thin card. Fold the card in two and staple the layers together at the edges so that you can cut out two exactly matching templates. Cut the boots out with scissors.

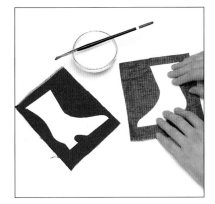

2 Separate the templates. Turn one over and glue each on to a piece of co-ordinating fabric.

3 Cut around each boot, leaving an allowance of barely 1 cm (½ in). Snip the excess fabric around all the curves and stick down firmly to the back of the card.

4 Glue a loop of cord to the back of one card for hanging, then glue the two sides of the boot together and leave to dry thoroughly.

Glitter Keys

A simple idea for transforming everyday objects into fantasy tree decorations. Once you've picked up the glitter habit, you may find you want to cover all kinds of other things – and why not?

YOU WILL NEED
old keys in various shapes and sizes
PVA glue
old paintbrush
sheets of scrap paper
coloured glitter
fine gold cord

old paintbrush

old keys

scrap paper

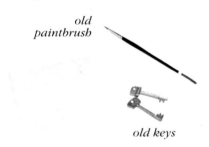

coloured glitter

PVA glue

fine gold cord

1 Using an old paintbrush, cover one side of the key with a coat of undiluted PVA glue.

2 Lay the key on a sheet of scrap paper and sprinkle generously with glitter. Repeat with the other keys, using a separate sheet of paper for each one. Allow to dry completely.

3 Remove the key. Pinch the paper to make a groove for the spare glitter to run into. Pour it back into the container. Glue the remaining areas of the keys and repeat the process. Add further layers to build up quite a thick coating. Tie a loop of gold cord to each key for hanging.

CRAFT TIP
PVA glue dries to a transparent glaze, so you can brush it on over glitter you have already applied when building up the layers on the keys.

Ornamental Keys

Gold paint and fake gems can turn a bunch of old keys into something truly wonderful – fit to unlock a fairy-tale castle or treasure chest.

YOU WILL NEED
old keys in assorted shapes and
    sizes
gold spray paint
gold braid
hot glue gun
flat-backed fake gems in
    assorted colours

gold spray paint

scissors

gold braid

old keys

flat-backed fake gems

glue gun

1 Make sure the keys are free of rust. Working with one side at a time, spray with gold paint and allow to dry.

2 Cut the gold braid into a suitable length for hanging the key. Fold in half and attach the ends to the key with the glue gun.

3 Cover the ends of the braid by gluing a jewel over them. Arrange two or three more jewels on the key and glue them on. Allow to dry thoroughly.

Carnival Mask

A stunning decoration inspired by the traditional costume of the masked Harlequin. Use the fragile foil from sweet wrappers for part of the design to mimic the expensive look of fine gold leaf.

YOU WILL NEED
tracing paper
thin white card
pencil
ruler
scissors
craft knife
metallic crayons in gold and lilac
glitter paint
PVA glue
glitter
foil sweet wrappers
sequins
gold doily
matt gold paper
glue-stick
fine gold cord
gold buttons

PVA glue

matt gold paper

glitter paint

gold doily

glitter brush

thin white card

metallic crayons

pencil

ruler

craft knife

fine gold cord

scissors

glue-stick

gold button

sweet wrappers

1 Trace the template from the back of the book and transfer it to thin white card. Cut out the mask shape and eye holes. Use a soft pencil to draw in the diagonals for the diamonds.

2 Decorate the diamond shapes in different colours and textures. Use metallic crayons, adding glitter paint on some for texture. Paint PVA glue on to others and sprinkle with glitter. When dry, coat thinly with more glue to fix the glitter. Cut diamonds from the sweet wrappers and glue these on last to cover any rough edges.

3 Trim the eye holes with rows of gold sequins and the edging cut from a gold doily.

4 Use the template to cut a second mask shape from matt gold paper. Glue this to the back of your mask. Attach a loop of fine gold cord for hanging, covering each end with a gold button.

Lacy Silver Gloves

Dainty Victorian ladies' gloves make a pretty motif for a traditional glittering tree ornament. Use translucent glass paints, which adhere well and let the foil shine through the colour.

YOU WILL NEED
tracing paper
heavy-gauge aluminium foil
masking tape
dried-out ballpoint pen
scissors
oil-based glass paints
paintbrush
fine gold cord

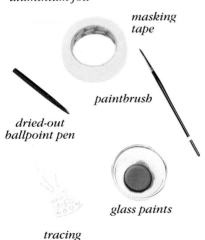

fine gold cord

scissors

heavy-gauge aluminium foil

masking tape

paintbrush

dried-out ballpoint pen

glass paints

tracing paper

1 Trace the template from the back of the book and attach the tracing to a piece of foil with masking tape. Draw over the design to transfer it to the foil. Remove the tracing and complete the embossing with an old ballpoint pen.

2 Cut out the glove, leaving a narrow border of about 2 mm ($^1/_{16}$ in) all around the edge: don't cut into the embossed outline. Make a hole in one corner of the glove with the point of the scissors.

3 Paint the design with glass paints, keeping the colours within the embossed outlines. Allow to dry completely for at least 24 hours.

4 Thread a loop of fine gold cord through the hole for hanging.

Gilded Rosettes

These flowerlike ornaments can be hung on the tree or used to decorate a sumptuously wrapped gift for someone special. Gold lamé makes an opulent setting for an ornate gilt button, but experiment with luxurious velvets too.

YOU WILL NEED
paper for template
small pieces of silk, lamé or dress-
    weight velvet
pins
scissors
matching thread
needle
fine gold cord
ornate buttons
hot glue gun

lamé and silk

fine gold cord

paper

buttons

thread

pins   *needle*

scissors

hot glue gun

1 Draw and cut out a circular template about 12 cm (5 in) in diameter, pin to a single layer of fabric and cut out (there is no need for a seam allowance).

2 Using double thread, sew a running stitch all round the circle, 5 mm (¼ in) from the edge. Pull the thread taut to form the rosette and secure the ends.

3 Thread a loop of fine gold cord through the top of the rosette for hanging the decoration.

4 Using a hot glue gun, attach a button in the centre to cover the raw edges.

Exotic Ornaments

These sequinned and beaded balls look like a collection of priceless Fabergé treasures, yet they're simple and fun to make. Hang them on the tree or pile them in a dish for a show-stopping decoration.

YOU WILL NEED
silky covered polystyrene balls
paper for template
pins
gold netting
scissors
double-sided adhesive tape
gold braid
sequins in a variety of shapes
    and colours
small glass and pearl beads
brass-headed pins, 1 cm (½ in) long

scissors

sequins

small beads

gold netting

gold braid

paper

double-sided adhesive tape

silky covered polystyrene ball

pins

brass-headed pins

1 Measure the circumference of a ball and make a paper template to fit around it. Pin to the gold netting and cut out.

2 Secure the netting to the ball using tiny pieces of double-sided adhesive tape. The tape and raw edges will be hidden later with sequins.

3 For an alternative design, cut lengths of gold braid and pin around the ball to make a framework for your sequins.

4 Thread a bead and sequin on to a brass-headed pin and gently press into the bauble. Repeat until each design is complete.

CRAFT TIP

Silk-covered balls are available as ready-made tree ornaments. When you are working out your designs, use simple repeating patterns and avoid using too many colours on each one, since this can look too busy.

A Country Angel

This endearing character, with her homespun clothes and tightly knotted hair, is bound to be a friend for many Christmases to come.

YOU WILL NEED
40 x 24 cm (16 x 10 in) piece
    natural calico
40 x 26 cm (16 x 11 in) piece
    checked cotton homespun or
    small-scale gingham
30 x 22 cm (12 x 9 in) piece blue
    and white ticking
tea
paper for templates
scissors
fabric marker pen
sewing machine
matching thread
polyester wadding
twigs
secateurs
fine permanent marker
stranded embroidery thread
    in brown
needle
garden twine
scrap of red woollen fabric
fabric stiffener
copper wire
all-purpose glue

1 Begin by washing all the fabrics to remove any chemicals. While they are still damp, soak them in tea. Don't worry if the colouring is uneven, as this adds to their rustic, aged appearance. Trace the templates for the head, dress and wings from the back of the book. Cut the head and torso out of doubled calico, leaving a 1 cm (½ in) seam allowance.

2 Machine the two body pieces right sides together, leaving the lower edge open. Clip the curves and turn to the right side. Stuff loosely with polyester wadding. Cut two twigs about 20 cm (8 in) long and stick them into the body to make the legs. Sew up the opening, securing the legs as you go.

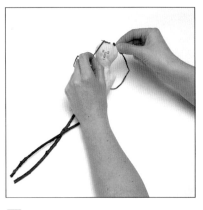

3 With a very fine permanent marker, draw the eyes, nose and mouth on to the face. Make heavy French knots with embroidery thread around the top of the face for the hair.

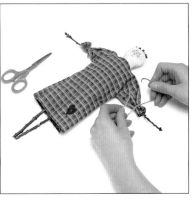

4 Use the paper pattern to cut out the dress from the checked fabric. Sew up the sides, leaving the sleeves and hem with raw edges. Cut a slit in the top for the neck and turn the dress to the right side. Cut a small heart from the red woollen fabric and attach to the dress with a single cross-stitch in brown embroidery thread. Put the dress on the angel, then place short twigs inside the sleeves, securing them tightly at the wrists with garden twine. The twigs should be short enough to let the arms bend forward.

twigs

wadding

garden twine

blue and white ticking

pins

paper

red woollen fabric

needle

natural calico

checked cotton homespun

thread

all-purpose glue

fabric marker pen

fine permanent marker

secateurs

stranded embroidery thread

copper wire

fabric stiffener

scissors

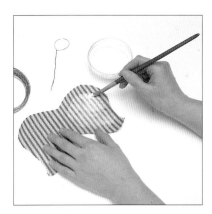

5 Cut the wings out of the ticking and fray the raw edges slightly. Apply fabric stiffener liberally to the wings to soak them thoroughly. Lay them completely flat to dry.

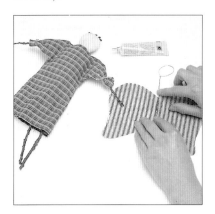

6 Make a halo from copper wire, leaving a long end to glue to the wings. Stitch the wings securely to the back of the body through the dress.

Silk Purses

Ribbons are available in a great range of widths and colours and you need only a small amount of each to make these delicate little purses to hang on your tree. Use luxurious satins or sheer organza, with contrasting colours for generous bows around the top.

YOU WILL NEED
an assortment of ribbons
pins
scissors
matching thread
needle
fine gold cord
polyester wadding

needle

thread

polyester wadding

pins   *fine gold cord*

scissors

ribbons

1 Cut enough ribbon to make a pleasing purse shape when folded in two, short sides together, allowing for the raw edges to be folded down at the top. To make a striped purse, pin and stitch three narrower lengths together using running stitch.

2 With the right sides together, sew up the sides of the purse by hand, or using a sewing machine if you prefer.

3 Turn the purse right side out and tuck the raw edges inside. Stitch on a loop of fine gold cord for hanging. Stuff lightly with polyester wadding.

4 Gather the top of the purse together and tie with another piece of ribbon, finishing with a pretty bow.

Gilded Glass Spheres

With a gold glass outliner, you can turn plain glass tree decorations into unique gilded ornaments. Don't be too ambitious with your designs: you'll find that simple repeating motifs such as circles, triangles and stars are best to begin with and can be the most effective.

YOU WILL NEED
plain glass tree ornaments
white spirit
gold glass outliner
paper tissues
jam jar
wire-edged ribbon
scissors

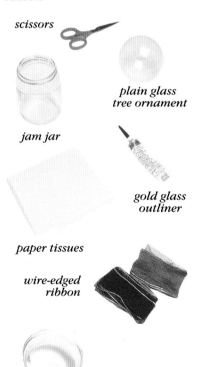

scissors

jam jar

plain glass tree ornament

gold glass outliner

paper tissues

wire-edged ribbon

white spirit

1 Clean the glass ornaments with detergent and wipe them with white spirit to remove all traces of grease.

2 Working on one side only, gently squeeze the gold glass outliner on to the glass in your chosen design. If you make a mistake, wipe the outliner off quickly with a paper tissue while it is still wet.

3 Rest the sphere in an empty jam jar and leave for about 24 hours to dry thoroughly. Decorate the other side and leave to dry again.

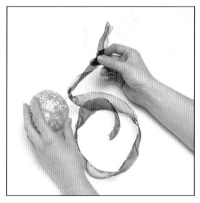

4 Thread a length of wire-edged ribbon through the top of the ornament and tie it in a bow.

NATURAL DECORATIONS

No country Christmas is complete without its complement of natural displays – the wreaths, topiaries and arrangements of organic materials that bring the smells and textures of field, hedgerow and woodland into the home.

Twiggy Door Wreath

Welcome seasonal guests with a door wreath that's charming in its simplicity. Just bend twigs into a heart shape and adorn the heart with variegated ivy, berries and a Christmas rose, or substitute any pure-white rose.

MATERIALS
secateurs
pliable branches, such as
  buddleia, cut from the garden
florist's wire
seagrass string
variegated trailing ivy
red berries
tree ivy
picture framer's wax gilt
  (optional)
white rose
garden twine

1 Using secateurs, cut six lengths of pliable branches about 70 cm (28 in) long. Wire three together at one end. Repeat with the other three. Cross the two bundles over at the wired end.

2 Wire the bunches together in the crossed-over position.

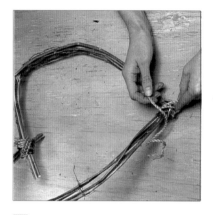

3 Holding the crossed, wired ends with one hand, ease the long end round and down very gently, so the branches don't snap. Repeat with the other side, to form a heart shape. Wire the bottom end of the heart. Bind the wiring with seagrass string at top and bottom and make a hanging loop at the top.

4 Entwine trailing ivy around the heart shape.

5 Add berries. Make a bouquet of tree-ivy leaves (if you like, gild them using picture framer's wax gilt) and a white rose. Tie the bouquet with golden twine. Wire the bouquet in position at the top of the heart.

Everlasting Christmas Tree

This delightful little tree, made from dyed, preserved oak leaves and decorated with tiny gilded cones, would make an enchanting Christmas decoration. Make several and then group them to make a centrepiece or place one at each setting.

MATERIALS
knife
bunch of dyed, dried oak leaves
florist's wire
small pine cones
picture framer's wax gilt
flowerpot, 18 cm (7 in) tall
small florist's dry foam cone
4 florist's stub wires
florist's dry foam cone about 18 cm (7 in) tall

1 Cut the leaves off the branches and trim the stalks. Wire up bunches of about four leaves, making some branches with small leaves, some with medium-sized leaves and others with large leaves. Sort the bunches into piles.

2 Insert wires into the bottom end of each pine cone and twist the ends together. Gild each cone by rubbing on wax gilt.

3 Prepare the pot by cutting the smaller foam cone to fit the pot, adding stub-wire stakes and positioning the larger cone on to this. Attach the leaves to the cone, starting at the top with the bunches of small leaves, and working down through the medium and large leaves to make a realistic shape. Add the gilded cones to finish.

Twiggy Stars

Buy a bundle of willow twigs or, better still, hunt for them in winter woods and gardens. These pretty stars would look equally effective hanging on the tree or in a window.

YOU WILL NEED
willow twigs
secateurs
stranded embroidery thread
checked cotton fabric
scissors
natural raffia

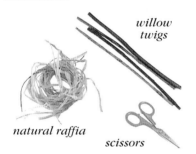

natural raffia   *willow twigs*   *scissors*   *embroidery thread*

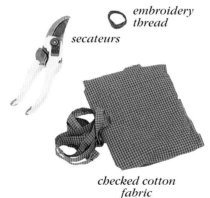

secateurs   *checked cotton fabric*

1 Cut the twigs into lengths of 15 cm (6 in) using the secateurs. You will need five for each star.

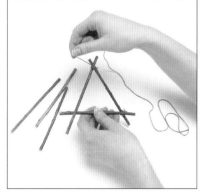

2 Tie the first pair of twigs together near the ends with a length of embroidery thread, winding it around and between to form a "V" shape. Repeat with the remaining twigs, arranging them under and over each other as shown in the photograph to form a five-pointed star.

3 Cut the fabric into strips approximately 15 × 2 cm (6 × ¾ in).

4 Tie a length of fabric in a double knot over the thread, securing each point of the star. Attach a loop of raffia to hang the decoration.

Clementine Wreath

The wreath will look spectacular hung on a door or wall, and can also be used as a table decoration with a large candle at its centre, or perhaps a cluster of smaller candles of staggered heights. The wreath is very easy to make, but it is heavy and if it is to be hung on a wall or door, be sure to fix it securely.

MATERIALS
.71 wires
27 clementines
plastic foam ring approximately
  30 cm (12 in) diameter
pyracanthus berries and foliage
ivy leaves

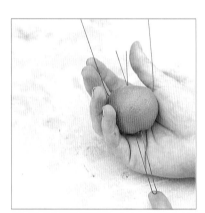

1 Push a .71 wire across and through the base of the clementine from one side to the other, and bend the two projected ends down. Bend another .71 wire to form a hairpin shape and push the ends right through the middle of the clementine so that the bend in the wire is sitting flush with the top of the fruit. Do the same to all the clementines. Cut all the projecting wires to a length of approximately 4 cm (1½ in).

2 Soak the plastic foam ring in water. Arrange the wired clementines in a tight circle on the top of the plastic ring by pushing their four projecting wire legs into the foam. Form a second ring of clementines within the first ring.

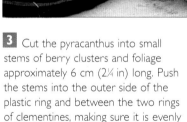

3 Cut the pyracanthus into small stems of berry clusters and foliage approximately 6 cm (2¼ in) long. Push the stems into the outer side of the plastic ring and between the two rings of clementines, making sure it is evenly distributed.

4 Cut the ivy leaves into individual stems measuring approximately 7 cm (2¾ in) in length. Push the stems of the individual leaves into the plastic ring, positioning a leaf between each clementine.

Front Door Wreath

Take a break from traditional red berries and ribbons with this fresh-looking arrangement. The vibrant orange kumquats are perfectly set off by the cool blue spruce.

YOU WILL NEED
fresh greenery: sprays of bay leaves
    and blue spruce
secateurs
florist's wire
kumquats
green chillies
pine cones
ready-made willow wreath
wire-edged ribbon
pins
scissors

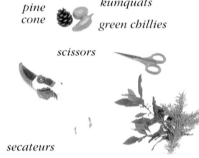

pine cone   *kumquats*   *green chillies*   *scissors*   *secateurs*   *pins*   *fresh greenery*   *wire-edged ribbon*

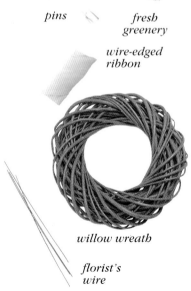

willow wreath

florist's wire

1 Trim the greenery into sprigs suitable for the size of the wreath, wiring pieces together here and there to fill them out.

2 Twist a piece of wire around each stem, leaving a length to insert into the willow wreath.

3 Wire the kumquats and chillies by sticking a piece of wire through the base then bending the ends down and twisting them together. Wind a piece of wire around the base of each pine cone.

4 Attach the greenery, fruits and cones to the wreath, twisting the ends of the wires to secure them.

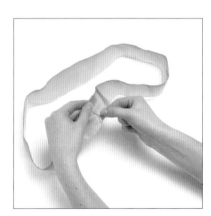

5 Reserving a short length of ribbon for the centre of the bow, join the ends together with a pin.

6 Fold the ribbon over on itself to make four loops.

7 Pinch the centre of the loops together and secure with a wire. Cover this with the remaining piece of ribbon and wire the bow to the wreath.

CHRISTMAS CANDLES

Perennially popular and nowadays
indispensible, candles furnish the purest
and warmest Christmas light – a final glow
that illuminates scenes of friendship
and love that will linger in the memory
throughout the year.

Rolled Candles

Rolled candles made from thin sheets of wax are the simplest candles to make. Wax sheets can be bought ready for use and need only to be warm and pliable before you begin.

YOU WILL NEED
sheet of beeswax
hairdryer
scalpel or craft knife
metal ruler
wick
scissors

1 To make a tapered candle, use a rectangular sheet of beeswax and warm it with a hairdryer. The short side of the sheet determines the height of the candle. Cut a narrow triangular segment off from the longest side.

2 Cut a wick that will extend about 2 cm (¾ in) above the height of the candle. Press the wick gently into the edge of this longer short side. Roll up the wax, checking that the wick is held closely from the first turn.

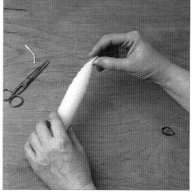

3 When you have finished rolling the wax, press the edge into the candle to give a smooth finish. Trim the wick, then wrap a tiny piece of wax around it so that it is primed and ready for burning.

Silver Crown Candle-holder

Masses of night-lights make a lovely glowing addition to your decorative scheme: dress them up for Christmas with these easy foil crowns. Make sure the candles you buy come in their own foil pots to contain the hot wax.

YOU WILL NEED
night-light
heavy-gauge aluminium foil
ruler
scissors
masking tape
dried-out ballpoint pen
glue-stick

dried-out ballpoint pen

glue-stick

masking tape

scissors

ruler

night-light

heavy-gauge aluminium foil

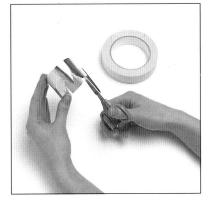

1 Cut a rectangle of foil to fit around the night-light and overlap by about 4 cm (1½ in). The foil should stand at least 3 cm (1¼ in) higher than the night-light.

SAFETY TIP
Candles and night-lights are a fire hazard. Never leave them burning unattended.

2 Wrap the foil in a circle around the candle and secure with a piece of masking tape. Cut the points of the crown freehand with scissors.

3 Remove the tape and lay the foil flat on a protected surface. Emboss a design on the foil with an old ballpoint pen, making sure that it will meet neatly when the crown is joined up.

4 Roll the finished design tightly around the night-light to get a good candle shape and stick it together finally with a glue-stick.

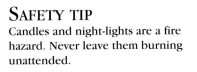

CANDLES

Stencilled Candles

Plain candles can be made to look more exciting for a party or Christmas celebration with stencils.

YOU WILL NEED
candles
tape measure
stencil card
pencil
ruler
scalpel or craft knife
spray adhesive or masking tape
non-toxic spray paints
lace or paper shelf edging

1 To make a stencil to cover the whole candle, first measure its height and circumference. Then draw your design on a piece of card to fit. Cut out the parts of the design that will form the pattern on the candle.

2 Fix the stencil firmly around the candle. Coat the back of the stencil with a light layer of a spray adhesive that allows for repositioning and stick it to the candle. Wrap the stencil tightly around the candle and then apply the paint, leave it to dry and remove the stencil.

3 An equally effective method that does not require you to make a stencil is to cut lengths of lace or paper shelf edging to fit around the candle.

174

Shaker Candles

Candles can be decorated with sponged patterns and motifs cut out of wax for a simple home-spun feel.

YOU WILL NEED
sponge about 2 cm (¾ in) thick
felt-tip pen
scalpel or craft knife
old baking pan
greaseproof paper
paraffin wax
double boiler
deep red wax dye
spoon or stirrer
heart-shaped biscuit cutter
plate
aquamarine water-based paint
washing-up liquid
candle
wax glue
fine paintbrush

1 On the sponge, draw one square and divide it into four small squares. Cut out half the depth of the sponge on two diagonally opposite squares.

2 Line the baking pan with grease-proof paper. Melt a small quantity of wax in the top of the double boiler and add the dye. Stir until well blended. Pour the molten wax into the lined baking pan. Tip the pan to spread out the wax evenly so that it forms a fine layer. While it is soft, use the cutter to stamp out as many hearts as you need.

3 Mix the paint with a little washing-up liquid to the consistency of double cream. Dip the sponge into the paint and then press it on to the candle to make a border. When the borders are complete, leave them to dry thoroughly.

4 Press a heart against the candle so that it becomes curved. Melt a little wax glue, paint one side of the heart with glue and then press it firmly to the candle. Add more hearts at equal intervals until the decoration is complete.

Filigree Candle Crown

Metallic candle crowns surround and protect the flames and make pinprick patterns of light through punched holes as the candles burn down inside them. You could place a group of them on a circular tray or platter, or sit single pieces on individual brass dishes or saucers, surrounding candlesticks or holders. Try experimenting with different patterns of pierced holes in straight lines and curly swirls. For further embellishment, glass nuggets and beads set into the metal take on a jewel-like quality with candle light behind them. To fix them in place, cut holes slightly smaller than the nuggets; spread glue around the holes and press on the glass or beads.

YOU WILL NEED
copper foil, .005 in thick/
   36 gauge
pencil
ruler
protective gloves (optional)
round lid or coin for template
bradawl
magazine or pile of newspaper
small pointed scissors
brass paper fasteners

1 Cut a rectangle of foil 28 cm x 16 cm (11 in x 6½ in). Use a sharp pencil and ruler to draw a line across the length of the foil, dividing it in half. Then draw parallel diagonal lines across the width of the foil, to make a lattice design. Using a round lid or a coin as a template, draw circles between the parallel lines along the top and the bottom edges.

2 Begin to punch holes, regularly spaced, along the pencilled lines, using a bradawl. Punch a single hole in the centre of each circle and triangle. If you like, place a magazine, or something similar, which will 'give' slightly and protect your work surface, underneath the foil.

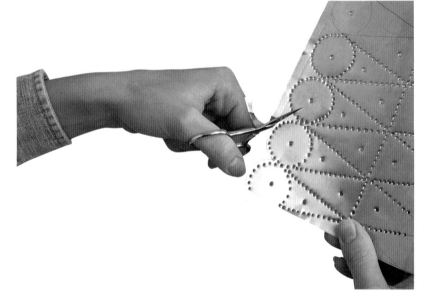

3 Cut along the top edge with scissors to leave a small border around the punched holes and make a scalloped rim.

4 Gently bend the foil round so that the ends overlap slightly, to form a cylindrical candle crown. Make three corresponding marks on both pieces of foil where they meet and punch holes through these. Push a paper fastener through each set of holes to hold the foil in place, opening out the ends of the fastener on the inside of the crown.

Painted Candlesticks

New wooden candlesticks can be aged and mellowed using simple paint techniques which instantly give a patina of age.

YOU WILL NEED
FOR THE ANTIQUE-FINISH CANDLESTICK
wooden candlestick
wax candle
off-white emulsion paint
small, flat and fine paintbrushes
fine sandpaper or wire wool
antiquing patina
rag
acrylic paints (smoke blue and jade green)
matt varnish
varnishing brush

FOR THE GOLD CANDLESTICKS
candlestick
gold paint
paintbrushes
craquelure base varnish
craquelure varnish
antiquing wax or raw umber oil pigment
soft cotton cloth
matt varnish
varnishing brush

1 For the antique-finish candlestick, rub the candlestick with the candle, applying a light coating of wax. Paint the candlestick with off-white emulsion and leave to dry. Lightly rub over the candlestick, using fine sandpaper or wire wool, to give a scuffed surface.

2 Apply a coat of antiquing patina with a brush. Lift off some of the patina with a rag to mellow the painted surface and add texture.

3 Using a fine paintbrush, roughly paint bands of smoke blue around the top and bottom of the candlestick as well as inside any grooves. Leave to dry. Roughly paint thin lines of jade green within the smoke blue bands. Leave to dry then varnish.

1 For the gold candlestick, paint the candlestick gold, taking care not to let the paint build up in any grooves. Spread the paint with even, regular brushstrokes. Leave the paint to dry thoroughly.

2 Brush on an even coat of craquelure base varnish and let it dry. Next, use a clean, dry brush to apply an even coat of craquelure varnish to the entire surface, making sure that the base coat of varnish is thoroughly covered. Smooth out the varnish and put the candlestick aside to dry naturally (this will take about 15–20 minutes). Colourless cracks will form over the surface. Take a cotton rag and rub on a little antiquing wax or oil pigment and then seal the surface with a coat of varnish.

Advent Candle Ring

An Advent candle ring makes a pretty Christmas centrepiece. This one – decorated with glossy green tree ivy, Cape gooseberries, dried citrus-fruit slices and bundles of cinnamon sticks – is a delight to the eye, while giving off a rich seasonal aroma.

MATERIALS
florist's foam
knife
florist's ring basket
4 church candles
moss
dried orange slices
florist's stub wires
secateurs
cinnamon sticks
golden twine
tree ivy
Cape gooseberries

1 Soak the florist's foam and cut it to fit the ring basket.

2 Position the candles in the foam.

3 Cover the florist's foam with moss, pushing it well down at the sides of the basket.

4 Wire the orange slices by passing a stub wire through the centre and then twisting the ends together at the outside edge. Wire the cinnamon sticks into bundles, then tie them with golden twine and pass a wire through the string.

5 Wire the tree-ivy into bundles.

6 Position the ivy leaves into the ring. Decorate by fixing in the orange slices and cinnamon sticks and placing the Cape gooseberries on top of the candle ring at intervals.

Candle Centrepiece

Even the humblest materials can be put together to make an elegant centrepiece. The garden shed has been raided for this one, which is made from a terracotta flowerpot and chicken wire. Fill it up with red berries, ivies and white roses for a rich, Christmassy look; or substitute seasonal flowers and foliage at any other time of year.

MATERIALS
18 cm (7 in) flowerpot
about 1 m (40 in) chicken wire
knife
florist's foam ball to fit the
  diameter of the pot
beeswax candle
tree ivy
white roses
berries
variegated trailing ivy

1 Place the pot in the centre of a large square of chicken wire. Bring the chicken wire up around the pot and bend it into position.

2 Cut the florist's foam ball in half and soak one half. The other half isn't needed.

3 Place the foam in the pot, cut-side up so that you have a flat surface. Position the candle in the centre of the pot.

4 Arrange glossy tree-ivy all around the candle, to provide a lush green base.

5 Add a white rose as a focal point, and bunches of red berries among the ivy.

6 Add more white roses, and intersperse trailing variegated ivy among the tree ivy.

Gold leaf Candles

Gold leaf is expensive if you use it in large quantities but it has a special quality all of its own. It can be used to decorate candles to give stunning results. English transfer leaf – the best kind to use for this job – can be bought in books which contain several sheets. If you feel confident, you can draw designs freehand, transferring a pattern directly on to the candles. However, although the technique is very easy, mistakes can prove quite costly. If you are trying this for the first time, you should draw your design on paper before you start. The safest method is to trace a pattern on to the gold leaf.

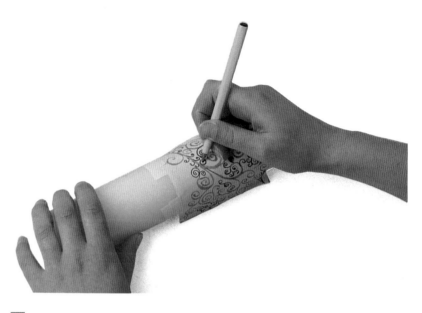

YOU WILL NEED
tracing paper
felt-tip pen
sheets of gold leaf
candle
masking tape
scissors
ballpoint pen or blunt-ended
  instrument

1 Draw your design on to tracing paper (the sheets from between the gold leaf transfer are ideal for this purpose because they match the gold leaf exactly in size).

2 Position a sheet of gold leaf transfer, gold side against the candle, and fix it firmly in place with strips of masking tape. Place the tracing paper with your design over the gold leaf. Fix it lightly in place with masking tape so that you can lift it off and reposition it later. Draw over the pattern with a ballpoint pen – there is no harm in embellishing your basic design at this stage if you want to.

3 Peel back the gold leaf transfer, checking that all the pattern has been successfully transferred. If necessary, replace it and trace parts again.

4 Using fresh sheets of gold leaf, and re-using your tracing paper design, repeat all the above until a gold pattern has been applied all over the candle. As more of the candle becomes decorated try not to stick masking tape on to areas where the pattern has already been applied.

TEMPLATES

*These templates are used in some of the projects in
the book. You can trace them direct from the page
and enlarge them to the size you want.*

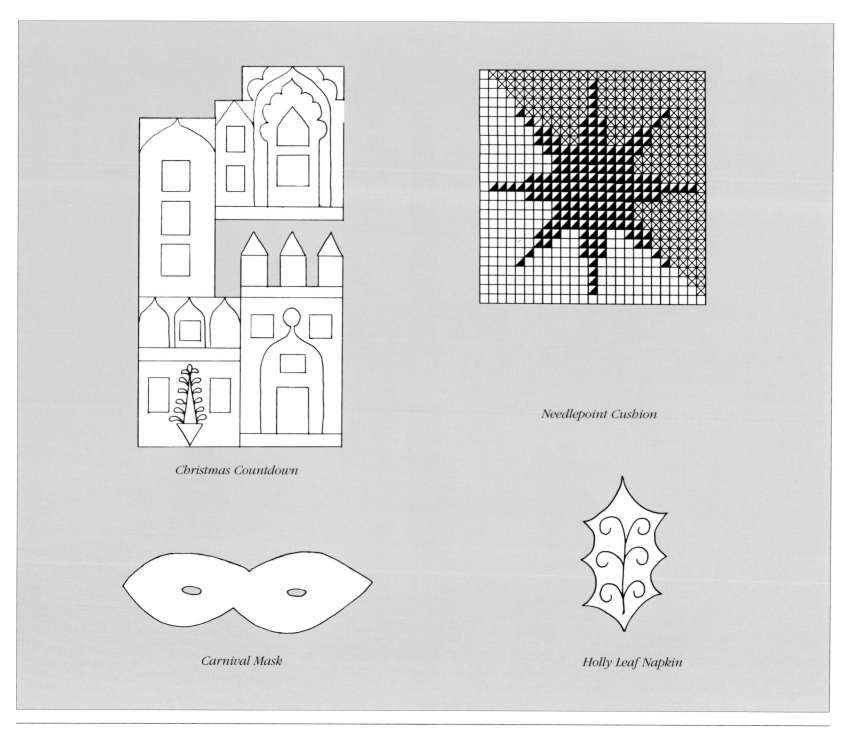

Christmas Countdown

Needlepoint Cushion

Carnival Mask

Holly Leaf Napkin

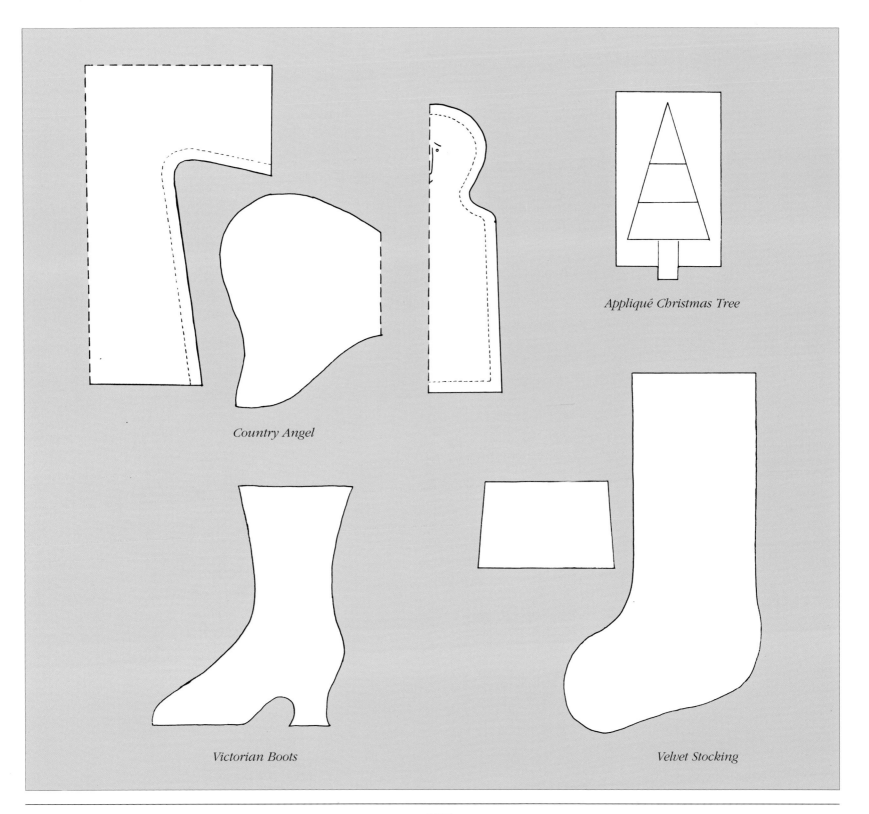

Country Angel

Appliqué Christmas Tree

Victorian Boots

Velvet Stocking

Lacy Silver Gloves

Gold Crown Tablecloth

Collage Gift-wrap and
Christmas Tree Gift Tags

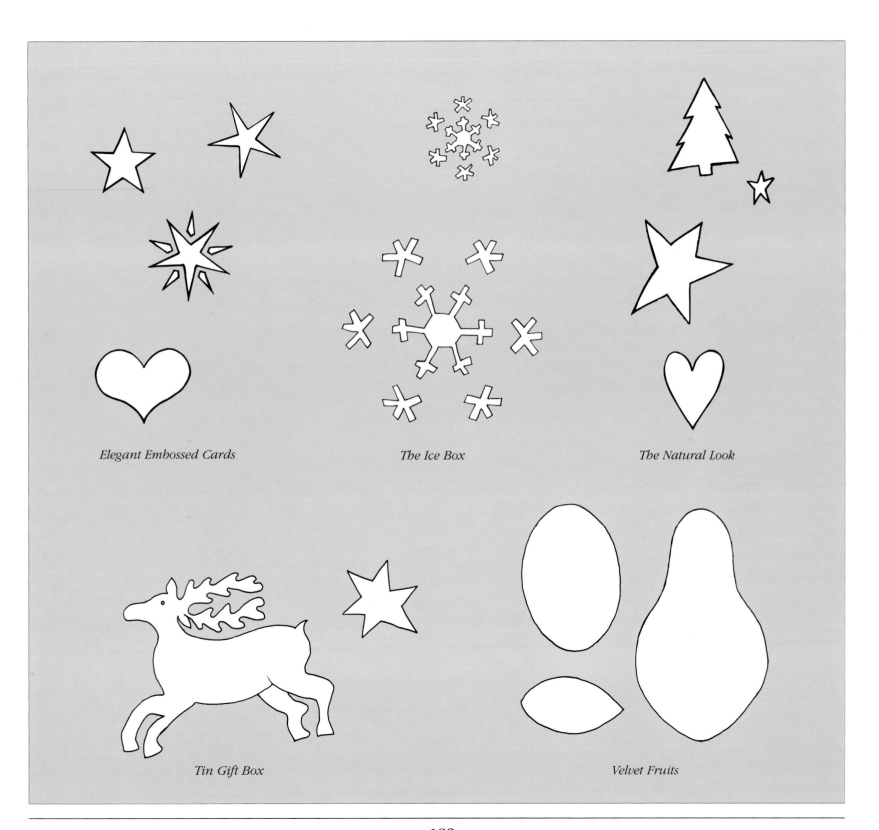

Elegant Embossed Cards

The Ice Box

The Natural Look

Tin Gift Box

Velvet Fruits

INDEX

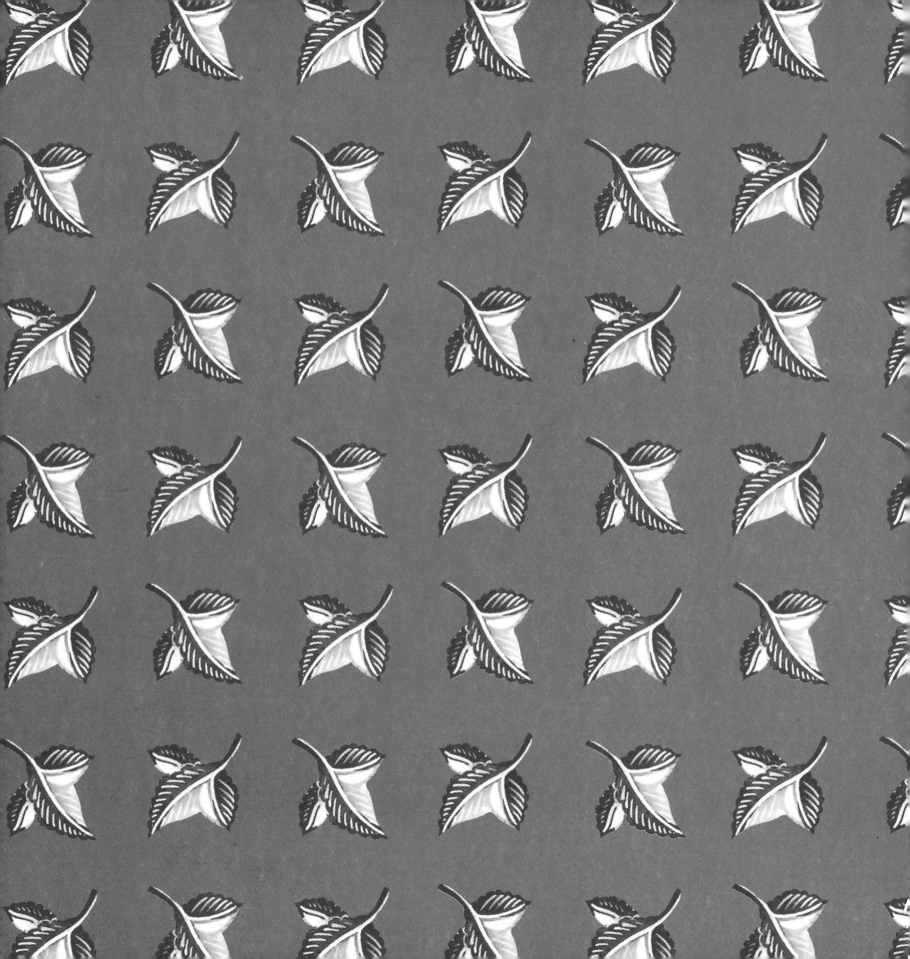

CATHERINE COOKSON COUNTRY

The photograph on the front of the book jacket was taken at the junction of Jarrow Road and Leam Lane near the house where, in 1906, Catherine Cookson was born.

OTHER BOOKS BY
CATHERINE COOKSON

NOVELS

Kate Hannigan
The Fifteen Streets
Colour Blind
Maggie Rowan
Rooney
The Menagerie
Slinky Jane
Fanny McBride
Fenwick Houses
The Garment
The Blind Miller
Hannah Massey
The Long Corridor
The Unbaited Trap
Katie Mulholland
The Round Tower
The Nice Bloke
The Glass Virgin
The Invitation
The Dwelling Place
Feathers in the Fire

Pure as the Lily
The Mallen Streak
The Mallen Girl
The Mallen Litter
The Invisible Cord
The Gambling Man
The Tide of Life
The Girl
The Cinder Path
The Man who Cried
Tilly Trotter
Tilly Trotter Wed
Tilly Trotter Widowed
The Whip
Hamilton
The Black Velvet Gown
Goodbye Hamilton
A Dinner of Herbs
Harold
The Moth

THE MARY ANN STORIES

A Grand Man
The Lord and Mary Ann
The Devil and Mary Ann
Love and Mary Ann
Life and Mary Ann
Marriage and Mary Ann
Mary Ann's Angels
Mary Ann and Bill

FOR CHILDREN

Matty Doolin
Joe and the Gladiator
The Nipper
Blue Baccy
Our John Willie
Mrs Flannagan's Trumpet
Go Tell It To Mrs Golightly
Lanky Jones
Nancy Nutall and the Mongrel

AUTOBIOGRAPHY

Our Kate

CATHERINE
COOKSON
COUNTRY

CATHERINE
COOKSON

HEINEMANN : LONDON

William Heinemann Ltd
10 Upper Grosvenor Street, London W1X 9PA

LONDON MELBOURNE TORONTO
JOHANNESBURG AUCKLAND

Conceived and produced by
Pilot Productions Ltd
59 Charlotte Street, London W1P 1LA

First published 1986

Copyright © Pilot Productions Ltd, 1986
Contributions by Catherine Cookson
Copyright © Catherine Cookson, 1986

ISBN 0 434 14254 9

Typeset by Dorchester Typesetting
Limited, Dorchester, Dorset
Originated by Bright Arts,
Hong Kong
Printed and bound in Great Britain
by Purnell Book Production Limited,
Paulton, Bristol

Pilot Productions wish to join with the author in thanking all the people who have
helped in the research and preparation of the book, in particular Professor Norman
McCord of Newcastle University for his enthusiasm for the project and considered
views on the history of the region; Anthea Zeman, Dee Dudgeon, Sarah Knowling, and
Carol Manderson for their editorial research; Doris Johnson and Keith Bardwell of the
Central Library at South Shields for their editorial advice and picture research; Posy
Harvey for her picture research; and Safu-Maria Gilbert for her design assistance.

We wish to thank all the picture sources, which include the BBC Hulton Picture
Library, the Beamish North of England Open Air Museum, the Bede Gallery, the
Borough of South Tyneside, John Cornwell, Jimmy Donald, Brian Duffy/the Daily
Express, Gateshead Libraries and Arts Department, the Gibson Collection, the
Newcastle Journal, the Newcastle University Library, North Tyneside Libraries
and Arts Department, the Northumberland Record Office, Paul Perry,
Vince Rea, Fred Mudditt, Edward Cowen, and the South Shields Gazette.
While every effort has been made to trace copyright sources,
Pilot Productions would be grateful to hear from any unacknowledged copyright holders.

Contents

In the garden of our house at Langley.

Foreword by Tom Cookson

'How do you do? Do you fence?'

I was being introduced by my landlady to her daughter Kitty McMullen; and I can still hear those words being spoken.

The voice was strong; it was vibrant with life. I had heard nothing like it before. No, I hadn't overlooked that this girl, this woman, was beautiful; but it was the personality through the voice that was affecting me.

The next day, on a trumped-up excuse, I called at her home. Would she like to go to the pictures? Yes, she would.

From then on, the more I saw of her the more I reflected: my landlady was a working-class woman from the North-East. Nothing surprising in that. Yet her daughter was living in . . . no, was the owner of what had been described by the estate agent as a 'gentleman's residence'; and what is more, she spoke in a manner which, in those days, would have been said befitted such a residence. Her voice sounded cultured: she articulated correctly; there was no deliberate effort whatsoever about her pronunciation. And there was something else strange to my ear, a lilt or inflection, an inheritance from the North, that added to its charm, at least for me.

From that very first meeting we have talked, or rather at the beginning she talked and I listened; and my admiration for her became threaded with amazement.

At University I had read Mathematics; before that, for the Higher School Certificate, I had studied not only Mathematics but also Latin and French. And perhaps from this my own reading can be gauged. But here I was, listening to a person who had left school before she was fourteen and who seemed to be consumed with a desire for learning; and (again to my surprise) to such an extent that she was wanting to discuss Voltaire's *Candide*. And yet the reason was soon apparent: she had felt herself to be alone in a fight against superstition, bigotry and intolerance. And she has never given up the fight.

It is as well to remember the period. This was the 1930's: this woman had, since she was twenty-three, been managing the laundry of Hastings Workhouse, having to supervise eleven paid staff and up to thirty inmates as well as a share of the daily casuals or tramps from the road, and at the same time she was endeavouring to run and to develop a home for epileptics.

That was the intention; but she was also willing to take a guest or two, and because, during my summer vacation, her mother had returned to the North-East, I became one of those guests. To me, the work and responsibility this young woman took on was mind boggling.

And yet, somehow she found the time to write; in fact, she had been writing for some years, in any spare time she had, during her dinner break in the laundry and often, bleary-eyed, in bed at night.

One day she presented me with evidence of her efforts. I was with her on the landing of The Hurst, her 'gentleman's residence', and she opened the door of the linen cupboard and took out a number of notebooks and a stack of sheets of paper all covered with pencilled writing, and handed them to me. They were short stories and sketches of life in the workhouse; and now, looking back, I realise they were written very much in the style of her recently published *Hamilton* series.

It should also happen that another guest was a TB patient, a man in his late thirties who, unfortunately, was soon to die, and much of his time was spent in reading and writing. Kitty had often had discussions with him, and she looked upon him as an 'intellectual', a word much used then. One day she asked him to read some of her work. It was a tentative approach she made, but behind it must have been a great longing for a few words of praise. But none was forthcoming. At that time she knew nothing about a man's egoism; her delving into Freud and Jung and the philosophies had yet to come.

Without more to do, she collected together every piece of writing from that cupboard and she burned the lot. I cringe when I think of all that humour and pathos that went up in flames.

Yet this did not stop her scribbling, as she termed her writing: nothing in the world could have done that then; and certainly nothing can do that today, not even age. She carried out then, as she still does today, her own advice to would-be writers: write something every day.

In her early twenties she had read *John O' London's*

The second question she asked me was, 'Do you fence?' Catherine is third from the left.

Weekly and *T.P. & Cassell's*; she had later also read *Books & the Man* by Sidney Dark, the editor of *John O'London's*; and for her, at that time, this volume was as important as *Lord Chesterfield's Letters To His Son* had been earlier. It whetted her appetite.

We were married in June 1940, and within a month the school was evacuated to St Albans, and for the first time in her life Kitty had leisure in which to read. We had found a flat opposite the public library, and she made out a list of more than 100 titles of books she must read, over the years, of course. She would not wish me to name them: I can only say the list was a comprehensive one in that it ranged over English Literature from Chaucer to the 1920s, a list which filled me with a form of envy in that I realised just how much I had kidded myself in the past with regard to my own knowledge of literature.

As in everything else she tackles, she persevered working through that colossal list. Even today this spirit is still exemplified in so many everyday ways: for example, she will answer all the awkward letters first. Get them out of the way, she says; maintaining that it is better to tackle obstacles straightaway, otherwise mountains invariably grow out of molehills. Most of us recite proverbs: she acts on them, and in doing so is enabled to get through an inordinate amount of work. To her, work is the essence of being; not the type of work, be it what might be termed lowly, or be it intellectual, it is work itself.

And it is this same drive probably that makes her read

time and time again Plato's *Apologia* on the trial and death of Socrates, for here, she says, is someone who stuck to his principles even unto death.

And of course, the development of her character has been fully in accord with that laid out by Lord Chesterfield for his son in his celebrated *Letters*. These were grasped by her at an earlier age, and they have been her bible ever since. In bed, at night, she will still occasionally read aloud to me one of these letters; and we will discuss it, and in doing so, I, too, have come to realise the wealth of knowledge of one's fellow man, still applicable today, that can be gleaned from Chesterfield's *Letters*.

In order to press on with her reading, she kept it to a chronological order: so that after much sweating she came to the nineteenth century and the Romantic Movement poets and writers. These immediately kindled the imaginative spirit that was already present within her: she was away from the critical, reason and wit, which she hadn't fully enjoyed, and was with imagination, humour and pathos, which was to form the basis of her own writing.

Had she been born twenty or more years later than she was, she would undoubtedly have profited from the formal education that would then have been available: 'winning a scholarship' to High School, and then proceeding to University; and even being the age she is, had she been born in better circumstances in the sense that books would have been readily to hand, as well as guidance from educated people around her, she would have taken full advantage of both. In either set of circumstances, having this urge within her to write, she would, at some time, have studied the form of the novel and its development, and then written accordingly. But she had neither advantage, and so had perforce to be self-educated. However, because of this her natural creativity was not channelled, as it might have been, along lines dictated by others. In consequence, she does not analyse and interpret, as the modern aspiring novelist might be guided to do, she constructs and describes through characters placed in particular environments.

In these days of advertising, she is often classified as a romantic novelist, which she certainly is not; at least in the loose way in which this word romantic is today applied to novels; she is a story-teller. And one must again

We were married in June, 1940.

remember her upbringing in the years prior to and during the First World War: no wireless – this came in the 1920s – no T.V.; only reading, if possible; but certainly there was the listening to tales told and retold by members of the family, detailing events which had occurred much earlier, perhaps going back even to her great-grandmother's time before the 1850s. And this only child amongst adults, with her imagination and sponge of a mind, would be transposing all she was hearing into pictures.

This it was that enabled her to tell the tale, and in her own way. And she has developed this into a highly skilled talent which, today, brings pleasure, not just to thousands, but to millions of readers throughout the world, and to many of them an understanding of themselves or perhaps of their near ones. And such discerning people would deny that she is a romantic writer. Her stories do not bring in a realism in which the worst is taken for granted, but a realism in which love, caring and compassion appear, and most certainly hope. And this type of realism does exist, as well as the other. If a character struggles against the odds in order to succeed, and this is called romance, then so be it; it is but a reflection of Kitty's own life, and that has certainly been real enough.

Apart from the long years of reading, study and discussion required of her in order to fit herself to write the stories that were presenting themselves to her, she still had to become conversant with the history of the nineteenth century, and to study this she was helped by those marvellous 'History story-tellers' G. M. Trevellyan and Arthur Bryant. In addition, she has been through many of the books and booklets that abound in this part of the country and which deal with coal, iron, lead, glass, farming, and the railways.

The writer she is today stems from the years of study behind her. And it is well to note that from 1945 right through to the middle sixties she was fighting out of a breakdown. As she herself says, the extrovert was fighting the inferiority complex.

Eventually the great day for her, and for me, arrived when the University of Newcastle upon Tyne informed her that they wished to confer on her the Honorary Degree of Master of Arts.

She has given much to charities and to hospitals, and to the University itself, particularly to the teaching side of the hospitals, and so it rather worried her that it might be this which had prompted the University's offer. She is well-known, if not famous, throughout most of the world. But this means nothing to her; it does not register: a letter from Japan, or an enquiry from Yugoslavia just makes her shake her head. However, at Congregation, the University Orator made plain that the degree was being conferred for her work dealing with the every day lives and vicissitudes of the people of this Northern area of England.

I had had no hesitation that she should accept. I, and only I, knowing all that has been here explained, considered her a fit and proper person to be adjudged worthy to receive this degree. She had earned it through her years of study; and she has earned it for proving to me that education begins after you leave University.

Had her autobiography *Our Kate*, begun in 1956 and published in 1969, not been written, had she not laid herself bare to the world, Kitty would have been accepted as a highly educated and intelligent woman; but since its publication she has continually been portrayed as the illegitimate child of a drunken mother, who left school at fourteen; in other words, as uneducated, with the unasked question always there: how then can she write novels?

This is why I have written this side of her life, a side known only to me, in order to answer this same question. I hope I have done so.

T.C. 1985

Introduction

When did I first begin to read and write? I can't recall the time when I could not read. There was the *Chatterbox Annual*, then *Rainbow Comic* every week and *Tiger Tim's Weekly*. The first book I owned was Grimms' *Fairy Tales*. I must have been about eight at the time. But at what age did I advance to Charles Garvice, Ethel M. Dell, and Ruby M. Ayres? Odd, but I did not read Elinor Glyn at this period. I was twenty when her *The Career of Catherine Bush* led me to Chesterfield and real reading. Yet I did read *T. P. & Cassell's Weekly* and *John O'London* during my workhouse years, and the impression I got from these papers was that there was a different world somewhere in which the Sitwells lived.

Elinor Glyn was banned by the Catholic Church. I was a strong Catholic in my teens and must have stupidly made my views verbal in the workhouse mess room, for there, as if placed by the hand of the devil, I found in my room *The Career of Catherine Bush*. I was tempted, and I fell. And in the middle of the story there were these enlightening words spoken by the Duchess to her secretary: 'The first essential of a lady is to be well read and the book you must get on which to base your education is *Lord Chesterfield's Letters To His Son*.'

Oh my! What a revelation. And what an irruption those words caused in the breast of Katie McMullen, for, although she was well aware that she was bound towards a writing career, and she longed to be a writer, an amusing one, there was something she desired even more, and that was to be a lady and to speak correctly. So I flew to the South Shields library – and it was the first time I had entered a library – and I took out the tomes of *Lord Chesterfield's Letters To His Son*; and they blew me from the narrow rivulet of my existence into the broad ocean of knowledge in which I've been swimming ever since.

Yet on looking back, I seem to have been treading water all the time, for the more I read and the more I learned, the wider the ocean seemed to become, and my regret now when the far bank is coming into view is I have learned so little. Yet I know that not one minute spent with Chesterfield was wasted time.

I have never wasted time, no matter how I have felt.

Having now to spend a great part of my time in bed, I have to be feeling very ill indeed not to be working on a story: taping it, revising it, deleting chunks of it – a most necessary art I learnt early – or answering my mail that gets heavier every day.

Katie McMullen Country

This book is called *Catherine Cookson Country* but I think it should have been called *Katie McMullen Country*, because Katie has been writing since she was eleven years old.

Altogether, I love my husband for many reasons, one

John McMullen with Rose, me grandma, and their son, Jack. Though he was my step-grandfather, as a child in East Jarrow I was known as old John's grand-bairn.

being that he made an illegitimate legitimate by giving me his name. Yet, I still wish I'd had my books published under Katie McMullen. Although that wasn't my name, not even a grandfather's name, but that of a step-grandfather, nevertheless, it is the name that holds for me all my early years. Those years that made me what I am. Catherine Cookson is merely a cloak covering the mind that developed during that raw period which harboured the inherited qualities and traits of Our Kate . . . and of *him*, traits of the one at times embarrassing those of the other, but all going towards the making of Katie McMullen.

So why did I want to get away from her and my early environment? Why did I lie and deny her and it? Was it simply because of the dream that I had been fathered by a so-called gentleman? Or was it the latent artist in me striving to turn my eyes to exterior beauty and softer, wider horizons from those grim, grimy, dock-bound river towns? Or was it really to escape from Kate? . . . Here, in my eighty-first year I still do not know. But what I do know is that all my hoodwinking could not cover up that girl from East Jarrow, and it took a breakdown to make me recognise her and the background that had forged her and fostered her talents.

So why didn't I give the name that portrayed my real self to this talent? Perhaps, as today, I was just so grateful to the man who gave me his name and behind whom I thought I could hide my real identity.

Perhaps a further reason why this book should have been called *Katie McMullen Country* is that, of the sixty-four books I have had published, only one is set wholly in an area outside that of the North-East, that is *The Fen Tiger* written while on a boat trip on the Fenland rivers and published under the pseudonym of Catherine Marchant.

Looked at from a distance, it seems impossible to write sixty-three stories about the same place, many set in shipyard, mining, and agricultural areas. Surely if you've read one you've read the lot? Well, there is a reason, I suppose, why I write solely about this small and esoteric part of the country, and I can best explain it by relating a true incident. I was walking along London Road in St Leonards in Sussex – I lived in Hastings for forty-six years

– when I saw a lady coming towards me with a finger pointing. I didn't know her. She looked a county type: tweeds, brogues, a Henry Heath hat and a collar and tie. I imagined she must be looking at someone behind me; but no, she stopped dead in front of me and, her finger still pointing, she said, 'Ah! Mrs Cookson the regional writer!' I had not before heard myself referred to as a regional writer. And then she went on in her high-falutin voice, 'I've read your books, but, you know, I've been made to wonder why you must always write about the North-East. Can't you write about any other place but that North-East? Why don't you write a book about Hastings and St Leonards? Look at the wonderful things that have happened here, especially in Hastings. There was the building of the castle, and the discovery of the caves; there were the smugglers; and there's the fishing fleet. Not forgetting 1066, mind you! Can't you write about any other place but that North-East?'

You know, it's very odd how you can come to hate somebody in two minutes flat.

I don't know what I said to that lady but I do know that when we parted I stumped away, thinking: write about any other place but the North-East, I'll show her. I can write about any place I put my mind to.

So I set about proving this to the lady, whoever she was. I got in touch with the men in the fishing fleet: I went round the boats; I learned about the wholesale buying and selling of fish; I rummaged through the ship-chandler's store. And then I set to work.

At this time I was still writing in longhand; in fact, I wrote my first sixteen books in longhand, the writing of each one taking me a year to accomplish. But one day, after having been on this story for six months, I suddenly stopped because I knew it was no good: I had to face up to the fact that the only thing in the story that had any guts was the fish. I was a regional writer; I couldn't write with any strength about any other place but that dirty backward North-East, as the lady had implied.

Why?

What's bred in the bone, they say; but in my case it was what I had soaked up during those twenty-two years spent in and around East Jarrow, Jarrow and South Shields. Like a great sponge I'd taken it all in: the character of the

people; the fact that work was their life's blood; their patience in the face of poverty; their perseverance that gave them the will to hang on; their kindness; their open-handedness; their narrowness; their bigotry, for there were those who couldn't see beyond the confines of the county of Durham, in fact little beyond Shields and Jarrow: to many a Shields man, a Sunderland man was an enemy; and, as I brought out in *Pure as the Lily*, a North Shields man would treat a South Shields man as a poaching foreigner should he cross the river to look for work . . . And the women. Stoics would be a better name to give to the females of that time, my early time, because for most of them along those river banks it was grind in one way or another from Monday morning till Sunday night.

Of course there was the upper working class and the lower middle class. I knew them too. Did I not work for them? Only for a short period, it's true, for there was

Like a great sponge I'd taken it all in: the character of the people; the fact that work was their life's blood; their patience in the face of poverty; their perseverance, their kindness, and their open-handedness; their narrowness and their bigotry . . . I couldn't write with any strength about any other place.

something in me that objected to servitude, that kind of servitude. And I hope my short experience with mistresses taught me how not to be one.

This, then, must be the reason why I cannot write about any other place but the North-East and why this North Country idiom – I rarely use dialect – is translated into foreign languages. How on earth do they translate 'I'll skelp the hunger off you', or, 'He's got a slate loose', or, to use stronger language, 'Bugger me eyes to hell's flames!'? But they manage to do so, and in seventeen different

languages, and I'm told that every book I've written is still being published and still selling all over Western Europe. This from the child who left school when she was thirteen. At what period during that year I don't know, but after a fall in the schoolyard something happened to my hip, and there I was, free from school.

When I discovered the beauty of words

In all, I attended four schools, starting at Simonside when I was four and a half. This school was situated in what, at that time, was called the country. I was happy there; but before I was eight, my granda commanded that I be taken away in order 'to learn the faith'. And so for a few months I attended The Meases school at East Jarrow, before being sent to the Catholic school at High Jarrow. After a year here, I was sent to St Peter and Paul's, Tyne Dock.

What did I learn there that would have gone towards making me a writer, because out of the six hours a day of education almost two were taken up with religion, and the rest, in general, with the three R's and sewing? I used to say I learnt nothing there; but I was wrong, I learnt poetry there. Miss Barrington, big Miss Barrington, kind Miss

The South Shields ferry, 1890: 'A waste of good coppers . . . I almost had to swim back. When we said we were from Jarrow, why man, you'd have thought we'd said we'd come from Russia to start another revolution.' Pure as the Lily

Barrington, and the younger Miss Caulfield who had taught me in High Jarrow, they both recognised that I was quick to learn poetry.

I can see myself standing on the mat on a winter's night entertaining me granda, Our Kate, and likely a lodger or two, and me doing me turn:

'Had I but served my God with half the zeal I served my King, he would not in mine age have left me naked to mine enemies.'

On and on it would go. Eeh! I was clever; at least so I had thought when Miss Barrington, pointing to the blackboard and looking at me, had said, 'Who wrote those words, Katie?'

'A fella called Shakespeare, Miss.'

Then I would follow this up on the mat with:

'There was a sound of revelry by night,
And Belgium's capital had gather'd then

Her beauty and her chivalry, and bright
The lamps shone o'er fair women and brave men;
A thousand hearts beat happily; and when
Music arose with its voluptuous swell,
Soft eyes looked love to eyes which spake again,
And all went merry as a marriage bell;
But hush! hark! a deep sound strikes like a rising knell!'

Yes, I did learn something at St Peter and Paul's, Tyne Dock: I learned the beauty of words, words I couldn't spell, or even understand. But there was the sound of them, the lilt of them, the pictures they conjured up in my mind. And so it was odd that, feeling for poetry as I did in those early years, my taste should waver from it, if not fall away altogether, and turn to the prose style, the story that had long lines.

Today, what I dabble in I do not call poetry but prose on short lines, because in those early years I formed an opinion of what I expect from poetry, and knew that I myself could neither aspire to produce anything acceptable to that opinion nor enjoy anything that fell below the standard instilled into me by Miss Barrington and the younger Miss Caulfield.

Making people laugh . . . or cry

I have been published now for thirty-seven years, and from the very beginning I have had what one would call fan-mail, and it's some long time now since it reached at least three thousand letters a year. But it was following the publication of my autobiography *Our Kate* that began the spate of so many different types of letters from so many different types of people. I imagine it was because my own life had touched on so many different aspects, including illegitimacy, drink, poverty, exploitation as a child, miscarriages, a breakdown with its myriad fears, and an inherited blood disease. This was why, I suppose, people identified with me: one or another of these things had plagued their lives too. And so, for many I became a mother confessor and, in some cases, a psychiatrist, which I must admit was heavy going . . . and still is, for it is difficult to answer questions when you do not know the answers.

When I read in a letter, 'I am devastated, and feel I'm going into a breakdown, because you see, I can't bear children,' I can certainly write back and say, 'My dear, I

The classroom of a Tyneside school of the period (1910). I used to say I learnt nothing at school; but I was wrong, I learnt poetry there. 'Some clever people would dissect it until it was gutless,' said Jimmy. 'Poetry is observation, Felton; observation put in a crucible and the essence that is drained from it is a something we can only describe as poetry . . . You, boy, have been given some essence; nurture it.' Pure as the Lily

know all about that devastation,' etcetera. Yet, it's odd that I've never really brought that particular feeling into a story, because in doing so I knew I should have to show a side of me that I want to forget.

I am a kind person, I wouldn't hurt a fly, in fact there was a period in my life, an intensely painful period, when even bluebottles, which I hate, would be assisted through an open window into life and liberty for their span. So how could this kind, caring, loving individual have the terrible desire to pick up a baby from a pram outside a shop and run off with it? But worse still to take hold of that baby and dash it to the ground. How often have I had to rush home to vomit and fling myself on the bed in an effort to beat this terrible urge out of me.

I lost my fourth baby in 1945 during the first year of the breakdown, and this baby syndrome kept with me for a long time afterwards, in fact, it was many years, ten, fifteen, before I could hold a child in my arms: I no longer had the desire to harm a child, but I still couldn't bear to hold one.

Oh yes, missis, I sympathise with you in being unable to bear a child.

And how does one work out of a breakdown?

Yes, how does one work out of it? Those who write to me asking me for help in this way have read *Our Kate*. This account was begun in 1956, the year my mother died, but it took twelve years to complete for publication for I rewrote it eight times, deleting a little bitterness at each attempt. And so it was 1968 before it was published.

In it I describe my own breakdown, and because I had already written a number of novels, it was imagined I must have got over it.

It must therefore be depressing for them when they are told that my breakdown lasted for fully ten years and more.

During this period I read every book (dealing with nerves) that I could get my hands on, and many on philosophy because I knew that I had to try to alter my way of thinking. So I aimed, not only to write myself out of it, but to talk myself out of it. I started to give talks; I got onto Woman's Hour; I was asked to 'open things'. But one thing I couldn't do, I couldn't stand up and talk, I had to sit. My excuse was I had rheumatism; you didn't own up to nerves when speaking to the W.I. or to Business and Professional Women in an endeavour to make them laugh . . . .

Odd that, but my main object in life at that time was to make people happy, make people laugh . . . or cry. Yet for most of the time I myself was in the depths and was desperately trying to work myself out of it by physical labour: I would cut down trees, haul them to the block, then saw them up – we had moved house to Loreto and started adding pieces of woodland that needed clearing – I would saw for at least two hours a day, then cart the wood into the house to keep the fires going. I also looked upon this as a form of recreation from all my other chores. In between times I cooked and I cleaned the house, did the washing . . . by hand – I didn't even have a dryer; I was once again saving every penny, for a certain purpose, to acquire £5,000 in order that Tom could retire early, as he

was tortured with migraine. Impossible now to imagine that around 1960 one could live on that amount augmented by a small pension – and, of course, I wrote.

The aim was to fill every minute so that I should not have time to think. Fourteen hours a day, seven days a week was the pattern. In between times, of course, I had to go into town to do shopping. It was then I saw the babies.

One occasion I can look back on and I can laugh about it. Being a schoolmaster's wife, I had to attend functions, such as the boys' and masters' cricket match once a year on the Central Ground. On that day, it was the aim of all wives to appear in their best bib and tucker. And I always tried to excel in this way, altering a dress or retrimming a hat. I favoured large picture hats with veils attached. I recall that I didn't want to go to the cricket match; I didn't like cricket and considered it a waste of time. But there I was, prancing down Queen's Road in a white linen costume, black shoes, black leghorn hat with veil, white gloves and a black bag. And I stopped at the Fifty Shilling Tailors. This is where I had to cross the road in order to enter the cricket field, where Tom was already playing.

Around the shop corner I noticed some men attending to the brickwork and there were a number of loose bricks lying in the gutter. Stopping to wait for a car to pass, I looked down, and there was this full-size pink brick. There were bits and pieces lying around it, they didn't interest me, but that pink brick did. I turned and looked at the Fifty Shilling Tailors' plate glass window, then at the brick again, and I had the strongest desire to pick it up and hurl it through that window.

Why? I don't know, except that it was one of the symptoms of the breakdown: I wanted to hit out at something or someone for the life that had been dealt me up till then, especially for the fact that I'd lost God, in fact, had thrown Him out of my life, together with the Virgin: for what had they done for me and all my praying? Landed me with a breakdown. It is strange how religion tends to simplify one's thinking.

As far as I can remember, one of the workmen came up to this smartly dressed young woman and, laughingly looking down at this brick, said, 'D'you want to take it home with you, missis?' And I answered something to the effect that, 'No, not really; but I could find other uses for it,' and I glanced towards the plate glass window. At this he laughed, while giving me an odd look and commenting, 'Aye, well!' And I laughed. Then I crossed the road and went into the cricket field and sat in the middle of a row of masters and made my near companions laugh at my *sotto voce* remarks on cricket.

Strange that it seemed to be my aim in life to amuse people and make them laugh. I have, I feel, many ingredients of the clown covering the solitary individual, the extrovert with the inferiority complex.

I often wonder, too, what a reader who begs me to help her – or him – out of a breakdown thinks about my advice, to stand in front of a mirror and give herself a damn good swearing at. In bad times, sick with self-pity, I would force myself to do just that, and I always found it to be therapeutic. It was as if Kate would answer me back from the mirror, never saying, 'Snap out of it!' because that's the worst advice anyone could give to another in this state, but, 'Thank God for what you have, lass, a man like Tom, and the fact that you can see, hear, walk, and talk, and that you're still alive. Many a one in their coffin would be glad to change places with you at this minute. So come on, lass, and use your gumption.'

Psychiatrists have a more scientific approach. I tried them, but they never worked like the mirror.

With regard to gumption. I think the greatest insult I have received in my life was being told I hadn't any gumption, and I've never forgiven the medical person who said it. I have always considered I was bred on gumption, having brought over from my birth the vascular disease of telangiectasia with its constant bleeding and accompanying anaemia, the latter state not being helped when I contracted lead poisoning from inhaling white lead during the two years I was pen-painting, and then the gradual deterioration in my spine following on the fall in the school yard – I am not whining, I am merely wondering, if it wasn't gumption that got me over these and other recurring hurdles, I don't know what did – No, I have never forgiven that medico.

Influences in the literary world
Concerning this writing business, I am continually being asked if at the start I knew anyone in the literary world, and was perhaps given a push. The answer is no; I knew no one in the literary world. And I've had help from no

Mrs Cookson, 'the regional writer'.

one, except from my husband, that is practical help. Before him there was Chesterfield, but I'll come to him later. Of course there are two other men, John Smith and John Foster White. John Smith was my first agent and John Foster White my first editor. They are both to this day my very dear friends. But in no way did they help me to get a start, or help me to write; what they did for me was done in the way of business.

The only one who has been of any help to me is Tom. And then I must admit it was a rough passage with him at first, because he was a ruthless critic and many were the nights I cried myself to sleep over his harsh judgement.

Tom is fortunate in being able to spell almost any word that is put before him. He is a mathematician, and he still enjoys his Latin. And so his English, at least when writing, is very good in its grammatical context, never a comma out of place, colons and semi-colons where they should be, verbs, adverbs and adjectives doing their stuff, and predicates affirming what they are meant to affirm. And what does it all amount to? Grammatically correct sentences in which, if I had adapted his style, my Geordie characters would have definitely become gutless as they aimed to speak grammatical English.

As I said in my autobiography, I went along with him for a time because I hated any dissent between us. I studied grammar each day under his tuition, with Fowler's English to my hand when he wasn't there. And what was the result? Certainly not a story that anyone would want to read, but stuff that could be broken up into good essays. As for my flesh and blood Northern characters they wilted under Tommy Cookson's correct but stilted English.

When I first started to write novels, I would tell Tom the story in order to set it in my mind. I would then put it down in longhand; then reassess and correct it, after which he would go over it. It was then that the battle would begin. And I fought him, oh yes, I fought him to do the thing in my own way because I knew my way was right. Yet at the same time I learned a great deal from his stilted English, I learned how to disseminate it as it were, while still using the Northern idiom.

I wrote my first fifteen books in longhand, and then I became troubled with writer's cramp and a frozen shoulder. This was a very painful period and I imagined my writing career to be finished; but Tom suggested I use a tape recorder. And the size of a tape recorder in the early sixties! I didn't know then what a new world was opening up for me, because while talking my Northern characters down I could see them acting: I could feel through my voice their emotions, their laughter, their humour, their sorrows and their joys, and I could catch the element of their origin, the origin that comes from far back and threads the people of this particular area.

A friend, so called, at a dinner party once exclaimed very loudly: 'Oh, Kitty is all things to all men.' I have met a great many men in my time, handsome, nice men, a number among my publishers. But I have never met any man to come up to my husband, and to him and him only I have been all things, wife, mother, mistress, and friend, all things to one man, all 5′ 4½″ of him!

It is now sixteen years since he retired early because of migraine. And from then he took over the cooking and the housekeeping in order to leave me free to do my work. He it is who sees to me when I am ill and on my emergency trips, often in the middle of the night, into Newcastle. He also plays the part of the chauffeur, and definitely that of private secretary, for between us we see to all the fan mail and so much correspondence connected with this writing business, not forgetting the charities that take up a great deal of our time now. Our life is still made up of the seven day week and a twelve or more hour day. And besides all this, Tom can turn his hand to any household job from painting to plumbing, which is really why we have always been able to live in large houses.

If he should go first what I'll do without him God Himself alone knows, I don't. Being six years older than him I could easily will myself to join him.

In the meantime I am writing two books a year, much of it dictated on the recorder from my bed, and as I have, at the moment, nine waiting to go to the publisher, it won't matter if I never write another one.

Having reached this far, I feel I have achieved one thing at least, I have my values right.

Over the last two or three years I've received a number of honours, the latest being the O.B.E. from Her Majesty. Previous to that in importance was the Freedom of the Borough of South Shields, the Honorary degree of M.A. given by the University of Newcastle – I don't know who felt the more honored, myself or Tom; he had always considered me worthy of it – then the Rotary Paul Harris Fellowship, not forgetting the Variety Club of Great Britain Writer of the Year, and the Personality of The North East.

In 1968 I was awarded the Winifred Holtby Prize for The Best Regional Novel of the Year, *The Round Tower*, given by The Royal Society of Literature, and on hearing this I bawled my eyes out. And this weakness was to be my usual reaction to later recognitions.

It was in 1974 that South Shields did me the honour to make me a Freeman of the Borough. I was greatly touched by this at the time because this doesn't often happen to authors. We were living in the South when this was bestowed upon me, and I think it was from then that the

Receiving the Honorary degree of M.A. given by the University of Newcastle.

urge to return crept into me. Yet I made no effort to do so; . it was Tom again who thought I should come home because, as he said, if anything should happen to him I'd be among my ain folk or, on the other hand, it would be better for me to die among my ain folk. Such an encouraging thought.

Over the years I made frequent visits back to the North-East to get the feel of the setting for a new story; and so in '75 we took a house in Jesmond and, having commuted to it on five occasions within a few months, Tom, an Essex man, fell in love with Newcastle, and that clinched the matter.

There is certainly something about this area that gets people. It is fortunate in a way that we don't have it over warm here else the two counties would be swamped.

A thing which seems to puzzle interviewers today is my having become a world famous writer – their words – without the apparent necessary university education. I should really let Tom answer this one because he waxes indignant and eloquent when he tells people that I've read more and perhaps more widely, too, than had I been to university. Of course this is biassed and an exaggerated statement, but I certainly have read a great deal; and this, as I've said so many times, stems from my reading of Chesterfield's *Letters*. What a lot I owe to that gentleman. And how amazed I was to find that everyone didn't acclaim him. Followers of Doctor Johnson, I found, openly sneered at him; so therefore I've never liked Johnson. Prejudice in its turn.

There were times during my striving to be intellectual when I would tactfully bring the conversation round to Lord Chesterfield, and some individual would counter me immediately by saying, 'Oh, Johnson said of Chesterfield that he had the manners of a dancing master and the morals of a whore.'

When this has happened, and it has more than once, I have known immediately that this person has never read anything of Chesterfield and, like many others, has simply picked up the quips of Doctor Johnson.

Chesterfield was a great man: first and foremost he was an educationalist; he was also a diplomat; he was a writer; he was a most eloquent speaker; he was a charmer of women. At first I accepted this trait in him because I imagined him to be a six-footer, terribly handsome, but I

19

couldn't believe it when I first saw his picture, for he was a dwarf of a man, rather ugly, and I understood he had a high squeaky voice. Yet here was a man who could not only charm women, but also hold Parliament enthralled. And what endeared him more than anything to me was his kindness. He left evidence of this in his will. Having allotted some money to his servants he added the following words; 'THESE MEN ARE MY EQUALS IN NATURE, THEY ARE ONLY MY INFERIORS IN FORTUNE.' Tell me of any gentleman in the eighteenth century who would voice such sentiments about his lackeys, because that's what servants were termed in those days, simply lackeys. If I loved him for nothing else I'd love him for that.

Why did he create such a fuss among the Victorians? Simply because he told his son how to deal with women, and in the nicest of terms. This, his illegitimate son, whom he sent touring the world with a tutor at seven years old, became for him a beloved pupil and he poured out his advice and his knowledge on him. And he poured it out on me too. All right, he hadn't a high opinion of women's intellect; likely, because women were clever enough to hide it in those days when men held the power, and that it was wise to know on which side you wanted your bread buttered. And he didn't like laughter. I admit that puzzled me. But then he wasn't exactly God and so was bound to have a few faults.

How delighted I am to this day when I receive a letter from a reader asking me to recommend books on Chesterfield. There have been so many written, but I think I like Willard Connely's *The True Chesterfield* best of all. Only last week a woman wrote, saying, 'Here I am seventy-six and you've opened a new world to me. Why haven't I heard of him before?' And I want to answer back, 'Well, missis, you never read the romantic story of Elinor Glyn's and heard the Duchess's advice to her secretary.'

Child of the Tyne

There is that word, 'romantic'. I don't like it, at least not in the sense it's tacked on to me. This didn't happen until my *Mallen* trilogy was made into a television series. Before that I was what the lady in St Leonards said I was, a regional writer. I can't imagine how anyone could tack the word 'romantic' on to *The Fifteen Streets* or *Colour Blind*, or on any of the others for that matter. Of course there are the Catherine Marchant's. Yet even these, in my estimation, do not fall into the category of romantic drivel.

Why did I write under two names, people ask. Simply because in those early days *Woman's Realm* wanted me to write serials for them: they wanted romances, but with the strength of my writing and my name (because even in those early days I was, fortunately, selling well). I would write stories for them, I said, but not under the name of Catherine Cookson; and so Catherine Marchant was born. John, my agent, thought her up.

Katie Mulholland seems to be the favourite of many readers, and it isn't strange how the idea for that book was born for most of my work stems from an incident in my past.

For instance *Colour Blind*. There was a black man called Black Charlie. He used to stand on the dock bank among the men waiting to be set on the boats, and I understood he was some kind of an interpreter for the foreign sailors who came into the port. He had a family and they lived in Bede Street, somewhere up above Bob's the pawn shop, and like many another man on the bank he witnessed my shame-filled trips to Bob's as I slunk into the front shop or darted up the back lane into the cubicles. I understood he was a very nice man and was well liked. He was known as having a 'respectable family'. I recall his daughters went to St Peter and Paul's at the same time as I did, but I cannot remember speaking to them; I can recall that in my eyes they were superior because me granda 'had a good word for Black Charlie', so he must have been all right.

I know that the family is linked, in my mind, with an incident that happened in the pawn shop. I can recall that there were two women standing in that dark well of a shop and one had put my parcel in because I wasn't of age to pawn and she had received from me a penny for her trouble. And as I was about to leave the shop she stroked my curls and said, 'Eeh! but you have bonny hair, haven't you lass.' And I, lifting my loose auburn hair aside, pointed to the dark thick rim of hair edging the bottom and back of my head, and looking up at her I said, 'That's nearly black, me Da must have been a nigger.' I don't know what age I was but I must have been aware that I had no Da.

Why should I say such a thing? To make them laugh like our Kate did even when she hadn't had a drink? I couldn't have been aware of the implication of my words, I only know I was pleased still to hear their laughter when I was well out of the shop.

Nevertheless, I knew at that time that there was a colour bar relating to the Arabs in Corstorphine Town. A woman had just to be caught looking at an Arab and her name turned to mud. But from those days and feelings, *Colour Blind* was born.

Then *Feathers in the Fire*. Definitely this had its origin in Jackie Halliday's coal cart. Jackie Halliday sat in the middle of the cart shovelling out buckets of coal at tuppence a time. I used to think his legs were buried under the coal, and when there wasn't much coal in the cart I imagined his legs must be sticking through but that I couldn't see them. He lived in Bogey Hill, half a mile away from the New Buildings, East Jarrow. One day I was up there and, crossing a back lane, was this man, this half-man moving over the cobbles on two stumps. I looked at him and he looked at me and the expression on his face was to remain with me for many years, in fact, it seemed to become more vivid with time: the horror on my face must have created the anger and hurt in his. So he became the central character in *Feathers in the Fire*.

And to go back to *Katie Mulholland*. I'm never stuck for a story; before I finish one, another is forming in my mind. But I recall this day in the kitchen of Loreto in Hastings. I was talking to Tom; we were both standing in front of the Aga. We had been outside working and we had come in frozen. He had put the kettle on and we were waiting for it to boil and I said to him, 'I've got this big story in my mind but I still don't know where to place it for the best.' I had been in touch with the two Johns and they were of differing opinions about it because my original idea was to begin it in the Roman times dealing with the occupation of the Wall. And I can see Tom now, lifting the kettle off the hot plate and mashing the tea as he said, 'You're always talking about Palmer's shipyard in Jarrow. Why don't you just bring the story to the last century and set it there.'

YES. YES. Of course. Palmer's shipyard, the life's blood of Jarrow for so long, and although it was now dead I could recall it vividly when it was alive. So Katie Mulholland was born.

Up till then I'd had little luck in being published in paperback. Corgi had turned me down twice – funny that, now I come to think of it, when to date they have sold well over thirty millions – and as yet I hadn't been in the American paperback market either, but a United States publisher reading this story saw how it could be adapted to paperback if, and the 'if' was big. IF it could be cut by one third.

It had been the most difficult story to write in the first place because I had done a great deal of research on Palmer's shipyard. I had been in touch with Sir Charles Mark Palmer's grandson; I had gone into Ellen Wilkinson's *Politics*; and in the end I felt I could speak for the working man . . . and also make pig iron. So the prospect of cutting it by a third daunted me. Yet everyone connected with me at this end saw the possibilities of getting into the American paperback world. And so I set about the cutting, which was much more difficult than writing the story in the first place. But it opened a new era to me: I was, so some people said, discovered.

The previous eighteen years and the seventeen books I had written might never have been. And yet some of my best writing was accomplished in those years: books that I considered were the social history of the North-East, readable social history interwoven into the lives of the people; and it is after all, simply the people who make history whether they are ascending thrones or fighting wars; it is the people who create not only replicas of each other, but atmosphere, environment, and the meat for writers.

And the people of this area have certainly provided me with the meat for my books. I may not be a Shakespeare, an Austen, a Brontë, or a Hardy, the one to whom I am often likened, but I am a product of the Tyneside and, cover me up as you may with the name of 'Cookson', gild me over with my thirty-six years in the scholastic world, O.B.E. and M.A. after my name, I am still a child of the Tyne whose far horizons reached only to Palmer's Shipyard in Jarrow and the sands at South Shields. And isn't it strange that from the wider world into which I escaped I have to return, like the eel to the Sargasso Sea, to die where I began, among my ain folk.

C.C. 1985

Palmer's Shipyard
In the 1850s Charles Mark Palmer's
personal industrial empire largely
called the town of Jarrow into being.
'There's always a chance I'll get set
on at Palmer's.' Rodney Mulholland
in *Katie Mulholland*

My Land

The nineteenth century saw an awesome growth in industrial activity in Tyneside, a development which attracted people to the towns from the countryside like iron filings to a magnet, the patterns of concentration roughly defining the sites of the most commercial Tyneside pits.

Among the most technologically advanced and productive coal mines in the early nineteenth century were Gateshead, Felling, Hebburn, Jarrow and South Shields, an area which forms the focal point of Catherine Cookson Country. The escalating population figures of these towns provide the scale for this incredible story of expansion and social revolution.

	1800	1850	1880
Jarrow	1,566	3,835	37,719
South Shields	11,171	28,292	55,875

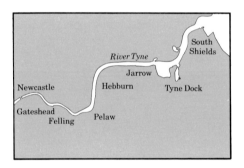

In 1841 the Royal Commission on the Employment of Children reported: 'Within the last ten or twelve years an entirely new population has been produced. Where formerly there was not a single hut of a shepherd, the lofty steam engine chimneys of a colliery now send their columns of smoke into the sky, and in the vicinity a town is called, as if by enchantment, into immediate existence.'

The population increase due to coal mining in the early 1800 s gathered pace in 1850 with the improvement of the river as an international port, the surge of activity in the chemical and glass-making industries, and the revolutions wrought in the ship-building and engineering industries.

South Tyneside, 1859

From a twentieth-century perspective it is almost impossible to imagine the sights, sounds and smells of this new powerhouse of activity as it was being formed.

Difficult too for Annabella Lagrange, who, being a young and impressionable member of the gentry of the nineteenth century, had been protected from the harsher realities of the industrial revolution.

Annabella had grown up in the sanctuary of Redford Hall, situated 'six miles from Newcastle and five miles from South Shields or Jarrow, depending on which path you took at the crossroads. Its grounds extended to sixty acres, ten of which were given over to pleasure gardens, the remainder to the home farm.' There Annabella lived with her father, Edmund Lagrange, owner of a now ailing glassworks, and the woman she thought was her mother, Rosina.

In this extract from *The Glass Virgin*, Annabella is swept through the south Tyneside of 1859, her experiences given a sharp edge when she is brought face-to-face with her real mother in the brothels of the Temple Town/Holborn area – that old, 'cosmopolitan' riverside stretch in which Katie Mulholland once founded a property empire and where *Colour Blind*, a novel of racial discord, is partly set.

George Boston, wealthy friend of Lagrange and unwelcome suitor of Annabella, is in the carriage with them.

The carriage turned out of the drive and on to the rutted road; the bumping disturbed Rosina but delighted Annabella. She looked first to one side and then the other, and everywhere the land rolled away in open fells, showing great sweeps of purple, brown and green. Then of a sudden, into her view came a huddle of

Being thrown out of a job meant destitution for a miner's dependants, whose only option was a makeshift shelter on the fells.

Above Left:
The Ordnance Survey map was published in November, 1864, just five years after Annabella Lagrange made her trip from Redford Hall, which might be said to be located in the area of Ulsworth by Hylton Moor in Durham County. Annabella's trip takes her to Palmer's Shipyard in Jarrow, just west of the chemical works on the map. Thence her route can be traced along the River Don (which becomes the Gut as it crosses the Jarrow Slake), past the site of St Paul's and the Slake itself, through Tyne Dock and into that built-up riverside area (which includes Temple Town) in South Shields.

make-shift shelters constructed from what looked like pieces of furniture, and scattered about them were a number of children who, on the approach of the carriage, ran towards the road.

'Oh, Mama, look! the poor children.'

'Sit back, dear,' said Rosina calmly.

Annabella sat back but she could still see the children running along the high bank keeping apace of the carriage. They were all bare-foot, and like the three distant children in her memory they were dirty and gaunt and none of them were laughing.

Edmund Lagrange now shouted to his coachman, 'Speed her up there!' Then in an undertone to Boston he said, 'Rosier's rabble; another strike. It took the militia to get that lot out; he's filled the village with Irish. There'll be serious trouble one day, mark my words. He can't handle the men, never could, neither he nor his father.' He spoke as one who could handle men.

Two miles further on they passed through Rosier's village. The dust flew up from the horses' hooves and smothered the women standing at the doors of the row of cottages.

There were children here, too, standing at the side of the road and some of them waved and shouted, and Annabella had the desire to wave back, but she knew she mustn't.

Another two miles further on and they entered Jarrow, and Annabella was again sitting on the edge of the seat.

In the past ten years Jarrow had emerged from a pit village and a small boat building community into a bustling, overcrowded town in the making. Two men out of every three had an Irish brogue; fighting and drinking were the order of the day; and the reason for the prosperity that enabled working men to drink frequently was the birth of Palmer's shipyard.

In 1850 there had been between two hundred and fifty and three hundred houses in Jarrow; now in 1859 there were three thousand and builders were working like mad grabbing at the green fields to erect row on top of row of flat-faced single bricked dwellings.

The carriage tour was to take in Palmer's shipyard, so they emerged into Ellison Street, so named after a man who owned a great deal of the land thereabouts. And the horses going at a spanking pace along the street brought women from the communal taps at the corner ends, customers out of shops, and even turned men's heads from their beer drinking to crowd at the public house windows and ask, 'Is it Palmer?' and hear the reply, 'No. Bloody gentry; bloody blood-suckers.'

When they reached the gate of the steelworks, Edmund Lagrange called a halt to the coachman; then standing by the side of the carriage door, he pointed out the great smoking chimneys, the mass of towering iron that was the gantries and cranes, the ships in the river hugging the staiths, and, of all things, a big, black looking boat sailing down the river with the smoke pouring out of a funnel in the middle of her as if the whole erection was on fire.

The wonder of it all struck Annabella dumb, but not pleasingly so. In her ten years the only place she had visited outside the perimeter of the grounds was Durham, and Durham was different from Jarrow; it had a wonderful cathedral standing on a rock towering over the river and it was very imposing and everything looked clean, except some of the men who were usually covered in coal dust and who, she understood, were miners. But this Jarrow, this was a different world; the great ships, the noise, the men scurrying about like ants, and the crowds in the streets all dressed in dark, drab clothes. She had noticed a dreadful thing outside one of the inns; she had actually seen a woman lying in the gutter . . .

The carriage had turned round and once more the horses were galloping down Ellison Street with children running on each side

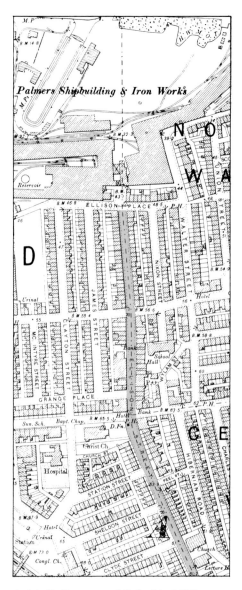

A detail of a map published in 1897, which shows Ellison Street, the route that Annabella followed to Palmer's.

of the carriage now, shouting in what sounded like a foreign language.

'Hoy a ha'penny oot!'

When no money was forthcoming the words, still unintelligible, took on a derisive offensive tone.

'Gan on, ya big gob skites!'

'Aal dressed up like farthin' dolls.'

'Sittin' up a height like bloody stuffed dummies.'

When Armorer's whip licked along one side of the carriage the children shied away, except one who yelled up at him, 'Go on you fat-arsed lackey. Come doon offa that an' Aa'll rattle your cannister for you. Go on, ya stink.' The boy hung on to the door of the carriage now and yelled at the company. 'Ya all stink; ya rift up me belly like a bad dinner.'

All this while Edmund Lagrange had been talking to George Boston as if the carriage was running through open deserted country and Rosina sat straight-backed, her eyes directed towards the coachman; but Annabella and Stephen stared at the children, Stephen with an amused smile on his lips, and Annabella straight-faced and troubled, especially when Armorer kept using his whip.

The carriage now passed the expanse of land where disused salt pans lined the banks of the River Don; it passed the church where St Bede had preached and taught; it crossed the river by a stone bridge, then on past the Jarrow Slacks, and down the long country road with farms and fields on one side and the River Tyne on the other, and so into Tyne Dock, where on the third of March in that very year the new docks had been opened.

Edmund Lagrange pointed derisively at the huge gates as they passed and remarked to George Boston, 'A white elephant if ever there was one; a new dock and the river so silted up you can walk across to North Shields at low tide! It's ludicrous, don't you think? Then they grumble about Newcastle getting all the shipping. Ten years they've been making that dock; you would have thought the '54 business would have deterred them, but no, somebody got an idea and they must carry it through.'

Rosina looked at her husband as he talked. Anyone who didn't know him would think that he had the town and its affairs at heart. His reference to '54, which Mr Boston likely knew nothing about, was the terrible day when sixty-three ships which were seeking refuge in the river were wrecked and many, many lives lost, and all in sight of people standing on the shore. But Edmund didn't really care if the town sank or swam; he talked to impress Mr Boston, and there could be only one reason why he wanted to impress this young man, for Mr Boston was a common man and ungainly in both manner and speech. She wondered to what extent her husband was in this young man's debt and what hope Mr Boston held out of being repaid.

Her eyes widened a little when her husband now directed the coachman away from the main road which led into South Shields and along by the river and through what she knew to be a most disreputable area which led to The Gut and finally to the Market Place. When he gave further instructions that Armorer should walk the horses she felt a protest rising in her but checked it before it escaped her lips. Annabella, she felt, had seen enough of sordid living for one day, but what she had witnessed in Jarrow would be nothing to what she would see if they went through Temple Town, which was obviously where Edmund was directing the carriage.

Armorer, too, was obviously surprised at his master's orders for he repeated, 'Through Temple Town, Sir?'

'Yes, yes; we'll see more of the river that way, and the ships.' He turned to Annabella. 'You'd like to see the ships, wouldn't you?'

'Yes, Papa.'

But she didn't see the ships for some time. What she saw were rough looking people, poor people, and lots of children, and mostly bare-footed. The towns seemed full of poor children, the whole world seemed full of bare-foot children. Of course, the weather was warm; perhaps that was why they were without shoes or stockings.

Sometimes she herself longed to take off her shoes and stockings and run in the grass with her feet bare, that is, when it was warm; but perhaps these children had no shoes and stockings on when it was cold, wet, snowing. She said to no one in particular, 'They have no shoes or stockings on,' and her papa answered, 'They don't need them, my dear; the soles of their feet are like leather.'

'Really!' She moved her head from side to side and smiled slightly at her father. His answer was very reassuring.

But the further the carriage went into the old town the more she became aware of the drabness, the dirt, the stench. All the people were odd looking. Perhaps, she surmised, they were from foreign lands. Then an awful thing happened; she saw a lady empty a chamber pot from an upstairs window and Armorer had to jerk the horses into a gallop to avoid the contents. She was amazed that the lady had aimed the filth at them and that she continued to laugh aloud.

Looking at her mama after this incident she saw that her face was very white and her mouth tight, as when she was angry. Her

Tyne Dock, 1890: 'It was one of those dull, cold days that you get in the North when the sky seems to be lying on the top of the ships' masts and the whole world is grey.' Our Kate

father swore, but Mr Boston laughed and when she looked at Stephen she was surprised that he, too, was almost laughing.

They now entered a street named Crane Street. It was facing the river and she didn't know whether to look at the ships or towards the pavement for a lady was walking in step with the carriage. She was different from all the other ladies she had seen because she was wearing gay coloured clothes. The lady was looking at her, staring at her, and when they were some way down the street the lady smiled, and she smiled back at her; then her gaze was diverted from the lady to a high window where there were a lot of ladies, and they were hanging over the sill and shouting. All their faces looked merry and happy and she saw her papa look up at them and smile slightly, and so did Mr Boston. But her mama was looking at the lady who was walking by the carriage; but the lady

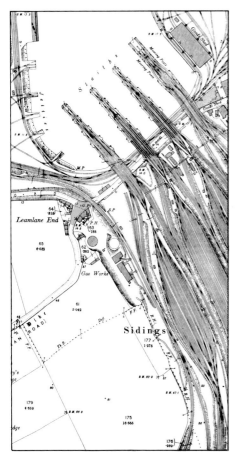

1894 is the date of this map which shows clearly the position of Leam Lane in relation to the 'five great slime-dripping arches' of Tyne Dock. Number 5 Leam Lane, where I was born, was on the east side, almost opposite the houses shown in the picture on the front of the book jacket. Just beyond the row of houses lay the gas-works: I used to run around the rim of the gasometer, fascinated and frightened by the foot of water dividing it from the enormous tank.

wasn't looking at her mama, she was looking at her. She had never seen a lady before with such a colourful face, her eyes were very dark and her lips and her cheeks were very red . . .

Tyne Dock and East Jarrow, 1906

Between the era described in *The Glass Virgin* and 1906 the population in Northumberland grew from 300,000 to 600,000; in County Durham it increased from 390,000 to 1,190,000 in the same period of fifty years.

I was born on June 20th, 1906, in Number 5 Leam Lane, at the bottom of Simonside Bank, Tyne Dock. Tyne Dock is, or was at the time, just what it says, a dock on the river Tyne. Where the river flows into the North Sea the towns of North and South Shields stand, one on each bank. South Shields is connected with Tyne Dock; up river Jarrow, Hebburn, Pelaw, Felling and Gateshead all follow; on the other side of the river is North Shields, then follows Howdon, Wallsend, Willington Quay and Newcastle. Both banks were lined with shipyards, chemical works and factories.

Simonside Bank was just a cluster of houses within three minutes walk, under five great slime-dripping arches, of the actual dock gates; and yet we were on the verge of what was known as the country. A few minutes walk up the hill from our house were the big houses. There were about half-a-dozen of them, and above them a farm and a little country school and church.

The first group of houses on the left going up the bank was confined between two house-shops, one at each end. One was kept by the Lodges, the other by the Lawsons. In the middle was a public house. I never knew it called anything but 'Twenty-seven', because I understand there were only twenty-six staiths in the docks and the bar being a place where the men eventually docked became twenty-seven. Our house was next to the bar. On the opposite side were two houses and a blacksmith's shop.

Simonside Bank was shaped like a bent funnel, the broad end opening on to the main road between Tyne Dock and Jarrow. Where the funnel curved and narrowed sharply to mount the steep bank, there was, on the right-hand side, a row of houses perched high on a terrace . . .

I must have been between five and six years old when we moved from Leam Lane to East Jarrow. We made the move on a flat cart. It would likely be Jackie Halliday's, for he was the coalman and the only one we knew who had a cart. And I remember I sat on the back, under the big arch of the mangle, swinging my legs.

East Jarrow lies between Tyne Dock and Jarrow. It is only about three-quarters of a mile from the dock gates and half-a-mile from Leam Lane.

The New Buildings as the two terraces and the three streets were called – and weren't new at all – faced the Jarrow Slakes, a huge timber seasoning pond into which the river Tyne came and went on its rise and

Where the Jarrow Slake meets the Tyne.

'For days after her da had been hanged, her mother would . . . stand looking across the expanse of the Jarrow Slacks, the great mud flat that twice a day was covered by the tide flowing in from the North Sea and swelling the river.' Katie Mulholland

Left:
Many routes taken by Catherine Cookson's characters, some referred to in this book, can be traced with reference to this 1920 street map of the Borough of South Shields.

fall. From the bottom of William Black Street, the street in which we went to live, you could look across the road – the same road with the single line tram track that connected Tyne dock with Jarrow – across the Slakes, to the ships in the river, and beyond them to Howdon on the other side of the water . . .

The slacks was an open space starting from the saw mill wall, and finishing at the wall of the Barium Chemical Works. Altogether I think about one thousand feet of open frontage. I'm not very good at measuring distances. I imagine that Howdon, across the river, was about three-quarters of a mile away. But much nearer to us, say four hundred feet from the actual road, lay the gut. And the space between the gut and the slack bank which bordered the road was used as the timber storing pond. The whole of the slacks emptied when the tide went down.

In the centre of this area, on a permanent floating raft, was a substantial hut. This was the headquarters of Mr Tulip, the man in charge of the timbers. Son followed father in this job and they lived in a nice

house on the terrace right opposite the slacks. One of the old Mr Tulip's unofficial duties was to keep the children clear of the timbers. He never chased me, but always said, 'Be careful, hinny, don't go over to the gut.'

Meeting him one day in my teens he looked at me and shook his head as he said, 'You know, hinny, you shouldn't be alive, you should have been drowned seven times a week. Somebody must have been looking after you or you wouldn't be here the day.'

I wondered too how I had escaped drowning.

I have always been afraid of water, yet I used to walk along a single rotten plank very much like a man on a tightrope, my feet splayed to get a grip. The pond was cut into a cross and this cross was formed by single timbers tied to posts at regular intervals. I would cling on to one post, take a breath, then make a steady dive for the next post. Most of the timbers that were beyond Mr Tulip's hut were rotten, green and slimy, and those bordering the actual gut were death traps. I very rarely got as far as the gut for I was terrified of the black creeping mud in it. It was in this gut, some years later, that one of our neighbours was drowned. He was a nice lad, Matty Kilbride. He had just recently married and had taken a boat

I must have been five or six when we moved from Leam Lane to East Jarrow.

'No one had ever been known to arrive with their furniture in a van. A flat lorry, yes, or a coal cart; at worst, a hand barrow, after dark. These were the general modes of removal.' The Fifteen Streets

The photograph, taken at the turn of the century from Swinburne Street looks across Morgan's Hall (the building with the spire, where Morgan the policeman lived). Round the corner to the right lay Simonside Terrace and the rest of the New Buildings, and to the left the Jarrow Slake.

along the gut to look at a ship lying in the main river over on the Howdon side. The tide turned and caught him in a whirlpool. His wife, if she had been looking, could, from her window, have seen him drown.

This childhood experience was drawn upon in the novel, *The Fifteen Streets*, in which another Katie is less fortunate, Katie is the daughter of an impoverished docker, John O'Brien; Christine is her great friend:

As John ran on down the pavement towards the middle of the slacks where the gangway of timbers led from the bank to the edge of the mud, he had to push his way through the people pouring out from the streets known as the New Buildings that faced a part of the slacks. He thrust at them with his arms, knocking them aside and calling forth hot exclamations. Those standing on the gangway jumped clear of him, and he took the timbers four at a time. The noise from the bank died down and there was only the wind, on which was borne thin wails, and the squelch of the water between the timbers beneath his pounding feet. Automatically he paused at the cabin, which was mounted on a platform of lashed

The gut, horribly polluted by the chemical works, flowed through the mud flat known as the Jarrow Slake and on into the Tyne. This is where Katie and Christine, in The Fifteen Streets, *meet their tragic end.*

timbers in the centre of the great square, and grabbed up a long pole with a hook on its end that the timber man used for pulling the timbers together. Now the race was to reach the end of the timbers bordering the gut before the boat came abreast of him. He could see it was being held stationary at the moment; but by what he couldn't tell. If it was stuck on the other side of the gut on the great mud flat that extended to the river then it was almost a certainty that it would be sucked into this oozing morass.

Arrived at the end of the roped timbers, he had to take to the narrow planks that formed a precarious gangway to the gut. Here, he couldn't run, but had to pick his way over the green, slimy wood. The pole impeded him still further; and once he slipped and the water swirled about his thighs before he could pull himself up again. He had managed to retain his grip on the pole; and as he regained his footing a great 'Oh!' came from the bank. The sight of the boat speeding towards him lent wings of sureness to his feet, and within a matter of seconds he reached the gut.

Clinging to the great post that was the last support of the foot timbers he shouted madly to the approaching boat, 'Grab the pole!'

*Me with my granny at the front door of 5
Leam Lane, where I was born. Sometimes
she'd sing her only song:*

*Love it is teasing,
Love it is pleasing,
Love is a pleasure when it is new,
But as it grows older and days
   grow colder,
It fades away like the morning dew.*

But the wind tore at his voice, carrying his words away from him and them.

The boat was now making swift circles; one second, he would see Katie's face over the gunwhale, her eyes staring in terror, the next he would be looking at the back of her head, her hat still on it. Christine was sitting in the middle of the boat, her arms still stretched taut, her hands gripping the sides in a pitifully vain endeavour to steady the tiny craft. She had seen John, for each time she fronted him her eyes held his for the second before they were torn away again.

It was not the wind that was driving the boat down the gut so much as the tide which was in full ebb; the locked waters between the floats of timbers were rushing madly back into the gut to meet the water draining from the mud flat beyond. Added to this, the suction of the cross channel, bordering the sawmill on the far side of the slacks, made the main gut a frothing boiling mass of water.

As the boat came abreast of him, John bellowed, to the very limit of his lungs, 'Catch the hook, Christine!'

Perhaps she heard him and was afraid to loosen her grip on the sides of the boat, or perhaps his voice became only part of the wind, for when he cast the crooked end of the pole towards the boat it fell close to it, and anyone on the alert could have grabbed it; but the fraction of time during which this could have happened was lost. The boat gave another mad turn and was away, past him. He saw Katie stand up. She seemed to stand perfectly straight and still, and he experienced the odd sensation that her face was floating to him . . . imagination! But it was not imagination when he heard her voice coming to him against the wind . . . 'John! Oh, John!'

The boat was now flung into the vortex of water where the channels of the gut crossed. It heaved and whirled. Then like a ball, held by some mighty hand, it became still, and John saw clearly the two figures, their arms wound tightly about each other, crouched together; the hand was lifted, and the boat, like a ball, was thrown up and over.

As John raised his arms to dive, two hands clawed at him and grabbed his belt. He half turned, screaming at the man behind him, but in wrenching himself free he overbalanced and toppled into the water. When his head broke the surface Peter Bracken grabbed his hair, and Peter's agonized voice screamed at him, 'It's no use! It's no use! They've gone. Don't make another.'

37

The gut was a treacherous place. Yet with my sack on my back I went within yards of it to retrieve some piece of wood. Sometimes I would find myself clinging on to a post terrified to return the way I had come, then having reached Mr Tulip's cabin at last I would tell myself I would never go past it again, but I did.

Great Aunt Maggie lived up the street next door to my Aunt Mary in number twenty-six, downstairs. She was near sighted, yet she read avidly until she was eighty, and often by the light of the street lamp that shone outside her window. It was years later when I really came to know her and like her, even love her. She had a wonderful sense of fun. But this day she was on the slacks gathering sticks.

Among the floating pieces of debris I noticed a sleeper. Sleepers were pieces of wood about three feet long and six inches wide that were used to hold the timbers together. This one had a staple in the middle from which led a length of rope. I pulled it out of the water and laid it on one side with the intention of coming back after I had got my bag full of little bits. But when I returned my Aunt Maggie was humping the sleeper up the bank. 'That's mine,' I said.

'What's yours?'

'That sleeper.'

'The whole slack's yours!' She looked down on me with her round piercing eyes.

I didn't dispute this but said, 'It is mine. I pulled it out an' just left it, I was comin' back for it.'

There followed a verbal battle which I must have won, for with the sack over my shoulder and pulling the sleeper by the piece of rope I went home, and me granda, seeing it was a nice piece of wood, used it to renew a post of the hen cree, without bothering to take the staple out.

Morgan, the policeman who lived in the Hall, wasn't exactly loved by the people in the New Buildings and he was hated by me granda. One day we had a visit from him. He was looking for sleepers; a number of them had been cut away from the timbers, and this was serious as the timbers drifted apart and took some getting together again. And there facing him, with the staple for proof, was a sleeper.

Eventually there was a summons and me granda had to appear in Court. It was a dreadful state of affairs. It was the first time me granda had been in Court in his life, which was surely a miscarriage of justice, and on this occasion, being innocent and indignant, he absolutely refused to plead guilty and they were for sending the case to the Assizes, for as the Magistrate said, 'How could a child of eight years carry such a piece of wood as this?' – the sleeper was no longer in the hen cree but now reposed on the bench before him.

To this me granda had replied, 'You don't know me granddaughter, sir.'

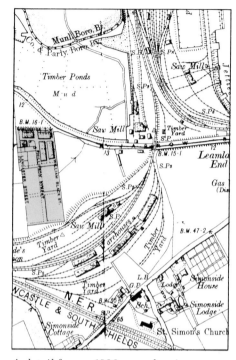

A detail from a 1920 map showing William Black Street, where we moved when I was five. As you went up William Black Street you were flanked on the left by black timbered palings behind which was a field of corn. The farmhouse and main farm were opposite my school at Simonside and at the top of the street was an open space that took in the top of Philipson Street. Opposite Philipson Street was another open space and beyond that a short street called Lancaster Street. At the end of these three streets ran the two terraces. The five streets formed a letter E... And it was in this small community, in this chequered world, that I lived until I was twenty-two.

Harton and Westoe

'Once a man wanted prestige he moved to Westoe or Harton.'

One day when I was five, and walking through the arches from the Docks – from a very small child I was used to going about on my own – I saw someone coming towards me whom apparently I didn't want to meet for I crossed over the road and, turning my face to the blank, black wall, walked sideways until I was passed them, for I knew that if I couldn't see them they couldn't see me. I was to follow this pattern for many years; whenever I didn't want to face up to some reality, I would turn my face to a wall; and always I would see a picture, which became the focal point of my striving, because it presented to me a different way of life. It showed me a big house peopled by ladies and gentlemen, and surrounded by cars, horses and servants. Of course, I was in the picture, dead centre.

The nearest reality to the picture, in the vicinity of East Jarrow, were the villages of Harton and Westoe. Katie Mulholland began, against all odds, to make her fortune in the old part of Shields. Despite wagging tongues she made the transition to Westoe in the best capitalist tradition:

In the fourteen years that had passed since the day Katie became the owner of 12, 13 and 14 Crane Street many changes had taken place in her life, and also in the town. The latter had spread itself far beyond the confines of the river. An 1827 map had shown wide

The first of the 'five great slime-dripping arches' and the one nearest to Tyne Dock itself.

'She turned into the main road from which the fifteen streets branched off; walked between the tram sheds and the chemical works, and came to the Jarrow Slacks, with the great timbers, roped together in batches, lying helpless on the mud like skeletons unearthed in a graveyard. She passed the New Buildings opposite, similar in design to the group she had just left, and walked on down the long road connecting East Jarrow and Tyne Dock, past the saw-mill, through the five slime-dripping arches, and into the heart of the docks. She passed the dock gates and stood on the pavement, waiting for a tram that would take her into Shields.' Kate Hannigan

Westoe Village where the owners of industry lived. Trees lined the roads, from which they were separated by white wooden railings, inlet at intervals to make a carriageway to the gates or doors of the superior dwellings.

stretches of open land between the town and the parishes of Westoe and Harton owned by a certain Mr Cookson, who in 1837 began the manufacture of sheet glass, but with the years Shields had encroached upon this land until now Westoe village, although clinging tenaciously to its aristocratic bearing, was no longer a separate entity but a suburb of Shields.

It was said that the better part of Shields was full of worthy people, but once a man wanted prestige he moved to Westoe or Harton. Here were to be found the owners of shipyards, foundries, glass-works, breweries, coal-mines, quarries, pipe factories, soap factories, candle factories, pottery factories, bankers and property owners.

The really big houses stood back from the roads, guarded by their high stone walls and stiff shrubberies, and titles weren't unknown in this quarter. The not so ostentatious but still grand houses were in rows or terraces, each house being of a different design, some being taller than others, some having porticoes over their front doors, and most having gardens with hedges to screen their lower windows from the public gaze, from the strollers who came in from Shields, to walk under the trees and gape at their betters, or watch the gentry riding in their carriages.

Trees lined the roads, from which they were separated by white

Westoe Village, where in The Gambling Man *Rory first called on Charlotte Keen with her father's slum rents.*

wooden railings, inlet at intervals to make a carriageway to the gates or doors of the superior dwellings.

Here and there you would find a small house called a cottage, which might have six to eight rooms. In 1880 Katie Mulholland, known now to some as Mrs Fraenkel, had bought six so-called cottages and had recently purchased a much larger domain in which she was considering taking up residence. Not that Mrs Fraenkel wanted to move into the heart of the élite, for she had been happy in her present home in Ogle Terrace for the past eight years; and Ogle Terrace, one of the best of the residential quarters in South Shields, had proved test enough to a woman who had made her money by buying tenement houses that lined the river; houses that were known by her name, Katie Mulholland's houses. And by the conduct of the occupants of her houses she had further gained an appendage to her name which was nothing to be proud of, but against which she was powerless to defend herself, for did she not live on the money she received in rents? Moreover, as was whispered in some parlours, did she not live openly with a Swede, and, whisper softly, had she not been in prison through running one of her houses as a place of infamy.

41

Catherine Cookson Countryside

There must have been a real urge among all the people in the New Buildings to get out into the country. I think there must have been a longing in me too . . . not for the country exactly but for a different view, something different from the streets, and the river and the ships. I say that yet the greatest excitement that I had in coming back to the North was crossing on the ferry from Shields to North Shields. I looked up the river and there were the cranes and all the ships; it was busy then.

There is a passage in *Fenwick Houses*, where the young Christine Winter, a child as yet unspoiled by fate, shares her sweet joy in nature with her mother. It is another world from the bustle of new Tyneside. Although Fenwick Houses is a composite picture (there is no real place) it is a typical pit village, and there were hundreds of pit villages in the sort of countryside described, on the edge of industrial Tyneside in the shadow of the fells.

There it is, the fortress of pain wherein you were a child and you learned to laugh, only it looks nothing like a fortress, it's just a

'Always a shadow of pity rose in him when he looked upon any town, even the great Newcastle, for he could never understand how men, given the choice, would want to live among the bustle and hustle.' Simon Brentwood in Tilly Trotter

'Some mornings I went into the fields or the wood to pick flowers to take to my teacher. There was always something to be picked at different times of the year, cowslips – not buttercups or daisies, they were too common – catkins, wood anemones, ferns, bluebells and may, beautiful, scented white may.

'This particular morning was bright golden, and soft and warm, and the birds were all singing . . . but I did not run up the street or hug myself and leap from the ground at the sound of a bird song as I sometimes did, but went into the wood and made my way to the place where yesterday I had been with Don . . . And there I saw Fitty Gunthorpe.' Fenwick Houses

solitary little street called Fenwick Houses. Six of them, six of the ugliest, two-story, flat-faced houses man could devise. Why did Mr Fenwick place them up there, on such a height, with the end one pushing its nose almost into the wood? And why did he cut down the trees to give the front windows a clear view across Fellburn, right to Brampton Hill on the opposite side of the valley, and place the back windows so that they could suck in the wide expanse of sky that roofed the fells and the river.

Christmas came but it did not seem so happy this year. Then eons of time passed until one morning I knew it was spring. The sun was hard and bright; I had run up to the edge of the wood and there through the trees I saw a wonderful sight. There had been no snow for weeks, but sprinkled around the roots of the trees was something that looked like snow. As far as my eye could see there was this sprinkling of purity white, each drop separate from its fellow and divided within itself, and each part shining. I took in a great gulp of air. I wanted to share this wonder with someone, someone who needed wonder, and who needed wonder at this moment more than my mother, for she was tired. And so, dashing back down the street, I flew into the kitchen where she was on the point of lifting the big black frying pan from the fire, and clinging on to her apron I cried, 'Mam, come up to the wood and see something, it's beautiful. It's been snowing in the wood.'

She turned very quickly and looked down at me with a surprised, almost frightened expression. Then she said sharply, 'Don't be silly, child, it hasn't snowed for weeks.'

Now I laughed at her and said, 'It has, Mam.' I turned my head to where Dad had come out of the scullery, his shirt neck tucked in and soap on his face ready for a shave, and after looking at my face for a moment he said to my mother, 'Go on, lass. Leave the pan, I'll see to it.'

'What!' she exclaimed. 'Don't be silly.'

Now my dad came forward looking as if he had grown old overnight, for the soap had formed a white beard, and taking the pan from her hand he whispered, 'Keep it up.' Then nudging her, he added, 'Go on.'

She looked at me impatiently. 'Oh, come on,' she said, straightening her apron and clicking her tongue.

Her attitude didn't dampen my spirits and I danced before her up the street and into the wood. Then from my vantage point I stopped, and when she came and stood by my side I pointed and she looked. Then her hand came slowly round my shoulder and she pressed me to her.

And as we stood like this, gazing spellbound at the first sprinkling of anemones, I said, 'They seem glad to be out, Mam, don't they?' Her hand drew me closer and she said, 'Yes, hinny, they're glad the winter's over.' Then much to my surprise she didn't turn homeward but walked quietly on into the wood, her arm still around me.

At one point she turned and looked back, and I did, too, wondering what she was looking for. Then she did a strange thing. She went down on her hunkers like my dad did and, taking me by the shoulders, she gazed into my face, her eyes moving around it as if looking for something, like when I've had a flea on me, and pressing my face between her large, rough hands she exclaimed softly, 'Oh, me bairn.' Then she said a thing that was stranger than her kneeling, yet not so strange, for I understood it in part. 'Keep this all your life, hinny,' she said. And she ended with something which contradicted a daily statement of hers, for she said, 'Never change. Try to remain as you are, always.'

The brake trips would be right into the country to some place where there was woodland and a stream.

Families ready for an outing to Shotley Bridge. A brake trip was often the only holiday that two-thirds of the population of the New Buildings ever had.

I was ten years old when I first accompanied my mother, Kate, on a brake trip. There would be brake trips every year, and these trips wouldn't be to the seaside, they would be right into the country to some place where there was woodland and a stream.

A brake trip was often the only holiday that two-thirds of the population of the New Buildings ever had. Somebody would get up 'a trip', usually one of the Powers. Old Mrs Power who lived across the road in Philipson Street ran most of the trips and money clubs. You paid a shilling to join a club, and I was sent to draw the lots. Sometimes Kate had two lots, hoping to get an early number so she could pay off this debt or that debt. Old Mrs Power kept hens and the back-yard gave evidence of this. And their kitchen wasn't like our kitchen, but dark and gloomy. I only went in on club days and was always glad to get out. When the lots were drawn you handed over your shilling or two shillings as the case may be, and then, when subsequently you drew your pound club you were always expected to give a little backhander in return for the privilege of someone keeping your money for you.

Every week when you paid your club you put sixpence or so towards the brake trip, then one day in the summer – with the sun shining if you were lucky – you clambered in with your neighbours and sat on the hard seats that lined the wagon-like structure. Then the man climbed up behind the horses, cracked his whip and amid a throng of running and yelling children you were off for the holiday of the year.

'Hoy a ha'penny oot!' The children would be screaming and yelling as they ran after the brake, and there were ha'pennies and pennies thrown at them, and some of the gay spirits in the brake would sing out:

We'll not be back till mornin',
We'll not be back till mornin',
We'll not be back till mornin',
A hip, a hip-hooray.

The brake would come rattling back at eight or nine o'clock at night, it all depended on the time of the year and the light, and the children would be waiting for it with their cry again of 'Hoy a ha'penny oot!' But now most of the pockets were empty and the cries went unheeded, although everybody would be singing:

We're back to canny awd Jarrar,
We're back to canny awd Jarrar,
We're back to canny awd J-ar-rar,
A hip, a hip hooray.

In *Feathers in the Fire*, Angus McBain's farm is set deep in the Northumberland countryside, high above the industrial landscape and further west along the Tyne towards Allendale, a setting it shares with other novels, such as *The Girl* and the *Mallen* trilogy.

From where he, Davie, stood he could see a great expanse of land beyond the boundary of the farm. To the right of him were hills, young mountains some of them; showing green and brown, with here and there great black patches, telling scars of dead lead mines. To the left the land rolled into moorland flatness on its way to Haltwhistle and the South Tyne. In front of him, eight miles as the crow flew, twelve miles by the twisting road, lay Allendale in its nest of moors.

Even in winter he always paused at this spot to breathe in the air; it seemed purer from up here. Today, a late hot summer day, it was thin and clean and scoured his ribs as he drew it inwards. It was almost as good, he considered, as the air you breathed from the top of Shale Tor.

When I left the North in 1929 I knew nothing of this particular part of my land. I had been half a dozen times to Newcastle, once to Durham, once to Gilsand, a few times to Birtley. My horizon encompassed Jarrow and Shields, and even in these places I knew only main streets. I existed mostly in the circle of Tyne Dock and East Jarrow.

My first job was in a workhouse in Tendring, Essex, and what I saw of the countryside there left me cold. Suddenly this girl, who had come from

I think there must have been a longing in me too . . . not for the country exactly but for a different view.

this industrial area where even at night-time you heard the horns of the ships and the background noises of the shunting trains, found herself in the midst of this desolate countryside. In fact it wasn't desolate, it was all farmland: a vast expanse of flat farmland; it was like a different country and I was so lonely. I was stuck there for nine months and I hated it.

And I think that that feeling has stayed with me. There's nothing pleases Tom more than to walk through a field; Tom loves flat Essex and also the fenland. We had a boat on the fens and those flat expanses nearly drove me mad.

But up here in the hills I know that I am in my own country, not soft like the downs nor flat like the fens. This countryside is raw, and it is with me and I feel it.

Tom must be tired of the times we have brought the car from Hexham to Langley and I have said that it is the most beautiful sight that I have ever seen. As you approach the 'top', as we call it, you can look across and see that you're surrounded by hills, and Langley seems to be in a great valley, and all the way, everywhere you look, there are hills coming down, all the way round, coming down to this valley.

Up here I know that I am in my own country. This is my kind of country, not soft like the downs but rugged hills broken up into soft parts, an expanse of sheer mystery. I first became afraid of hills up here when Tom took me up Shap Fell and over Alston.

The Tor in *Feathers in the Fire* was set just at the back here, but Jackie Halliday was the real reason I wrote that story.

Jackie Halliday used to sell coal, tuppence a bucket, off a flat cart and I thought his legs were buried in the coal. As a child, I didn't work it out that I should have seen them sticking through the cart.

Then one day I went up Bogey Hill – I very rarely went up Bogey Hill – and I saw this 'thing' going across the back lane and I recognised his face and it was Jackie Halliday and for the first time I realised that the man had no legs, and I stopped and stared at him.

Well, a child's horror can affect someone, and I saw it in that man's face. And for years when a tragedy came up or someone was hurt very badly by someone else – not necessarily physically – I recalled the look on that man's face. It was misty: the face had gone but the feeling remained. And I felt that I had to portray that in some way, I felt that I was really experiencing what Jackie Halliday must have felt when as a young man he found that he had no legs. Just imagine . . . in a tough area like the Tyne, where they are all he-men. It seemed so unfair, but then ask yourself, is there anything fair in Nature? Ask yourself, when a mountain can come down and bury people in its mud. Is there anything fair in Nature, when a volcano can burst and burn people to death? Is there anything fair?

48

ANOTHER FACE OF MY LAND

My land of deep lakes
With mountain shadows
Like ancient cities
Buried and at rest in their depths.
My land of hidden valleys
Dotted with homesteads,
Solitary, aloof.
My land of barren fells,
Scree slopes gripped by hooves of sheep
And rams, protective of their own.
My land of skies stretching to infinity,
Blue high sheets of sheer clear light.
My land of mists,
Grey, wet, body-soaking mists
That shroud you to a trembling halt.
My land of tones
Fan-lit and sombre,
Heather purples and autumn golds.
Winter white,
Black frost laden nights
Driving hard to spring
And new born grass
And released water
Rushing from its prison of ice.
Oh, my land of sturdy men,
Short, stumpy men in part,
And women, warm of heart
And worth
And laughing lips,
My land of the North.

Here Amos appears on the Tor with his half-sister, Jane.

'The sun was going down and I stood on the top of High Fell straining my eyes into the dazzling rose and mauve light trying to make him out against the shades of the hills . . . I was so high up that I felt on top of the sun, and as it slipped over the brow of the hill yon side of the river it seemed so near that I had but to bend forward, put out my hand, and I could press it into the valley beyond.' Fenwick Houses

The sky was endless, seemingly without horizons. The bracken on the right of the Tor was shoulder high, some already tinged yellow, forerunner of the reds and purple that would turn the fells and hills into a warm flame. At the foot of the Tor were clusters of bilberry bushes, their fruit standing out like black and purple stains, and she pointed this out to the boy. But he didn't seem interested, for his gaze was directed to the top of the Tor.

The easiest way up was through the bracken, but the child would be enveloped in it, the fronds would impede him, and they could easily cut, so she led the way along the narrow road that skirted

49

the foot of the Tor on the north side, where it was mostly shale, giving place to rough rock. Starting from the road was a path, cut diagonally, and slowly mounting its way to the summit, and she took this. Picking Amos up in her arms with the order for him to hang onto his crutches and not get excited for fear he overbalanced them both, she began to ascend. The end of the path was out of sight on the east side of the Tor and away from the road, and when she finally reached it, she dropped the boy to the ground, then sat down on a rock and, panting and laughing, said, 'Well, here we are.'

The child was standing supporting himself on his crutches. She stared at his face; it was wearing the strangest expression. He was looking towards Whitfield Moor and the hills beyond. She watched him look from one side to the other, taking in the great range of space; then his head went slowly back on his shoulders and he gazed up into the sky.

'Isn't it beautiful?' She put out her arm and encircled his waist, and he turned and looked at her and smiled. And he was beautiful too. This face often made her sad, but not today; it was as if she also, like him, were seeing the world outside the farm for the first time. She gripped him to her and he dropped his crutches, and as she had been wont to do since she was a small child, until she was twelve years old, she rolled on the grass, but now with him pressed tightly to her. When she stopped they lay, their faces close together, laughing; then like an eel he was away from her, scrambling over the grass on all fours, his body, from his waist to his hips, wobbling from side to side. When he reached his crutches he began to run wildly here and there like someone demented, and she chased him, laughing as she called, 'Amos! Amos! Stop! Keep away from the edge! Be careful. Be careful.' Everytime her hands went to grasp him, he ducked or slithered from her hold.

The agility on his new-found legs amazed her; it was as if he had used the crutches from birth. It seemed that Parson Hedley was right, he was going to be very adaptable. Parson Hedley said he was the brightest child he had ever come across. For a moment a cloud passed over the bright day as she thought, if only her father could see him as Parson Hedley saw him; or for the matter, if her mother had viewed him as a human being; if only one of them had taken him to their hearts. Anyway, he had her, he would always have her.

50

The Tyne (c. 1890) from Hexham, Northumberland, the Hexham of A Dinner of Herbs. *Just east of the spot lies the setting for the novel,* Martha Mary Crawford: *'The Habitation was situated seven miles from Hexham and almost twenty from Newcastle; the nearest places to it being Riding Mill to the west and Prudhoe to the east. The house itself stood at the end of the hollow with a hill rising sharply at some distance behind it, and about a hundred yards from the river. The far side of the river was banked in most places by woodland, the trees coming almost down to the edge of the water, but apart from one or two copses, the land on this side of the river merged into meadows, almost up to the tollbridge two miles away.'*

She lifted up her skirts and raced towards him, for now he was some distance away and nearing the edge of the Tor where it dropped almost sheer to the road below. This part was strewn with loose rocks and boulders and, as he went twisting in and out of them, she had a job to outmanoeuvre him. When at last she caught him, she sat down with her back to a boulder and laughed as she rocked him. Then quite suddenly, as he was apt to do, he asked a most disconcerting question, 'Why haven't I got legs like you, Jan?' He sat back from her straight up on his buttocks, then with a swift movement he lifted her skirt and petticoats back up to her knees.

'Amos!' Her voice held a sharp note. 'You mustn't do that.'

'Why?'

'Well, just because.'

'But why have you got legs and I haven't?'

'You . . . you had an accident.'

'When?'

'Oh.' She closed her eyes and swallowed. 'It was before you were born.'

'What . . . what kind? Did I fall?'

'No.'

'Well, what kind of an accident?'

'You . . . you mustn't ask such questions.'

'Why?'

She couldn't say to him 'because she didn't know the answers', for he expected her to know all the answers. She was saved from further embarrassment by the sound of a pony trap below them. It was coming around the bend of the road. Jumping to her feet and pulling the boy with her, she raised her hand and shouted, 'Parson Hedley! Parson Hedley!'

The man in the trap stopped and looked about him, then lifted his head. She waved down to him again, and at this he waved back, then he lowered his hand and stared at the small figure by her side, and she knew that he was very surprised at what he was seeing. She put her hand to her mouth and shouted, 'We'll come down,' and at this he called back, 'No, stay there, I'll come up; just let me fasten Toby.'

She watched him drive the trap to where the ground levelled off sufficiently for him to take it off the road and where there was grass for the pony to nibble; then she followed his movements as he made his way up the winding narrow path, and when he was below them, she laughed down at him. Then with Amos stumping by her side, she ran back towards where the path came out on the summit. They reached the spot simultaneously and their greetings were high and pleasurable as if they hadn't met for some long time, instead of twenty-four hours previously.

The parson was a man of medium build. He had flat rather blunt features, none of which had any claim to good looks, except perhaps his eyes; even these were nondescript in colour, being of a flecked grey. But it was the eyes that gave interest to the face; perhaps it was the kindliness and understanding in their depths, and a certain sharp keenness in their glance, which rarely held censure, that made them attractive.

He gazed down at the boy who had become a deep interest in his life, as also had his sister, but whereas he could express his feelings on the former, he had to hide them on the latter. For all her capabilities, he still considered Jane a child, and even if she hadn't been, there remained circumstances which prevented him from presenting himself as anything but a friend, pastor, and tutor. But with the child it was different, and now he exclaimed loudly, 'Well! Well! A day of miracles. What is this?' He stood back and surveyed the boy standing erect, shoulders hunched, on the

Right:

The Girl *is set in the area around Allendale in the 1850s.*

'She was in the middle of the belt of trees when she heard Ned calling her name. "Hannah! Hannah! Don't be a bloody fool. Hannah! come back I say."

'The grassland in the valley gave way to ploughed fields, and the soil stuck to her shoes. Ned wasn't far behind now and intermittently his voice came to her, just calling her name, "Hannah! Hannah!".

'There was the wood ahead. Once in there he'd have a job to find her . . . the stone wall to the Buckley Estate was only about four feet high . . . if she could get in there she could lose herself . . . and as she rolled over it Ned's voice came from just yards behind her and his tone was different now and held the sound of a gasping plea. "For God's sake, Hannah, stop! Stop! Not in there. Not there, you bloody fool you . . ."

'She was about ten paces beyond the wall when his next words, screaming high above her head, brought her to a freezing standstill. "It's trapped! Mantrapped. For God's sake listen to me!" ' The Girl

small crutches; and when Amos, in his forthright manner, stated, 'I've got legs,' he had to pause before answering, 'Indeed, indeed you have, Amos. Now why didn't we think of this before, eh Jane?'

Jane smiled widely at him. 'That's the very thought that came to me a short while ago, Parson. Perhaps it's because I thought he couldn't manage them. . . .'

'I can manage them, look, look,' Amos interrupted while he demonstrated, going round in small circles, and she laughed as she caught him, crying, 'We can see. Yes, darling, we can see. But you'll make yourself dizzy. Come along, sit down.'

When they were seated on the grass, Arnold Hedley gazed before him for a moment in silence, then said, 'It's years since I was up here; I'd forgotten how magnificent was the view.' Then glancing at the boy who was sitting to the side of Jane, he said low, under his breath, 'It was good for him to see the world for the first time from this spot. It was like you to think of bringing him up.'

'It wasn't my idea, Parson, it was Molly who suggested it.'

53

He looked into her face. She was so honest, she would not even take a little credit to herself when it rightly belonged to someone else. Her face to him was beautiful, for it held the beauty of honesty, the beauty of an unselfish nature and a kindly heart. True, she was given to bouts of temper, but then she was but human. And she was young, so young, too young to have the responsibility of mothering this boy and running that disemboweled tortured household. He was often amazed at the gaiety she managed to maintain. But then her charge, although terribly handicapped, was a lively, intelligent little fellow, too intelligent, he considered at times, for his age. But he supposed God in His wisdom had given him the gift of memory and and keen perception to make up for his lack.

He was bending forward towards Jane to make a further comment when he was pushed aside by Amos's roughly forcing himself between them from behind. The force levelled by the child's arm into his ribs was of a strength one would associate with a boy of ten or twelve. He held back his head and surveyed the child as Jane admonished him, saying, 'That's naughty, Amos. You mustn't push like that. That's very naughty.'

Amos was now sitting upright between them. There was a slight smile on his face, and with a lightning movement he turned to the parson, raised his hand, and viciously nipped the lobe of his ear.

When Arnold Hedley actually cried out with equal amounts of surprise and pain, Jane, snatching the boy's hands, slapped them hard as she cried, 'That's very wicked, Amos, very wicked. How dare you!'

Amos stared wide-eyed up at her, and, his smile sliding into a grin now, he said, 'He pulls my ear.'

She exchanged a glance over his head with Arnold; then she swallowed and said, 'Parson does it playfully, he never hurts you. There is a difference between pulling and nipping. If you ever do that again, you'll get a sound smacking, a real smacking.'

The smile slid from the boy's face, his eyes clouded, and his lips fell firmly one on the other. In another child of similar years this might have been a prelude to tears, but he showed no signs of crying; instead he threw himself forward onto his hands and knees, crawled swiftly to where his crutches were, stood up on them and, looking from one to the other, said firmly, 'I'm going down to the farmyard.'

From Muck to Millions

Since the beginning of the 1840s when the railways had come into existence the North had known a growing prosperity; villages, like Jarrow, through its steel works, had mushroomed into towns. Middlesborough, only a few miles away, had in 1830 been a hamlet housing just over a hundred people but by the year 1853 it was a thriving port with nearly twenty thousand inhabitants. Names had become synonymous with places. Henry Bolckow of Middlesborough who was actually a German by birth; Stephenson of Newcastle; the Lehmans of Sheffield; and not forgetting John Brown, who from an apprentice in a cutlery firm rose to be the owner of a large steel works; Vickers, Armstrong, and Ramsden were names that spelt steel, names upon which thousands upon thousands of men depended for their livelihood; names that were carved in stone at the base of statues and busts, representing the gratitude of thriving towns to the benefactors who had erected gigantic municipal buildings or who had donated a public bath or perhaps a library.

The North at this period was an empire, an empire of coal mines, steel works, and railways, not forgetting glassworks. It was a time

By 1850 a network of railways was established, to be amalgamated in 1854 as the North Eastern Railway.

T021260

when a few outstanding men rose from muck to millions and having done so housed their families in palatial establishments. A percentage of lesser men made a good deal of money and they, too, lived well. And then there was the gentry, and they, as they had always done, lived high.

The Glass Virgin

Coal was the single most significant area of industrial growth in the first part of the nineteenth century and the most important in the way that it encouraged the growth of other industries. It provided the fuel, and the other industries returned the favour in their own way: the railways by decreasing the cost of moving coal to the ports; iron and steel by shaping

Puddlers at the puddling furnace in which scrap iron would be prepared for the steam hammer to work it free of impurities.

Above Right:
Iron workers known as 'shinglers' working up wrought iron; the steam hammer had been invented in 1851.

the ships that carried the coal to foreign lands; glass by its ability to employ otherwise unsaleable coal; the chemical industry by its use of brine, which was a nuisance in the pit but invaluable in the manufacture of alkali. In its turn the chemical industry provided essential ingredients for the glass, pottery, paper, soap, and textile industries.

Coal was thus at the basis of a network of interrelated industries, and the glory of the North Eastern Coalfield was that between 1850 and 1914, either directly or indirectly, it provided vital energy for the urbanisation and industrialisation of Western Europe.

The River

On some days in the early nineteenth century you might see a few hundred sail in the harbour at Shields, where the main collier fleet would

57

lie. And by 1848 there were thirty-six shipbuilding yards along the banks of the Tyne, though none were very large: small wooden ships, little complex equipment, small work forces – 'mostly scum down there' was Janie's opinion when Rory (the gambling man), with his brother Jimmy, shows his fiancée the boatyard he is about to buy:

The river was the gateway to the world export markets which were the making of Tyneside industry. Supported by the shipbuilding industry and seafaring traders were a whole host of secondary industries including rope-makers, biscuit-makers, fish curers and, under some threat with the advent of steam, the sail-makers pictured here.

All the while she kept looking from one to the other of them, but they remained smilingly silent. Then she burst out, 'But the money! You've got the money to buy this?' Flinging both arms wide as with joy she gazed about the long room.

'Well –' Rory pursed his lips – 'enough, enough to put down as a deposit.'

'He didn't get in till six this mornin'.' Jimmy was nodding up at her, and she turned to Rory and said, 'Gamin'?'

'Yes. Yes, Miss Waggett, that's what they call it, gamin'.'

'And you won?'

'I wouldn't be here showing you this else.'

'How much?'

'Aw well' – he looked away to the side – 'almost eleven pounds at the beginning, but' – he gnawed on his lip for a moment – 'I couldn't manage to get away then, I had to stay on and play. But I was six up anyway when I left.'

'Six pounds?'

'Aye, six pounds.'

'And this place is costin' thirty-five?'

'Aye. But five pounds'll act as a starter. Jimmy's goin' to get the address of the son and I'll write to him the morrow.'

There was silence between them for a moment until Rory, looking at Janie's profile, said, 'What is it?'

'The waterfront, it's . . . it's mostly scum down here.'

'Not this end.'

'She turned to Jimmy, 'No?'

'No, they're respectable businesses. You know, woodyards, repair shops, an' things like that. An' there's very few live above the shops. There's nobody on yon side of us, an' just that bit of rough land on the other. Eeh!' he laughed, 'I'm sayin' us, as if we had it already . . .'

'What do you think?' Rory was gazing at her.

'Eeh!' She walked the length of the room, put her hand out and touched the chest of drawers, then the brass hinges on the oak

Pan Ash Quay around 1900 showing the busy waterfront with its marine stores, shipsmiths and pump manufacturers.

The picture gives a sense of nineteenth-century hustle and bustle in the crowded moorings of Shields harbour.

'As she stood on the bank and looked at the different kinds of ships, forming a panorama that stretched away along both banks and made up of scullers, keel boats, barges, small sailing vessels, and large ones that looked gigantic to her eyes, she had been speechless.' The Whip

59

'Having about reached the Lawe she stopped an old riverside man and asked him if he could direct her to Connor's boatyard.

"Connor's boatyard? Never knew no Connor's boatyard along here."

"It's a small yard, I understand. Mr Connor has only recently taken the yard over."

"Small yard, taken it over?" The old man rubbed the stubble on his chin and said, "Oh aye, now I heard tell of a young'un starting up there. Takes some grit and guts to start on your own along this stretch.' The Gambling Man

chest, then the table, and lastly the rocking chair, and her eyes bright, she looked from one to the other and said, 'Eeh! it's amazing. You would never think from the outside it could be like this 'cos it looks ramshackle. But it's lovely, homely.'

'Look in t'other room.'

She went into the bedroom, then laughed and said, 'That'll come down for a start.

She was pointing to the hammock, and Rory answered teasingly, 'No. Why no. Our Jimmy's going to swing in that and we'll lie underneath.'

'Aw you!' Jimmy pushed at the air with his flat hand, then said, 'I'll be upstairs, I'll make that grand. Come on, come on up and have a look. Can you manage the ladder?

Janie managed the ladder, and then she was standing under the sloping roof looking from one end of the attic to the other and she exclaimed again, 'Eeh! my! did you ever see so many bits of paper and maps and books and things? There's more books here than there are in the master's cases in his study.'

In those days the route up river to Newcastle was dangerous. Sandbanks, shelves and nasty projecting points of rock helped make the Tyne a real problem of communication and at times impossible to navigate. It was not unknown for people using the Tyne ferries to take meals with them in case they were stranded, and just west of Newcastle there was an island (King's

The greatest excitement that I had in coming back to the North was crossing on the ferry from Shields to North Shields. I looked up the river and there were the cranes and all the ships; it was busy then. . .

'Andree said that, with the new innovation of the dredging to clear the channels and the new piers of the North and South towns forming a safe harbour at the mouth of the river, Shields would soon be a first-rate port.' Katie Mulholland *in the 1850s*

Meadows), big enough to have sheep on it and to support fairs, before it was dredged away later in the century.

The only magistrates able to exercise authority on the water were the Mayor and Aldermen of Newcastle. For years other Tynesiders had campaigned against the town's monopoly of the Tyne, the state of the river, and the high, port dues levied: in the first half of the nineteenth century Newcastle took £1,000,000 in dues. But it was only after the Reform Act of 1832, when Gateshead and North and South Shields were given their own MPs, that voices outside Newcastle began to be influential. From that date, whatever party a politician belonged to, he had no chance of being elected in these towns unless abolition of

'It was ten minutes walk from Pilot Place to Creador Street, and it was a nice walk, Emily considered, when like today the sun was shining on the river to the left of her and a big steamer with the smoke coming out of its two funnels was making down river for the opening between the piers . . .'
The Tide of Life

Two women chatting as they prepare to embark on the ferry.

The old direct ferry landing at South Shields. To the right, the public house known as Sisterson's, a regular haunt for rivermen and seamen.

Newcastle's monopoly was part of his manifesto. Finally, in 1850, authority was transferred to the Tyne Improvement Commission, a body which transformed the Tyne in the second part of the century and gave industry a doorway to fast developing export markets. For Katie Mulholland from South Shields and her Swedish sea captain, Andree, this vital turning point in the fortunes of the river would have been a common talking point:

The John Bowes, built by Palmer and carrying the auspicious name of the family whose mining interests so favoured the Palmer/Bowes partnership, wrought a revolution on Tyneside after it was launched in 1852. 'What she had done in five days would have taken two sailing colliers a month to accomplish. Palmer was set fair.' Katie Mulholland

Palmer's Shipyard in 1899, looking west. To the left are the 'stocks', upon which the boats were built.

All she had known about Newcastle before this visit was that it was the city that kept the rest of the towns on the Tyne poor, taxing them for the use of their own river, refusing them independence, and after her visit she could, in a way, understand the attitude of the city to the towns that crowded the river, because she saw them as servants to a master. But one servant, Shields, spat when the name of Newcastle was mentioned, for had not the vessels bound for the mouth of the Tyne to go all the way up to Newcastle to check in at the quayside so that the Newcastle Corporation could have its toll. The Shields men hated the

'They were iron men, steel men; they talked of hardly anything else, for only by iron and steel could they eat. Once a man had worked in Palmer's for some years he felt he would be no good for anything else; nor did he want to be.' Katie Mulholland

Newcastle men. But part of that particular strife had ended in August when Shields, after a long, bitter fight, had been created a separate port, and Andree said it was a fine step forward.

Perhaps the most dramatic turning point of all, because it affected both the coal and shipbuilding industries as well as virtually every industry in its wake, was the launching in 1852 of the *John Bowes* from Palmer's Shipyard in Jarrow. The *John Bowes* wasn't the first iron collier to be built; all the ideas that it embodied had been tried out before, but it was the most successful iron collier and the first that would make money — which, after all, is what made any event a turning point in an industry's evolution:

Bernard Rosier was a youth of eighteen, eight years ago, when on a June day in 1852 he had stood with his father in Palmer's Yard and watched the launching of the *John Bowes*; and many besides his father thought it was money being thrown to the wind on nothing more than an expensive experiment, for up to this time

sailing vessels were the cheapest form of transport. But they were to be proved wrong. On her first voyage the *John Bowes* carried six hundred and fifty tons of coal to London, discharged it and was back on the Tyne in five days. What she had done in five days would have taken two sailing colliers close on a month to accomplish. Palmer was set fair.

Katie Mulholland

So successful was the *John Bowes* that by 1862 more than ten shipyards on the Tyne were building iron ships and employing more than 4,000 men between them. By 1889 tonnage built on Tyneside was 280,000. At the beginning of the twentieth century more than a quarter of the world's

'It had been stimulating just to be in Palmer's company . . . There was enthusiasm, drive and the Midas touch if ever he saw it. Palmer was no age yet, only thirty-eight, and the yard had only been going nine years, but he was coining money, making it hand over fist; not only was he building ships but he was making the materials on the spot to build ships. Jarrow was booming. He had turned it from a village into a literal iron and steel goldmine . . . Oh, he was no fool was Charles Palmer, this fast-rising star, who was cunningly making a name as a philanthropist. We could all be philanthropists if we could dig gold out of steel.' George Rosier in Katie Mulholland

By 1862 more than ten shipyards on the Tyne were building iron ships and employing more than four thousand men between them.

tonnage was built in the shipyards of the North East.

The Men of Industry

The concept of interdependence, one industry depending on and supporting another, was reflected in the make-up of the boardrooms of the big companies. The Consett iron and steel company included directors closely involved in the railways and shipbuilding, for example. Charles Mark Palmer's secondary involvement in coal through his directorship of the John Bowes Partnership enabled him to benefit from easy access to economical quantities of fuel for his blast furnaces and his ships, but also provided him with direct profits from shipping Bowes coal to London. Again, when Cookson's glassworks, the single biggest glassmaking enterprise in the whole country, changed hands in 1854 the business

consortium which took charge comprised men with coal, railway, engineering, banking and commercial interests, as well as managerial and technical expertise.

The industrial entrepreneurs largely rose from the mercantile class, a brand of man that had been infiltrating the landed gentry for centuries, exploiting what lay beneath the land, and using the money to capitalise on both farming and a variety of industrial interests.

A mercantile background was a likely breeding ground for commercial skills, though not perhaps for the development of overscrupulous personalities.

'She was walking into a world that didn't belong to any kind of life she had yet imagined. She was going along what appeared to be a tunnel with ironrails down the middle, and she went to step in between them for easier walking when Kate with a bawl that nearly took her head off cried, "Do you want to be run over afore you start? Don't be so bloody gormless, lass, that's the rolley way. Look." She pointed ahead to where a young lad was coming towards them leading a horse, and as they came nearer, Tilly could see the three bogies ful of coal rattling behind the horse.' Tilly Trotter

'Davey felt the old man turn away from him and his voice re-echoed round the walls as he cried, "This one should have been condemned years ago; but no, no, they wanted their last drop of blood. The whole country's riddled with pits now. The whole kingdom they call the Tyne. Aye, the coal kingdom. Aye, the kingdom of slaves, the kingdom of the blind, the kingdom of long everlasting light.' Our John Willie

The Kingdom of the Blind

Me granda used to say that all pitmen hewed more coal at the corner end, or at their games of quoits, and pitch and toss, than they ever did down the mine. Added to this was my own experience of miners, derived more from the way they treated their wives and families, the females thereof, than from the men themselves.

It wasn't until about 1952 (long after I had moved to Hastings) that my opinion of miners turned a complete somersault. I was meeting my seven cousins from Birtley for the first time for about twenty-eight years. The four boys had always worked down the pits, and I angered them with my remarks about the price of coal in the South. The result of our verbal

69

battle was that they challenged me to go down the mine. The thought petrified me, but what could I do with those four indignant men facing me. I went down with Peter – he was a deputy at the Betty Pit in Birtley – and was down about three hours. I almost embraced the daylight when I stepped back out of the cage, and from that moment wanted, sincerely and genuinely wanted to pin medals on every pitman. The outcome of my nerve racking experience was my fourth novel, *Maggie Rowan*. Maggie has challenged Ann to go down the pit in order to face up to her irrational fear for David's safety:

As they dropped into the earth, the light from their lamps showed the rough-hewn surface of the walls not more than inches from the sides of the cage. The movement was slow, almost gentle, and in no way to be compared with the drop she had heard the men speak of. And when with a slight bump the cage reached the bottom her terror for a moment was stilled; only to return with sickening force when she stepped out in to the 'road'.

The road. How often she had heard her father speak of the road, when unconsciously she had created her own picture of it: a broad road, leading from a kind of hallway in which the cage landed; the road might narrow later on and men might have to crawl, but at its beginning the road was broad and high. But now she was standing in it, and it was little broader than a passage, about ten feet wide at most and seeming to be filled with a row of small trucks, which stretched away into the blackness and were lost.

The leather straps across the man's shirt kept in place a pad that protected his back when 'righting' waggons that had come off the tracks: a strenuous job, but judging by the size of his wrists, one that he was equal to.

Above Left:
A pit pony during one of its brief periods at the surface: 'Stick to your pony, lad, and it's ten to one you'll escape half the accidents; the pony knows what's afoot minutes afore you do. It's a sixth sense they have. Many's the life that's been saved by a pony.' Maggie Rowan

This pony looks as if it has been prepared for a show: there was great competition between pits for the best pony.

Mechanisation of the mines was slow and the hewers at the face were in constant conflict with the coal owners because they were part-paid per tub of coal, and there would always be argument about the amount disqualified as stone.

Above Right:
Nineteenth-century women workers tipping a 'tram' of coal in to the 'screen'. The coal would slide down a chute to be sorted by other workers.

She raised her eyes to the roof, about three feet above her head, and could scarcely believe what she saw: criss-crossed pieces of wood holding up huge boulders of rock, and these pieces of wood kept in place by pit props – just pit props – seeming to form a straight wall to the passage as they disappeared in the distance; and behind them lay masses of loose rock, not coal as she had surmised, but rock.

She moved away in the wake of the others; and her attention was suddenly taken from herself, for, to avoid stepping into pools of water, she had to keep her lamp playing continually around her feet.

They were walking single file in no more than a breadth of three feet, for the coal tracks overhanging the track took up most of the room. But once past the end of the trucks the ground became fairly even and the deputy's voice came to her as if he was speaking through a funnel, saying, 'We'll turn off here for a minute and see the ponies.'

She stopped. Oh no; that was one thing she couldn't do, she couldn't bear to see the ponies. She would let them go on. But this escape was denied her for a man coming up behind said, 'You'd better not dawdle, lass; you'd better tag along. What you trying to do, get lost?'

'No. They're looking at the ponies: I don't want to go in.'

He brought his blackened face down to hers in genuine surprise. 'Why, miss? Why not for? They'd like to see you, they don't often see a lass.'

He took her arm, determined to prove his point, and led her off the main road and along a passage. And she saw the ponies in their stables.

They looked fat and well-kept; but oh, the poor things! Down here all their lives, after having known the freedom of running wild. Oh, it was awful. Never to see the light of day again!

Ann walked silently past the man who had brought her in, and this time he made no effort to impose his will on her. She stood at the corner of the passage adjoining the roadway, and words of her father talking to Tom came back to her: 'Stick to your pony, lad, and it's ten to one you'll escape half the accidents; the pony knows what's afoot minutes afore you do. It's a sixth sense they have. Many's the life that's been saved by a pony.'

Yes; but to keep them down here all the time. Oh, dear God! She looked about her, but her eyes could travel no distance at all before being checked by stones or props. And not only the ponies, but Davie and all those men spent half their lives in this place, and in others like it; and were really terrified, too, of being stood off – so many pits were idle. Yet she wished at this moment from the

Among the priorities in the first part of the nineteenth century (as Sopwith is here reminded by Rosier in Tilly Trotter*) were waggonways to transport coal efficiently and economically to the ports: "'You know, you've always been behind the times. Why you're one of the few pits that's been running solely on horses for years. You thought you could go it alone. All pits are joining up their waggonways, some going straight to the ports . . . You're a bloody fool, Sopwith," he said. "That's what you are. You're sinking."'*

Left:
It is incredible to think that men and boys would go down the pits with naked-flame lights and nought but rats to tell them there were no gasses about. The Davey safety lamp was double-edged progress, however, 'for the owners looked upon the safety lamp as if it were Aladdin's very own, and after its inception they took even less safety precautions in the mine than they had done before.'
Katie Mulholland

bottom of her heart that the Venus, and this one too, were idle, for then her Davie would be up above, and he'd get another job somehow. Yet this she knew was a vain hope; he'd always go back to the pit; his dream was of the day when they'd get extra shifts in and earn more money to make living a little easier . . . It wasn't right somehow.

The deputy was now pointing out the pit props, which were no longer brown but white; and this was nothing, he was saying, to what they would see when they got into the mothergate. There, fungi as big as their hands grew on the props.

Ann ceased to listen to the deputy's voice, nor was she interested in those things which were apparently peculiar to this mine, she was weighed down by the overpowering terribleness of it all; but when the party again stopped and the deputy suggested that to see just how dark the mine was they should cover up their lamps, a protest escaped her and she cried, 'Eeh, no'; whereupon Maggie took the lamp from her hand and within a few minutes they were standing in darkness, the like of which she had never imagined possible – thick, heavy, clinging darkness, that hurt the eyeballs, that became alive and pressed on you.

'Don't speak for a minute,' said the deputy.

Now silence was added . . . the darkness and silence of the eternity of the damned. It flashed through Ann's brain that the roaring flames of hell would be preferable to this, for in hell there would be sound and colour; here there was nothing yet everything, everything that was needed to bring the dark terrors of the soul to the surface.

'Oh no!' Her own suppressed scream added to her terror. And as the lamps twinkled again, their small lights appearing brilliant in contrast to the blackness, she wanted to be sick. She turned to Maggie to make yet another protest, but her words and supplicating outstretched hand were checked, for Maggie was looking queer . . . white and sickly, almost as if she were about to faint. She stood gaping at her for a moment; then strangely she began to draw comfort from her sister's apparent weakness. She did not feel so alone in her fear now that a person of their Maggie's stamina could be afraid.

She said, 'What's the matter? Are you bad?'

For a moment Maggie seemed to peer through her, then shook her head in a sort of bewildered fashion before walking on, and she,

'Often when he had gone down the mine
with the manager they had come across
couples sporting and more in a side
roadway on the bare rock earth, and
while Yarrow scattered them, crying, "I'll
cuddle you! Begod, I'll cuddle you!" he
himself had been filled with envy. He
often thought about the word "cuddle". It
was a beautiful word, warm in itself.'
Maggie Rowan

pressing her teeth down into her lip, followed, until the deputy
ushered them through a low trapdoor and into a passage, then
through a similar door and into the mothergate which led to the
coal face.

Here it was even darker and the atmosphere was so moist and
warm that the road they had just left was, in comparison, as cool as
though it were swept by a sea breeze.

Stumbling along in the rear and bent almost double, Ann
followed on the heels of Maggie.

'All clear there?' The deputy's voice ricocheted from the walls.

And the answer came, 'Aye, Peter, all clear and respectable.'

A laugh issued from a section where no light was showing, and it
appeared as if the rock itself was speaking.

Ann, still on the outskirts of the group, saw a number of men in
trunks and singlets. Even from a distance most of them looked shy
and awkward. They continued with their work, just lifting their
heads at intervals to take a peep at the visitors.

'So this is where you get the coal?' Miss Wentworth spoke to one
of the men.

'Some of it, missis.'

'And how do you get it out? You actually pick it out?'

'He don't; a hard day's work would kill him!'

The humorist, now discerned as a huddled heap doing something in the corner of the road, seemed to be the only member of the workers or party who was enjoying the situation.

'Thoo better shut the gob. What do thoo say, dep?' The man indicated his mate with a nod of his head but spoke to the deputy.

'Divvent ask the impossible, Joe.'

Now the deputy was speaking in the same idiom as the men, and Miss Wentworth, looking from one to the other, made the embarrassing statement, 'There's no master and man; you work as a team, I suppose?'

There seemed to be a rustling of bodies. The deputy did not answer, and the man said, after a short while, 'We're all workers, miss, one way or another.'

'But some are more other than owt else.'

'Shut the gob, Joe.' It was the deputy speaking now, and for answer the man in the corner began to chuckle.

'Are they going to dig this coal out?' Miss Wentworth pointed to the seam and looked at the men.

'No. These are the stone men,' said the deputy. 'They are advancing the mothergate; they work with the pullers in there.' He pointed to an opening to the side of their feet. It was not more than

75

twenty-one inches high. 'These are the backshift men who get ready for the nightshift and the cutters.'

As Miss Wentworth looked down at the opening she was made to explain, 'Not in there, surely!'

'Aye, surely,' said the deputy, now feeling more himself that at least he had astonished this hard-boiled dame. 'Get down and have a look. Get down on your . . . stomach.'

'No, no. I can see all right from here.'

But now Ann, who had been standing on the outskirts of the group, felt herself compelled to move forward. She must see the place, or a similar place to where her Davie, for nearly seven hours a day lay on his stomach or at best crouched and swung a pick as fast as his strength would allow him.

The deputy said, 'That's right, miss; you want to see?'

Ann bent down. In the gleam of the lamps she saw what she knew to be men, but who appeared like strange, contorted animals from another world. She knew what they were doing; they were pulling out the chocks to let the roof fall.

The light gleamed on a naked arm. She could see it clearly because the sweat running down it streaked it as it went.

The deputy shouted, 'Hi, there, Michael!' and the arm stopped and the body moved round on the ground, and a face showed, all teeth and eyes. It was joined by another, and the deputy shouted again, 'I've three ladies here. Would you like them to come along?'

'Aye. Oh, aye. This is the very place for them.' The men laughed, and into Ann's tortured mind a sense of pride and wonderment forced itself for a fraction of a second. These men working in the lilliputian halls of a living hell were still able to laugh. But the wonderment fled on the thought of her David. He lay like that every day, with nothing but those little pit props to hold up the roof, to keep the thousands of tons of rock from crushing him . . . a few inches of wood defying that mighty weight! It couldn't do it, not all the time; it would give way; it would all give way; it could this very minute, now, while she was standing here! The fear for David became lost in the fear for herself . . . the place was closing in on her; she couldn't breathe . . . My God! We'll all be crushed to death; we'll never get out! Even the whispered words spelt panic, and the deputy said, 'What is it, miss?'

She turned to him and clung to his arm. 'The place'll fall in; I want to get out!'

Two men, with early electric lamps issued only to rescuers, prepare to descend after a pit disaster. The canary's job is to test the air for dangerous gasses. The miners themselves in the mid-nineteenth century would rely on the rats, which inhabited the mine shafts, as sensors: 'She learned to trust Charlie. This happened on the day one of the men, seeing the rat standing on his hind legs sniffing before scurrying away up the road, cried to them, "Run for it!"' Tilly Trotter

She clasped one hand suddenly over her mouth, and the deputy said sternly, 'Now, miss, take hold of yourself. It strikes me you should never have come down, but we'll be going in just a minute. The men are showing the lady how a charge is set.' He nodded towards Miss Wentworth.

A charge! An explosion! She knew what a charge was: a hole was made in the rock and the explosive put in, and then it blew up.

No power on earth, or under it, at that moment could have stayed her flight. With the fleetness of a stag she turned and ran up the roadway, skipping over the rocks, missing the roof beams as if by a succession of miracles.

The startled deputy shouted to the man who had been talking to Miss Wentworth, 'Bring them along to the cage, Joe,' as he set off after the fleeing figure.

'Now, now!' He caught hold of her arm and pulled her to a stop. 'Steady on.' He was breathing hard himself. 'There's no need to run like that.'

She stood swaying on her feet. 'I want to get out.' Her mouth was hanging loose and saliva was running over her lower lip.

'You'll get out; come on. Only go steady, else you'll likely as not break your legs, and then you'll be in a worse fix. You should never have come down. Hadn't you any idea what it would be like?'

'Yes . . . no. Well, not like this. I want to get out.'

'There now, take it easy. You see, you are in the main road now and it won't be long.'

They passed an old man, a solitary figure, standing as if he was part of the inanimate depth wherein he worked.

Without preliminary explanation the deputy said, 'She shouldn't have come down,' and the old man answered 'No, God fits the nerve to the need.'

As the cage moved upwards the light from above grew stronger, and she peered at the walls of the shaft, gathering to herself the rays of light . . . Oh, to be out in the light and the sun! The sun. To see the sun again. How many aeons of time had passed since she saw the sun! . . . and David. He didn't see the sun or light for over seven hours of each day, and then in the winter when he came up it was dark . . . Darkness. For days and days, darkness. Oh, David!

The cage bumped to a standstill, and with Bert's hand on her arm she stepped out on to the platform, and right to the feet of David!

The Cost

The cost of industrial expansion was measured in the employment conditions and the lives of the men, women and childen these industrialists employed.

The most dangerous period for miners was in the nineteenth century when colliers were mining deep pits in areas where they had no real knowledge of the level of danger from water or gas. As the size of shifts increased, numbers of dead would be measured in hundreds from a single incident. The situation came to a head in 1862 with the New Hartley disaster in which more than two hundred men and boys were killed.

When I was researching *The Menagerie* I wrote to the Ministry of Mines. They sent me white papers, huge maps depicting everything that had happened after an explosion. They were a fearful sight: even a man's bait tin or the exact site where another man's head was blown off, were pinpointed. I worked *The Menagerie* from these records:

The town was still, the shops were closed, and no traffic moved on

Among local mining disasters were Stanley, pictured here in 1909, in which 168 people died, and New Hartley in 1862 where there had been one shaft for all purposes – men, coal and ventilation – making rescue impossible. When finally the rescuers reached their destination, they discovered notes written by the men before they died, describing the scene as it had been, describing the prayer meetings that had taken place towards the end.

For those fortunate to have survived other disasters, the experience left its mark: 'From that time William had suffered from nightmares, nightmares in which he was suffocating among mangled bodies and blood.'
Katie Mulholland

Scene of funeral following the Stanley pit disaster of 1909.

the main road. The day had started quietly and the quietness had grown with each hour. When people stirred they did so softly; when they spoke, their words, broad as they might be, did not rise with the sing-song intonation and fill the air, but hovered close about them as if loath to jar this day of sorrows. The funeral route was black with people; and as the long line of hearses moved slowly to the cemetery, women cried, men cried, and small children were unusually silent.

Larry was the only representative of his family. The one uncle and three cousins he had were scattered over the country. The uncle was confined to his bed, and the cousins for varying reasons could not attend. Cables bearing frantic messages had come from Australia, but no one expected anyone from there. Neighbours and friends flanked him, but seemingly he was alone. Of his father and Jack, he did not think 'I am walking with them for the last time' because for days now they had been strangely nearer to him than ever they had been when alive. Some part of each of them had burrowed into his being; he felt he was no longer one but three men. But he would recognise the responsibilities of two only, his own, and his father's. His mother was his responsibility; so was Aunt Lot; but Jack's child... Here his particular self was constantly proving the point against Jack's pleading. The child was Lena's; she should be found and made to take it. Yet within himself he knew that Lena had gone for good, and that what was finally to become of the child would rest with him. And at the moment these three people represented his world, and their combined pressure lay on his shoulders like a roof fall.

The cemetery lay on a rising fell on the outskirts of the town, and from any part of it could be seen the shafts of the two pits. As the heart-breaking service went on, and names were called and the coffins lowered, and flowers sprinkled and muffled sobs and moans filled the air, heads would be lifted to the pit wheels, and like monster eyes in which was reflected nothing but indifference the wheels stared back and seemed to say, 'You asked for it. Who started me anyway? You want coal and more coal. You must pay for it.'

Frank and Jack were laid side by side, and as Larry stepped blindly back from the grave, he too seemed forced to raise his eyes over the mass of heads. The wheels looked at him. First the Venus then the Phoenix, and at the sight of them he yelled in his head, 'Damn you! Blast you!'

A woman near him quietly fainted, sliding down between two relatives as if she had just decided to sit, while another, unable to control her sobs, verged on hysteria. A man, whose son had just been lowered, gave a cry like a wounded animal and, turning from the grave, his hand shielding his face, he pushed his way aggressively through the crowd.

At last it was over, the dead were left in the bower of flowers. And it was of the flowers that Larry was thinking as he walked out of the gates. Never in his life did he want to see or smell another flower. Always would he be reminded of that grave when he saw a bunch of flowers. The smell of them was strong in his nostrils now and filling his head with a sick ache. He felt their scent would remain round him for ever.

Recession, Depression and Collapse
Quite suddenly on a May day in 1866 the empire of the North

80

A reflection of post-World War I poverty: children queue outside a soup kitchen.

shuddered and collapsed as if struck by an earthquake, and small men, middle men and those in high places felt the tremors.

There was panic in the City of London. Banks failed; railways went out of business; steel companies had to join forces in order to survive; businesses that had been held jealously within families were either bankrupt or were merged with companies that had been fortunate enough to escape the earthquake.

This one and that were blamed for the disaster but the fault seemed to be with the company of Overand and Gurney, who financed a great deal of the Northern industries at the time, and were overspent by many millions; and so the flame of panic spread from the banking houses in London and swept the North.

The Glass Virgin

81

Alongside Palmer's Shipyard, the Battleship Queen Mary built there in 1913. It was sunk during the battle of Jutland in May 1916.

Gurneys were part of a great Quaker group which had built up enormous financial business in the course of the nineteenth century. No one thought for a moment that this giant had feet of clay, and when the Bank of England deemed collapse inevitable, it was a catastrophe. Of course 1866 did not see the collapse of the entire industrial scene in the North, but its importance cannot be underestimated because it marked a loss of confidence on a grand scale in a world where confidence was essential.

The great export boom from about 1850 saw coal, iron, steel, engineering, shipbuilding in an ascending spiral of interdependence. But after the end of the First World War, with few warships being built, few new railway systems, and fierce foreign competition in other areas, the spiral

The launch of H.M.S. York, July 17th, 1928, at Palmer's by the Duchess of York, later Queen of England.

was put in reverse, and suddenly the interdependent structure of industry proved to be a fundamental weakness.

The terrible picture of Jarrow in the process of collapse is described towards the end of the novel, *Katie Mulholland*, when Bridget shows her friend, Daniel Rosier the Third, around a once proud Palmer's:

It was on the Wednesday, after tea, that Catherine suggested that Bridget should show Daniel around the town; he must see Marsden Rock, the mile-long pier, and the grand Town Hall, outside which, Tom had laughingly said, 'There stood the only natural women in

1934, the dismantling of the huge cranes at Palmer's. 'As long as you could see the cranes you felt that your job was secure' had become a saying of the past.

Shields.' Later, he found out that these natural women were outsize nude figures which he considered a brave gesture on someone's part. He enjoyed the evening. They laughed a lot. Bridget had a sense of fun not unlike her father's, he thought.

When he bade good-night to his great-grandmother she asked him to be sure to come down the following day for lunch.

By the 1860s more than half the nation's production of alkali and bleaching powder came from 24 chemical works along the banks of the Tyne. But by 1914 the industry had sunk, beaten by technical advances and other forms of competition from abroad.

Workers at the chemical plant with primitive protection from pollution.

On Thursday he came for lunch, and Katie kept him with her most of the afternoon and he learnt all about Mr Peter Conway, Bridget's fiancé. Mr Conway was ten years older than Bridget, but that was nothing. He was a splendid man and serious-minded. He had, when the works were in operation, been well up in the offices of Palmer's. He had been one of the men, too, who had represented the staff when the Duchess of York had come to launch the cruiser *York*. He had been very well thought of by the management and had fought hard, like all the staff, to keep the yard going. Katie had quoted this great Peter as saying that in 1930, when the razor of nationalisation had started at the end of Palmer's throat, and Sir James Lithgow of Port Glasgow, the strong man of steel, had chewed at the other with his plan for a nationalised industry, the blood had flowed so quickly that Palmer's became like an anaemic giant.

This Mr Peter Conway, Daniel decided, sounded like a stuffed shirt. Had the quoter been any other than his great-grandmother he would have squashed Mr Peter's simile about the death of the shipyard. He knew of Sir James Lithgow; his father had often spoken of him and the Lithgow firm, which was one of the greatest in Britain. Lithgow came of a shipbuilding family, and the idea of the great steel and shipbuilding industry being taken over by the government was anathema to him as it was to all shipowners. . .

85

Capitalists, as this Mr Peter Conway apparently dubbed them.

He was more than a little relieved when, after tea, he once again found himself being escorted on a tour by Bridget.

'I'm going to show you Jarrow,' she said. 'You won't like it, but I think you should see it.'

And he didn't like it. In fact he was appalled. The town looked dead, it even smelt dead to him. The district around the station had appeared dreary enough, but these dejected grey streets with groups of men leaning against the end walls, all attired in similar uniform, cap, muffler, and greasy-looking oddments of suits, were depressing to say the least. Men who smiled thinly, and chatted, and said at intervals, 'Watcher there,' yet who looked bewildered and numb, and at the same time aggressive. He knew this country was suffering under a slump; he wasn't unused to it in his own country, but here in this town the poverty was so stark, so raw, it was like looking on a body from which the skin had been ripped.

As they walked up the long road towards the dismembered shipyard that was once the proud Palmer's, she said, 'Did Aunt Katie tell you Peter was away helping to organise the march to London?'

'Yes, she did say something about it.'

Yet what echo do I hear?
Palmers of Hebburn
Is to close.
Is this the prelude
To fear
Resurrecting the
Slump
That was never to return?

They were silent until they came to the shipyard itself where the great gates had stood, and she stopped and, pointing to the vast jumble of contorted iron that the oxy-acetylene burners had made of the steel girders and cranes, and the great heaps of bricks where the blast-furnaces and their chimneys had once stood, said quietly, 'I never come into Jarrow but I am drawn here to watch this. I suppose it's because this whole business – I mean the closing of the yard – hit me personally.' She slanted her eyes at him, and there was a shyness in her look as she said, 'You see, it stopped my wedding. Peter losing his savings, all twelve hundred pounds of it,

87

and being responsible for his mother and the house; his father's dead. Then the fact that if we married I would lose my job . . .'

'How's that?'

'Oh, they don't allow you to teach after you are married, not the women. We, too, are dead if we marry. But I suppose it's to be expected. There aren't enough jobs for the male teachers. We know a friend of ours who put in for a post down South; he's a maths master. Do you know how many applicants there were for the job? Two hundred and fifty.'

'You don't say!' His brows were drawn together. Then he said 'Your fiancé – he . . . he didn't get any of his money back from the firm?'

'No, but he was just like hundreds of others in the town. There were families who had saved and saved for years and put it into Palmer's; perhaps it was only a couple of hundred pounds or so, but to them it was a fortune, and they lost every penny, and now they're on the dole and stunned by the hopelessness of it all.'

He looked hard at her as she looked at the gigantic wreck, and he had the strange disturbing urge to grab her by the hand and run pell-mell from this place. He had a picture of them tearing down the main street never stopping until they reached an open space where they could see nothing of tangled iron, dreary grey streets and hopeless-looking men and women.

'Come,' he said, his voice brisk-sounding. 'Let's get out of this.'

The key factor in the story of industrial growth proved to be the export boom and the lack of foreign competition. Once the rest of Europe began to catch us up and undercut our production prices, the end was in sight. Weak companies found no support from the government in the form of subsidies or tariffs on imports – none when the Belgian glass industry threatened; none when the German chemical industry came through . . . and no one felt the effects of the government's resolute non-protectionist policy more than the workers.

In fact even when the spiral of industrial growth was in its ascendancy there had been eddies in the opposite direction, depressions which resulted in large numbers of unemployed. And besides unemployment there was the problem of *under*-employment, which often left people worse off than being on the dole. Today dockers have a substantial minimum wage to sign on, but until the decasualisation of the docks they were paid by the shift. How many shifts in a week was completely unpredictable, for while the regular steamship traffic could be forecast fairly accurately, there was

Right:
"'I'm not broke, but I'm not going to let the blasted government get off with anything. No, by God, I'm going to get some dole out of them."

"You won't get any for a fortnight, anyway; they don't recognise the first week and then there's three days lying on." Dan was talking quietly.

"Tell me something I don't know, man. Anyway I told you I'll be at it again next week and I'll tell them what to do with their dole. But look," his manner changed abruptly and his voice became serious as he turned to David. "Don't let on to me mother, mind."' The Blind Miller

88

an enormous amount of ship traffic coming in and out of the Tyne which could not be. To service it required a pool of labour hanging about the docks and not getting paid.

The cancer of unemployment was eating the country, and the Tyneside in particular. It was eating into initiative and hope, and doubling despair. A man, becoming unemployed, went on the dole; and he would sign on each day before vainly doing the round of the shipyards. And in the evening he would stand at the corner with his pals, who were in the same predicament as himself, and they would hide their feelings in jokes. If he lay in bed at night and wondered what was to become of him and the wife and bairns once the dole was finished, he gave little sign of it during the day.

It is said that man can get used to any condition if he is in it long enough, and it would seem there was truth in this, for, as the years went on and the dole bred the Means Test, most of the men on the Tyne had forgotten how it felt to carry a bait tin – in fact they doubted whether there had ever been a time in their lives when they had worked. The younger men didn't have to wonder about this; those born just prior to or during the 1914 war never knew what it was to be employed. Even those apprenticed to the few small firms still in existence were stood off immediately they reached the age of nineteen.

It was strange, too, how stark poverty changed the flavour of the jokes from sex to food.

'Well, I'm off for me dinner.'

'What's it the day, lad?'

'Chicken.'

'Chicken agin?'

'Aye . . . I'm so bloody full of chicken I've got the urge to gan an' sit on a clutch of eggs.'

And so it went on. Here and there a man suddenly ended the struggle, and the effect on his mates, oddly enough, was such as to stiffen their fibre. 'It's no use taking things like that,' would be their attitude; 'things can't get any worse; the bloody Government will have to do something if they don't want trouble. Hang on a bit longer.'

Colour Blind

End of the Road

During one period of great depression – this was when my mother was a child – me granda worked in the workhouse, breaking stones at a shilling a day. The shilling was paid as a voucher which had to be taken to a grocery shop, and if anyone dared to ask the shopkeeper to put in a penn'orth of baccy he was likely to lose the voucher altogether. The utter degradation of the workhouse is described in *Our John Willie*.

'Come on.' He tugged John Willie into step with him, and it was only when, half an hour later, he came within sight of the workhouse walls that he stopped, and the effect of what he was about to do overwhelmed him.

Slowly he dropped on to his hunkers, and now in elaborate sign language he explained. Pointing first to the formidable grey

NOSTALGIA

Oh would the North were as it was
When I was little Katie
When ships were born from Palmer's
womb
And slag lit scarlet and black night sky
And rivets flew like sparks from stars
And men were proud to work and sweat.

And yet?
This is just reminiscing talk
No – I would not have the North
As it was
When I was little Katie
For then no workman owned a car
Or took a holiday across the sea
Nor dare he stand and say to THEM
'Lad, I'm as good as thee.'

Oh, little Katie of long ago
Of long, long ago.

90

buildings, he then pushed his finger into the young boy's chest, after which he placed the flat of his hand on his own breast, bowed his head, then rose to his feet and did a standing march.

John Willie understood, he understood only too well. His eyes screwed up, his mouth opened wide and from it was tumbled a rapid succession of 'Huhs' that grew louder in protest.

'Look! Look!' Davy rose to his feet and taking John Willie by the shoulders shook him as he cried, 'Listen. Listen.' He always said listen, even while he knew it was a silly thing to say.

John Willie now became quiet, still. His mouth closed, his eyes stretched wide, there was no movement in any part of his thin body while he stared into Davy's troubled face.

'I've got to go to . . . to find work.' Davy now demonstrated digging with a shovel. After this he pointed in the direction opposite to the workhouse, then counting on his fingers, 'One, two, three, four, five,' for that was one thing he could do, he could count up to twenty, he brought his arm in a wide circling movement, finishing up by once more placing his finger on John Willie's chest. And although John Willie made no signs whatever, Davy knew that his brother was aware of what lay in front of him.

Slowly now they went towards the gates. When he rattled the chain a man came out of the lodge and, looking through the bars, said, 'Aye, what you after?'

'I've got a ticket for bread.'

'Another one of 'em!'

The porter took a key that was hanging from his belt and unlocked the chain and pulled open the gates, and they went inside, John Willie walking so close to Davy's side that he almost impeded his movements.

'Go along there to the clerk, he'll see to you.' The man pointed into the distance, and they went towards a door, then through it and into a bare flag-stoned corridor. There were windows on one side of the corridor and through them he looked on to a big yard that was walled on all sides by high buildings. The yard was full of people, men, women, and children, and they were all doing odd things. Some were standing with their faces to the walls, some were jumping up and down as if skipping but without ropes; others were laughing. But there was one woman near the window almost within arm's length of him who had her face turned up to the sky and the tears were washing her cheeks. Then there was the noise.

Little hope reflected in the faces of men in the male infirm ward of the workhouse.

It was chattering noise, a mixture of all kinds of noises like that made by birds in a cage.

'They're the dafties.'

He swung round startled to look up at a big gangling woman who had a wooden bucket in one hand and a scrubbing brush and dirty cloth in the other, and she nodded her head towards the window as she grinned widely, saying, 'They're all daft, barmy. I'm not daft. I'm Emma Steel, and I'm not daft.' At this she turned and walked away to the end of the corridor where, putting the bucket on the ground, she knelt down by it and started to scrub the stones.

It was seconds before Davy realized that he was still staring at her, his mouth slightly agape. She said she wasn't daft, well, she wasn't among that lot but he had never seen anybody look dafter.

'What do you want?'

He swung round in the other direction now and looked at a woman in a kind of uniform dress with a starched cap on her head. The woman scrubbing the corridor had a cap on her head too but it was a different one; and all those women out in the yard, they were wearing caps, like bonnets, dirty white bonnets.

'I've got a ticket' – he held out the slip – 'for bread from . . . Par-

Above Left:
Harton workhouse, where I worked in the laundry. The asylum was to the right. The stone-breaking yard was at the back where my grandfather broke stones for a shilling a day.

'But God was good, and had showered his special blessing over them, when all around, weeping women and grim-faced men had watched their last sticks of furniture being carried out by the bums before wending their heart-breaking way down the Jarrow Road to East Jarrow, through Tyne Dock and down Stanhope Road, to where Talbot Road showed the grim gates at the far end, which, once entered, a family was no longer a family but merely segregated individuals, with numbers on each of their garments.'
Colour Blind

92

son Murray.'

'Go in the end door.'

'Ta.' He nodded at the woman as she walked away, and it was some seconds still before he could make his feet move towards the door at the end of the corridor.

When he opened the door he found he was looking into a room where four men were seated at high desks, and all were writing rapidly. The one nearest the door lifted his head and stared from Davy to John Willie, then back to Davy before saying, 'Aye, what is it?'

Davy repeated that he had a ticket for bread and held it out. The man looked at the slip of paper. Then raising his head and looking from one to the other again, he said, 'For the two of you?'

'Yes, sir.'

'You'll have to do four hours stone breaking you know.'

'Yes, sir.'

'I can't see him breaking many stones.'

'I . . . I can do enough for us both.'

'No, no, it doesn't work like that; a man can only work to his full capacity, as can a boy. You are expected to give full capacity in return for your food.'

'I'll work extra hard, sir.'

The man was again looking at John Willie. 'What is the matter with him? He's puny. How old is he?'

'Ten, sir. He's . . . he's deaf and dumb, sir.'

'Deaf and dumb? Ten?' The man gave a little shake with his head as if he didn't believe it, then added, not unkindly, 'If you work all day you can have a mid-day meal.'

'If . . . if you don't mind, sir, I'll . . . I'll just take the bread.'

There was rising in Davy a desperate urge to be away from this place.

The man now took a metal disc from a drawer and, handing it to Davy, said, 'I'm only giving you one 'cos he'll be no good at it. Go to the yard. See Mr Rider, the officer; he'll show you to the road where they're breaking.'

Davy looked down at the disc. There was an anger rising in him against the injustice of not giving John Willie a disc that would enable him to have his share of bread. Before he should give vent to it, however, he turned sharply away, dragging John Willie with him.

Out in the corridor again, he walked back to the woman who was scrubbing the floor. 'Where's the yard?' he asked her.

'Yard? Through there, you daftie.' She pointed to another corridor going off the main one.

Quickly he turned from her and went down the corridor which led to the yard. This yard, too, he saw was full. Women of all ages were shovelling coal into buckets while others carried them away. At one side of the yard under a wooden awning women were bent over poss tubs, wielding the heavy poss sticks up and down, up and down, on the wet clothes. There were great mounds of mole-skin trousers and grey twill dresses near every tub.

He passed by a low building from where the smell of hot irons issued. Some of the women peered up at them, others looked too lost in despair. These latter were generally those who had small children around them. When he asked where he could find Mr Rider he was directed to a short fat man who was hustling two small boys who were attempting to push a barrow of broken stone over the rough uneven flags of the yard.

'Bread. Four hours?' The man's small eyes scrutinized Davy. 'Only four hours and only one of you?' he said; then looking down on John Willie, he added, 'He can help push the barrows.'

'No, no; he can't, he's not goin' to. He's not earnin'. The man back there said he's not earnin' so he'll stay with me.'

'Be careful, young 'un, be careful, else you'll get me fist in yer mouth and me toe in yer backside, an' that'll be in place of bread.'

'Just try it on.' Davy was past caution now; all he wanted was to get out of this place. He had heard about the workhouse, he had heard terrible things about the workhouse, he had seen the poor apprentices from the workhouse in the pit; they were always given the worst jobs and received the worst treatment.

The man glared at him and Davy glared back.

Then from between his teeth he said, 'You young scut, you! get goin'!' And he pointed in the direction of an opening in the yard.

But Davy took his time in going; he out-stared the man for some seconds before turning away. And then he made his step slow and steady, which was difficult as John Willie was pressing so closely against him. When he left the yard he saw the men and the stones; they were making a kind of road leading across some farmland.

The man in charge of the work took the wind out of Davy's aggressive sails by saying, 'Four hours is it, lad? Aw well, just carry on in that corner. He hasn't got a disc, the young 'un?'

'No.'

'Well no, I don't suppose they'd give him one. Anyway, just carry on over there next to that big fellow. All right?'

Davy nodded, then went towards the tall man. He was redheaded and looked in his mid-thirties.

'What do I do?'

The man stopped his rhythmical hammering of a chisel into a block of stone. 'Same as me. Take the pick of your tools.' He nodded towards the edge of the road. 'And don't hurry or else you won't last.'

And that's all the man said for the next hour.

But his silence did not affect Davy, who was too full of his own thoughts. Every now and again he would look in the direction of John Willie, where he sat by the heap of broken stones, his head bent, his back bowed, his whole attitude showing his dejection, and he wanted to explain to him it was all right; for if it meant them starving he had no intention of leaving him in this mad hole. But he couldn't explain without attracting the notice of the other men at work, and pointing out to everybody that his brother was a deaf mute.

When the man did speak it was about John Willie. 'What's the matter with him?' he asked. 'Is he sick?'

'No, not really; he's deaf and dumb.'

'Poor devil.'

'Are . . . are you in for good?'

'In for good?' the rhymthic hammering stopped and the red head went back and the man laughed aloud before he answered, 'Not me, son, not me. It was only that me tongue hadn't licked food for three days that brought me in here.'

'Are you from these parts?'

'Near enough, Durham.'

'Oh, Durham. In the pits?'

'Aye, in the pits, or was.'

'Everybody's out these days.'

'Oh, it wasn't a case of being out; plenty of work in my pit.'

Now Davy gave the man his full attention. 'Then . . . then why are you here?'

'They got rid of me. Ever hear of unions?'

'Aye; aye, I've heard of unions.'

'Well, if you get started in the pit in future, lad, and want to keep your job don't agitate for unions. That's my advice.'

'They put you out for that?'

'Aye, they put me out for that. I'm on the black-list. But not for long, no, not for long.' He changed his rhythm and hammered three successive quick blows on the chisel. 'Come the day when we'll be on top. Do you know that, lad? We, the pitmen'll be on top. Not all the bosses, or gods'll get the better of me.'

Davy said nothing to this. He knew that the man wasn't referring to working at the pit-head but to getting one over on the bosses, and if there was ever wishful thinking that was wishful thinking, imagining you could get one over on the bosses. But it was a wonderful idea, although it would never come to anything. His mother had always said, 'There'll always be bosses and there'll be workmen,' and he believed she was right. However could a man be paid for his work if there weren't men with money to pay him? Yes, there'd always be bosses. He wished at this moment he was working for a boss, any boss, but preferably one who gave orders above ground in the daylight. Aye, it would be wonderful to be able to earn his living in daylight, even in a job as he was doing now. But not in here. Oh no! not in here.

Time went on; then a whistle blew and the man in charge shouted, 'Time for grub!'

The red-haired man laid down his tools and said, 'Well, stop that and come on.'

Davy stopped his hammering and, looking up at his companion, he said, 'I'm just workin' for the bread, four hours.'

'Oh, I'm sorry. Be seeing you then.'

'Aye, be seein' you.'

But Davy didn't see the man again for when those who had eaten returned there was whispering and laughing along the road, and without being told, Davy knew what had happened. The man had done a bunk, he'd had his meal and done a bunk. He'd heard of workhouse boys doing a bunk, but they were nearly always caught and brought back and lathered.

Under other circumstances Davy would have laughed aloud, but all he said to himself was, 'He might have been starving but he must have had some strength left to climb over that wall,' because it was higher than the one surrounding Miss Peamarsh's grounds and had broken glass bottles along its top.

It was an hour later when Davy left the road, and he almost had to drag John Willie with him for the boy was so dejected. At one point he put his doubled fist under his chin in an effort to raise his head and tell him it was all right. But John Willie still kept his chin tucked into his chest.

The man who was doling out the bread had a quirk to his lips as he said, 'One disc, one loaf,' then thrusting his hand to the back shelf he brought out a small loaf and banged it onto the wooden table. Davy picked it up without looking at it, for he was returning the man's stare.

The loaf held in the crook of his arm and tugging John Willie with him, he threaded his way among the milling inmates across the yard to the corridor, where in vain he tried to keep his eyes

97

from the windows and the mad specimens cavorting in the yard beyond. Then he was walking towards the iron gates, and as he went he felt the tension running from his brother's hand and without looking at him he knew that his head was up and his face alight.

Not until they had passed through the gates and the feeling of freedom was on him once more did Davy look down on John Willie, and then that girlish weakness that would assail him at times came over him now and it was all he could do to stop his own tears from flowing, for his brother's face was awash. But when the boy threw himself at him and his thin arms gripped his thigh, the lump in this throat threatened to choke him and, shaking himself free from John Willie's hold, he gabbled down at him, 'Stop it now! Stop it. You're all right. You understand? You're all right. Never, never.' He jerked his thumb over his shoulder towards the gates, then repeated, 'Never, never.' After which he thrust his forefingers into John Willie's chest and then into his own and then crossed his fingers, and John Willie gazing up at him almost with a look of adoration nodded his head and smiled. And Davy smiled back at him.

Now to assuage both their appetites he went to break an end off the loaf, but his fingers became still on the crust. The smile slid from his face; the loaf was hard, stale. He remembered the man stretching into the back of the shelf. He likely kept a number of such there as the means of venting his spite. Eeh! some people were awful, awful. He tore and twisted at the end of the loaf until he managed to break off a piece. This he broke in two and handed one piece to John Willie. Then they walked slowly back along the road home. Home that would only be theirs for another two days.

My Ain Folk

Our Kate, aged about forty, standing at the back of Number Ten. Kate's troubles hung over her head like an avalanche about to plunge down and bury her.

I was born when Kate was twenty-four and the life she was made to endure because of me would have driven anyone less strong not only to drink but into the madhouse. The cruelty of the bigoted poor has to be witnessed to be believed. It has to be lived with to be understood.

When my mother, sick to the depths of her soul, as I know now she was, had to come home from 'her place' (my mother's first spell of service was for a butcher in Stanhope Road) and say she was going to have a baby, The Fathar, as he was always called, was for killing her – she had committed the unforgivable sin. Yet when I was born and she had milk fever and her breasts swelled to bursting, the fathar was supposed to have saved her life by sucking the milk from them. It seems incredible to me that she should have looked upon this act as something almost heroic for, remembering him as I do, I can see that he would have enjoyed this operation – he was a frustrated, licentious man. His antidote against this, which the ailing health of me grandma could not alleviate, was drink and a dirty tongue, which he used against all women. Yet I must say that only on rare occasions did he let himself go in my presence, at least when he was sober. I feel grateful to him for this, for he had been known to make even the toughest women in the New Buildings blush.

As the years went on I think that of the two, me grandma was harder on Kate than the fathar, because, when coming home from place on her rare days off, if she'd attempt to take me in her arms me grandma would grab me from her, rearrange my clothes and almost dust me down as if Kate's hands had contaminated me in some way.

At the time she met my father she was working in an inn in Lamesley. She was working in the bar, and had been for two or three years. Her sister, Mary, who was three years younger, was a housemaid, and a very haughty, hot-tempered housemaid at that. I am not quite sure of the name of the owners of the inn at that time but I do know that the daughter was Miss Jenny. Kate often spoke of her. Also of the pitmen who used to take the long trek past the inn to the mine, and on pay day, which was once a fortnight, have a blow up in the bar and a pay up for the odd pints that had gone on the slate. She must have been a favourite with them, for she was an attractive woman in those days, gay, warm, large-hearted.

My father, I understand, first set eyes on her when she served him in the saloon.

Kate never told me anything about him until six years before she died. It was my Aunt Mary who, when I was sixteen, gave me the sketchy outline of my beginnings and set up in my mind an inordinate pride, a sense of false superiority and a burning desire to meet this wonderful

The Inn at Lamesley where Kate worked behind the bar and met my father; it features in my recently published novel, The Moth: *'In the inn at Lamesley he had met an old gaffer and paid for the history of the district in two half-pints of ale.'*

creature who had shocked me into being. This man. This gentleman. Oh, yes, he was a gentleman. My Aunt Mary stated this with emphasis. She had no love for her sister, Kate. Later in life when Kate became the object of her scorn, she still remained jealous of her, for people liked Kate, loved her in spite of everything. Mary did not have a nature that one could love, and when she imparted this news to me it was to hurt Kate, make me more ashamed of her. Yet deep in me I knew that my Aunt Mary wasn't a patch on 'Our Kate'. But Mary was often kind to me, it was only her scorn of Kate that made me dislike her. Anyway, Mary said this gentleman went head over heels as soon as he saw Kate.

What did this gentleman do for a living?

Nobody has ever been able to tell me.

How did Mary know he was a gentleman?

Well, he wore a black coat with an astrakhan collar. He had a high hat and carried a silver mounted walking stick and black kid gloves, like 'The Silver King', she said. 'And he spoke different . . . lovely.'

For two years the gentleman courted Kate. He did not come regularly but when he did he took her out, arranging his visits to her day off. She looked at no one else in the way she did at him. She was deeply in love. What did she expect from this association? She never said. But, knowing her level-headedness, I feel that she knew from the beginning that it was hopeless and therefore she kept him in his place, except for once; and once was enough. It seems pitiable to me at this distance that it wasn't until she was twenty-three that she first went with a man. I say first; it was the one and only time she had this kind of association with my father, and it's more pitiable still that she never had this association with anyone else until over sixteen years later when she married David McDermott, because she was of a loving nature. I can feel myself getting angry when I think that she was branded as a fallen woman – and you needed to make a mistake only once and give evidence of it in order to acquire this prefix in those days – while today girls still at school indulge in intimacy for kicks. If I hadn't stopped believing in God this injustice would surely have acted as a springboard against believing in a benevolent father, a controller of destinies, someone who has our welfare at heart, for such a deity must surely have had his favourites, and Kate wasn't one of them.

My bitterness is not for myself because I realise now that in being part of 'the gentleman' – and I have my tongue in my cheek even as I write the word – I have a great deal to be thankful for, for he provided the norm at which I aimed. It was him in me that pushed and pulled me out of the drabness of my early existence.

Big Houses Peopled by Ladies and Gentlemen

In the television series of *The Mallens*, a house in Derbyshire was used for High Banks Hall. But none of my big country houses – High Banks,

Langley Castle, Langley, before its restoration by Ted Cadwallader Bates.

'The boy stared long and hard at the pile upon pile of stone, and when he made no comment his father said, "Well, what d'you think?"

"It's old."

"Aye, lad, it's old."

"And it wants mendin'."

The tall man burst out laughing as he said, "Right again, it wants mendin'."'

A Dinner of Herbs

101

'The drive was wide and could take three coaches abreast. It was bordered directly in front by an ornamental privet hedge, not high enough to obscure the view of the gardens beyond. Yet the view was checkered by the contrasted mass of sculptured trees.' The Glass Virgin (Redwood Hall)

The lovely ceiling is like the one in the novel I am working on now, called Year of the Virgin. With all the clutter it is clear the amount of work for the maids.

'As John gazed about him, the room took away the ease and self-possession the little maid had momentarily given him. It was a melody of colour. He had never imagined colour as part of a room – good, strong furniture, yes, but here was russet and green, gold and white . . . Mary Llewellyn came in smiling, and as he looked at her he wondered at his nerve in daring to come and see this woman.'
David in The Fifteen Streets

Greenwall, Redford – are based on real buildings. They are all products of the imagination, and perhaps more than a little, a part of my 'picture on the wall', the focal point of my striving.

By the age of twenty-seven I had worked and saved sufficiently hard to be able to afford a 15-roomed, former gentleman's residence called The Hurst, and that was years before I began to write, and three years before I met Tom. As a teenager, after a childhood in the cramped conditions of 10 William Black Street, I remember promising myself that I would never marry but would, instead, give myself what the kind of man I should marry would give me: a very nice house with plenty of space.

So perhaps I owe my descriptions of big country houses to the gentleman

A very posed picture which in itself places this as a middle-class interior: notice the mantle border, the pull curtains beneath and the picture rail – few working class homes had picture rails.

The house of my imagination: The Hurst, Hoadswood Road, a fifteen-roomed gentleman's residence.

in me, 'the other half' which knew just what was needed.

Whatever is the case I have no doubt that my houses are realistic, for one day I received a telephone call from a man living in Scotland who had read one of my books. He was convinced that I had described his house and asked me when I had been there. When I told him that I had only been to Scotland once, on a day trip to Edinburgh when I was twenty-two, he said, 'But you have described my house in great detail, from the kitchen up. Have you seen pictures?' Of course I hadn't, but during our conversation I believe he mentioned only one feature of my description that wasn't quite the same!

The velvet over the mirror reminds me of Aunt Mary's house. When I was carrying my first baby we came through to visit my mother, who was suposed to be ill but wasn't, we came on the Friday night and on the Sunday we went to tea at Aunt Mary's. Tom couldn't believe it – she had knitted leggings for the legs of her enormous mahogany table. Uncle Alec was a crane driver then.

The Kitchen in Number Ten

Since returning to Tyneside I have had six houses and redesigned three of them. But of all the rooms I have ever lived in, the kitchen in William Black Street is the most important. Everything that I have written since seems to have been bred in that kitchen. Other things have been bred in me – the niceties, if you like – but the rawness of life came from that kitchen. The kitchen is the heart of the matter, for the kitchen was the axis about which revolved the lives of those nearest to me – my people, be they what they may . . .

We did not live in number ten when we first went to the New Buildings but in an upstairs house further up the street; but we did not live there long. Number ten was a downstairs house and had three rooms. The front room, into which you stepped from a tiny hallway that allowed only for the opening of the door, held a green plush suite – two stiff-backed armchairs, four single ones and a long couch – an oval table standing on a centre leg and a double brass bed. The bed lay in an alcove and you walked down the side of it to get to the door which led into the kitchen.

How a room the size of our kitchen could hold so much I don't know, for in its centre stood a large kitchen table of the better kind, with a leather covered top. Under the window that looked into the backyard stood another table, an oblong one, which was used for cooking. The fireplace was the old fashioned open black range and on the left of it for many years stood a great ugly unused gas stove. In front of the range was a massive steel fender, four feet long, and a conglomeration of steel fire irons, none

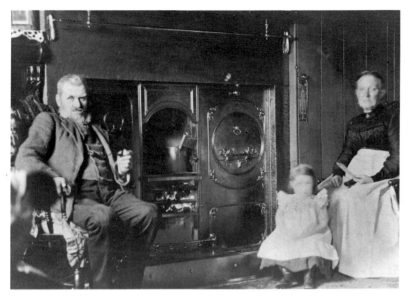

'The kitchen was bright and gleaming. From the open fireplace the coal glowed a deeper red in contrast with the shining blackleaded hob, with the oven to its right and the nook for the pans to its left. It sent down its glow onto the steel-topped and brass-railed fender, where its reflections appeared like delicate rose clouds seen through a silver curtain.' Kate Hannigan

I like this picture, nice, respectable people! The fender is just like ours, but ours had no rail; it's top was polished steel . . .' There's me sitting on the fender, Kate bustling around me. "Move your backside out of that," she says. I shuffle along the steel fender away from the black-leaded oven door, quickly past the fierce blazing fire, . . . and when I reach the far end of the long fender, I say, "A . . . w!" for the steel is always cold between the end of me knickers and the tops of my stockings.' Time and the Child

standing less than two feet high. On the floor, along the length of the fender was a clippy mat, a great heavy affair that I couldn't lift even when I was fourteen. On this mat stood a high backed wooden chair, 'the fathar's' chair, on which no one dared to sit but himself. Standing against the wall opposite the door that led out of the kitchen into the scullery was a chest of drawers. A six foot long wooden saddle – like a settee or couch – was set against the wall opposite the fireplace, but to get on to it you had to pull the table out or scramble over the head. Above it hung a picture of Lord Roberts sitting on a horse with a black man standing at his side. For years I believed the rider to be me Granda when he was in India, and when he levelled abuse at the picture, which he often did, I thought he was speaking to the black man.

What we called the scullery held two shelves and a backless chair, on which stood the tin dish used for all purposes that required water. Beyond was the pantry, a narrow slit with one long shelf. The tap was at the bottom of the yard, where also were the two lavatories. In this latter we were fortunate, there being a lavatory to each house. The back door leading to the upstairs house was on the left of our kitchen window, and opposite, running the complete length of the wall from our bedroom window to the coal house doors, were hen crees, always full of hens and ducks.

You reached the door of the bedroom by edging between the oblong table, the kitchen table and the head of the saddle, the bedroom in which I slept with my mother on a flea-ridden feather mattress, against which, with my conscripted assistance, she waged a fruitless war for years. Why didn't we get rid of the mattress? What! Get rid of a mattress that had supported countless births and a number of agonising deaths all because of a few fleas? And what would we have to lie on? There wasn't enough money for beer, let alone new mattresses.

The Pawn
The kitchen was the hub of my life; it was the centre of the universe from which all pain and pleasure sprang. In it would be enacted battles both physical and mental. One particular battle happened at least once a week between Kate and myself. It would begin with her saying 'I don't want you to go to school this mornin'.' This should have filled me with joy but it didn't. For it meant only one thing, she wanted me to go to the pawn. I would stand nearly always at the kitchen door leading into the scullery, from which you went by another door into the backyard. I would take up this position as if ready for flight. She would not look at me as she told me why she would have to send me to the pawn but would go about her business of clearing a table, or preparing food, or lifting up the mats, or throwing a great bucket of slack to the back of the fireplace in preparation for the tea leaves that would be put on it to clag it together. And she would be saying, 'It's the rent, I've just got to have it. This is the second week and they could put us in Court.'

Collecting rent cannot have been a very rewarding occupation in Jarrow in the nineteenth century, and being a cash business it must have carried its own temptations for the collectors. Certainly it did for Rory, the gambling man, as readers of the novel by that name will recall. Here the rent man's patter comes natural to Rory, though very likely his words will have held the same horror for this tenant as being taken to Court for arrears did for our Kate. Kate's debts hung over her head like an avalanche about to plunge down and bury her:

Rory shivered as he walked up the church bank and entered Jarrow. He passed the row of whitewashed cottages, then went on towards the main thoroughfare of Ellison Street. He hated this walk; he hated Saturday mornings; Saturday mornings meant Pilbey Street and Saltbank Row. Pilbey Street was bad enough but the Row was worse.

He had six calls in Pilbey Street and fifteen in the Row, and as always when he entered the street he steeled himself, put on a grim expression and squared his shoulders, while at the same time thinking, Old Kean and those other landlords he represents should

An enquiry into Child Welfare in 1909 claimed that 'Many children were very poorly clad and their clothes showed no signs of being repaired and lacked any method of fastening except pins. It was even found at times that a child's underclothing was sewn on . . .'

be lynched for daring to ask rent for these places.

For four years now he had collected the rents in these two streets. In the ordinary way he should have collected them on Monday, Tuesday or Wednesday because on these days he came this way collecting, and right on into Hebburn, but you couldn't get a penny out of anybody in Pilbey Street or the Row on any other day but a Saturday morning. And you were lucky if you managed to get anything then; it was only fear of the bums that made them tip up.

He lifted the iron knocker and rapped on the paint-cracked knobless door. There was a noise of children either fighting or playing coming from behind it, and after a few minutes it was opened and three pairs of eyes from three filthy faces peered up at him. All had running noses, all had scabs around their mouths and styes on their eyes. The eldest, about five, said in the voice of an adult, 'Aw, the rent man.' Then scrambling away through the room with the others following him, he shouted, 'The rent man, Ma! 'Tis the rent man, Ma!'

'Tell the bugger I'm not in.'

The woman's voice came clearly to Rory and when the child came back and, looking up at him, said, 'She's not in,' Rory looked down

'"Hallo, there Davie, man. Come and have a game." The hail came from a side street that was packed with children, and organising a game was one of his men. David stopped and shouted back, "Why, Phil, this is a new line, isn't it?" He laughed as he moved through the press of children and women, and Phil called, "Aye, it's harder work than hewing, this."' Maggie Rowan

on the child and as if addressing an adult said, 'Tell her the bugger wants the rent, and somethin' off the back, or else it's the bums Monday.'

The child gazed at him for a moment longer before once more scrambling away through the room, and when his thin high voice came back to him, saying, 'He says, the bugger wants the rent,' Rory closed his eyes, bowed his head and pressed his hand over his mouth, knowing that it would be fatal to let a smile appear on his face with the two pairs of eyes surveying him. If he once cracked a smile in this street he'd never get a penny.

It was almost three minutes later when the woman stood before him. She had a black shawl crossed over her sagging breasts, the ends were tucked into a filthy ragged skirt, and in a whining tone and a smile widening her flat face she exclaimed, 'Aw begod! it's you, Mr Connor. Is it the rent you're after? Well now. Well now. You know it's near Christmas it is, and you know what Christmas is for money. Chews it, it does, chews it. An' look at the bairns. There's not a stitch to their arses an' himself been out of work these last three weeks.'

Without seeming to move a muscle of his face Rory said, 'He's in the rolling mills and never lost a day this six months, I've checked. You're ten weeks in arrears not countin' the day. Give me five shillings and I'll say nothing more 'till next week when I want the same and every week after that until you get your book clear. If not, I go to Palmer's and he'll get the push.'

Kate would not have been put in court for two weeks rent, but often we had outstanding arrears of something between four and five pounds, and as the rent was only about four and six a week they represented many unpaid weeks.

So I would be sent to the pawn.

I would go out of the front door with the parcel. It is impossible to imagine the stigma of being seen by the neighbours. Nearly always there'd be somebody in the street doing their step or their windows, and they'd know where I was going. But this was nothing; the real agony started when I reached the bottom of the dock bank where the men waited to be signed on for work. They all knew who I was, old John's grand-bairn, as I was known. Opposite to where the men stood, Dock Street, Bede Street and Hudson Street went off at right angles. Gompertz the pawnshop, known as Bob's, was situated in Bede Street. To get to it I had to pass this gauntlet of men.

'Candy rock for stocking legs!' the rag man would shout, and mothers had to stop the children pinching their dads' clothes and running after him.

How do you assess the agonies of childhood? How do you go about putting them over? As a child I had not acquired the words to fit the pain. But by the time I wrote *The Fifteen Streets* I could give the problem to little Katie:

Katie moved the parcel on to her other hip. It was heavy; but not as heavy as the weight inside her; the weight was leaden. To go to the pawnshop with any parcel filled her with shame; to walk up the dock bank, under the knowledgeable stares of the men idling there against the railings caused her throat to move in and out; and to meet any of her schoolmates on the journey made her want to die; but when it was John's suit she was carrying every tragedy of the journey was intensified a thousandfold.

When her mother asked, 'Will you go down to "Bob's", hinny?' Katie had stared at her, speechless. She wanted to say, 'Our Molly

I had been going to the pawn for some years and was about eleven I think when I asked myself, "Why can't our Kate go herself?" and it came to me that she was as ashamed as I was to be seen going to the pawn. She didn't want to run the gauntlet of eyes either.

should go, she's bigger,' but she knew from experience that Molly always got less on the clothes than she did, and generally too, she lost something, the ticket, or worse still, a sixpence. And because her mother looked so thin and white when she asked her she remained silent, and watched Mary Ellen go to the box under the bed and take John's suit out.

It seemed such a shame that it was John's, because he had started work only that morning. They all had, after being off weeks. But there was nothing in the house now to make them a meal, and although they would get subs, her mother was relying on these to pay the three weeks' back rent. Katie felt that once the rent was paid, her mother would look less white.

Going through the arches into Tyne Dock she met Mrs Flaherty.

'Oh, ye're not at school the day?' Peggy greeted her.

111

'No, I was sick.' Katie stared up into the half-washed face, criss-crossed with wrinkles, and her tone defied disbelief.

'Oh, that's a pity, it is. Ye shouldn't miss you iducation. Some day, when ye're old enough, I'll lend ye one o' me books; they'll iducate ye like nothing else will. When ye're old enough that is.' She snuffled and caught the drop from the end of her nose on the back of her hand.

'Thank you.' For as long as she could remember Katie had been promised one of Mrs Flaherty's books, and the promise meant

Tyne Dock arches, the Slake Terrace end: the big building on the right is a dock storehouse, and this side of it, a police box and the dock gates where, as a child, I used to stand.

'Waitin' for your granda?' the policeman would say. On the left you can just make out the public lavatory where once, while waiting for the tram, I heard laughing and then to my horror saw a woman come out with some men!

nothing to her now. She said, 'Ta-ta, Mrs Flaherty,' and walked on, the parcel now pressed against her chest and resting on the top of her stomach.

Although she thought impatiently that Mrs Flaherty was always on about education, she wished her mother was a bit like her. She had almost given up talking to her mother about the examination and what Miss Llewellyn said, for her mother didn't believe Miss Llewellyn meant what she said – last time, she had stopped her talking, saying, 'Oh, hinny, you mustn't take so much notice of things; your teacher's only being nice. The examination she's on about is likely the one you have every year.' And when Katie had sat quietly crying, Mary Ellen said to John, 'Look, lad. I can't go down to the school and see what she keeps on about, I only have me shawl; will you go?'

'What! Me? Not on your life. Now that's a damn silly thing to ask me to do, isn't it! What could I say to the headmistress?'

'Well, will you go and see her teacher, then?'

John had just stared blankly at his mother, then picked up his cap and walked out of the house.

Katie thought the only one who understood was Christine. She liked Christine nearly as much as she liked Miss Llewellyn, but not quite. Life had taken on an added glow since Christine came into it; for Christine made her pinnies and dresses out of her own old ones. She gave her and Molly nice things to eat, too; and she had even given them money, real money, half a crown each. But only twice, for when they took their half-crowns into their mother the second week she made them take them back.

Katie could not understand her mother's attitude of not speaking to Christine and her grandfather. She allowed her and Molly to go next door, but Mr Bracken and Christine had never been into her house since that terrible day some months ago when their mother was taken bad. John and Dominic, too, went next door; and she often sat on John's knee while he and Mr Bracken talked. They talked about funny things, one of which stuck in her mind: Mr Bracken said you could have anything you wanted if you only used your thoughts properly . . . There were so many things she wanted, but she wanted above all to be a teacher. Should she do what Mr Bracken told John, lie on her back with her arms outstretched and think of being a teacher until she felt herself floating away? Eeh no! she'd better not, for there were some people who said Mr

Bracken was the devil. He wasn't; but anyway, she'd better not do it.

She always had a queer feeling when Dominic was next door, when she would wonder if he were trying to do what he was doing that night she went in unexpectedly. He had Christine pressed in the corner and was trying to kiss her. Her blouse was open, and the ribbon of her camisole was loose. Katie knew that Christine was frightened, for she held on to her until Dominic went out. Then she told her not to mention to John what had happened; and Katie only too readily promised.

At last she reached the dark well of the pawnshop, and listened, her eyes wide and sad, as Bob said, 'Only three-and-six, hinny. It's

This is Hudson Street. Off to the left is Dock Street, Bede Street (where Gombertz, the pawn was), and – shown here – Lord Nelson Street. Off to the right is Boldon Lane leading to the station (you can see the railway at the end of Hudson Street).

At the end on the left is where Miss Caulfield, my teacher, lived; nearer, the chemist shop where Uncle Jack got his flea powder to take with him back to the trenches in the First World War, and on the corner of Hudson Street and Nelson was the paper shop where once I pinched a comic.

Immediately on the right were the dock offices where the men queued up to be taken on. They were the reason why I took the tram from the Dock Gates to the end of Hudson Street when I was going to the pawn. Up the top on the right was the Crown cinema, to which I joyfully escaped on a Saturday afternoon.

getting a bit threadbare.' He turned to a woman and asked, 'Will you put it in for her?' And the woman nodded, taking the penny Katie offered her. Katie wished she were fourteen, then if she had to come to the pawn she wouldn't have to pay somebody for putting the stuff in – a whole penny just for signing your name! It was outrageous, and she disliked the woman intensely for being so mean as to take the penny.

As she was leaving the shop with the money tightly grasped in her hand, Bob said, 'I've got something here that might interest one of your brothers. It'll fit nobody else round these parts. It's a top coat, and it's a bobby-dazzler. Ten shillings, it is. And I only wish I had what it cost when it was new. Tell one of them to have a look in.' Katie said she would.

Dominated by Drink

In those days the New Buildings held a very mixed assortment. In some cases the contrast was striking, as with the once rich Larkins, who had owned the Barium Chemical Works, further up the road, and who still occupied the two large houses that took up most of the first terrace, and the Kanes who lived at the top of William Black Street – not sixty feet away – and who were so destitute that the daughter not only borrowed our Kate's boots but the mother used to borrow the gully – a bread knife.

Then there were, as in any community, the social climbers. These managed to employ a daily, or send their washing out, or have somebody in to do the washing and the housework. Perhaps I am wrong in calling them social climbers. Perhaps these were just outward signs of their respectability.

Then there were the strivers, those who neither drank nor smoked, and whose one aim was to keep their heads above water, water in this case being debt. Then last and by no means least came the hard cases. And there weren't so very many of these cases in the New Buildings in those days. But among them were families dominated by drink, as ours was.

From when I was about eight there was scarcely a day of the week that I didn't go down to Hudson Street or even as far as Brinkburn Street in Stanhope Road for the beer. During the War it was scarce and of an evening I would have to stand in queues. By this time I was carrying the grey hen. The grey hen was a large narrow necked stone jar; it was heavy when empty, much heavier full. I carried it on my left hip. True I was given my tram fare back, but I would often walk the whole distance from Tyne Dock to East Jarrow carrying that great jar to save the ha'pennies.

There was a great deal of comment in the New Buildings about my being sent for the beer. It was looked on in some quarters as a disgrace; in

The Alkali where I went for the beer.

The Alkali (now called the Zenith), was originally named for its proximity to the Barium Chemical Works.

the less refined quarters it was termed openly 'A bloody shame, sendin' that bairn for the beer with that great jar.' I think I was the only child in the New Buildings who was sent on such an errand.

As the years went on I became filled with shame at having to carry the grey hen.

Constitutionally my mother was as strong as a horse, yet in some strange way this constitution refused to carry drink, for, from the first glass of spirit she drank, her personality changed for the worse. After three glasses she became, not our Kate, but someone of whom I was deeply ashamed, whom in my early years I came to fear, then hate; then wish dead, yet all the time loved, loved because she was the only thing that was mine; even while I disowned her in my mind I loved her. This clash of emotions presented itself to me for the first time one Saturday.

I tried to express this clash of emotions in *Fenwick Houses* through Christine Winter and her illegitimate daughter, Constance:

It was a Saturday night and it was summer. I had sat in the back room of the Crown until closing time. There was the usual Saturday night crowd and we had laughed and joked until we parted. Mollie wasn't there, Mollie was never there now. I must tell you about Mollie. But this Saturday night I felt particularly carefree and happy. This wasn't always the effect that drink had upon me now. At one time I could rely on it obliterating all my worries and transforming me, as it were, on to another plane where cares were non-existent and whatever future there was was rosy. Then for no reason for which I could account, every now and again the effect of whisky would be to make me want to argue and to pick a row with somebody, and this feeling would always be accompanied by a spate of swearing in my mind. I would think in swear words – Mollie's vocabulary wasn't in it compared with the words that presented themselves to me.

The night that Constance brought up my past again was a Saturday night, but I was feeling happy and at peace with the world. I was crossing the bridge in the late twilight, humming to myself the song they had been singing in the back room earlier on: 'Now is the hour when we must say goodbye,' and then I saw Constance. She was standing talking to two girls and I saw her deliberately turn her back towards me. But that did not deter me from crossing over to her and demanding in words that I tried to separate, 'What . . . what-you-doing-out at this time anight? Eh? Come on now, away home.' She did not turn and look at me as I mumbled my order, but the other two girls stared at me in a sort of surprised way. I was about to add, 'You, too, you should be at home in bed,' when Constance darted away. I gave an admonitory nod to the girls and walked off, trying to keep my gait steady as I knew their eyes were on me.

There was no evasiveness from Constance once I entered the kitchen; she was standing waiting for me. Her pale skin looked bleached and her brown eyes black and staring, and she greeted me with, 'You! . . . you! You're a disgrace – acting like that on the bridge and Jean and Olive in my class. Oh . . . h.' The 'Oh' had a weary sound, and she followed it up with, 'I hate you. I hate you. Do you hear?'

Somewhere in my head words were gathering fast but I couldn't get them to come down into my mouth. It was as if there was a gap across which they couldn't jump. . .

I knew that the greatest disgrace in life was to have a ma who drank. It didn't matter so much if your da drank, most da's did, but to have a ma that drank made people talk about you; like they did about some women in the docks. 'They could drink it through a dirty rag', only the word used wasn't as ordinary as 'dirty'.

Now I must go back to Mollie. She had played quite a part in my life and she was to play even a bigger part. The simple reason I didn't see Mollie any more was that she had married. Not Jackie, but a very respectable man, a greengrocer, a Mr Arkwright. He was fifteen years older than her and had not been married before, and he didn't like me. It was really laughable when I thought of it, for whatever blame there was attached to Mollie's past he put it down to my influence. There was evidence of my sinning but none of Mollie's. I cannot think that she'd had any hand in forming this opinion, but apparently she could do nothing to alter it, and when she had to choose between becoming Mrs Arkwright and respectability, which position I am sure she never dreamed would be her luck, or keeping our friendship, Mollie, being human, chose Mr Arkwright. She tried to soften the blow by saying he was a bit fussy like and wanted her to himself for the time being. She had laughed and nudged me, but I couldn't see the funny side of it. I had met Mr Arkwright three times, and he did not hide his opinion of me. In Mr Arkwright's mind I was one of the fast pieces left over from the war. Moreover, when I had a drink I laughed a lot, which only proved to the greengrocer that he was right in his opinion of me. So Mollie and I no longer met in the back room of the Crown on a Saturday night. Nor had I been invited to the wedding. The excuse given me was that it was to be very quiet in the register office. And I wasn't invited to her new home. I liked Mollie; next to my mother, I think I loved her. She had been good to me, she had been my stay in my time of trouble, and her rejection of me hurt more than a little. It absolutely amazed me that she, of all people, could allow herself to be dominated by any man, and it seemed that she was paying a high price for her respectability. But that was the way she wanted it.

Then this particular week, because I had felt so miserable and down, I paid a visit to the Crown on a Friday night, which I had never done before. I had my week's wages on me intact as I had just left the doctor's. It was half-past six when I entered the back room and I noticed immediately that most of the people present were not the Saturday night crowd. There were only one or two that I knew, the remainder being strangers.

I sat down next to a woman called Mrs Wright. She was always a bit of a sponger and soon she was telling me her woes, and I was paying for her drinks. After my third whisky, one of which was a

double, I stopped listening and I began to talk. I told her about my job at the doctor's, my clever daughter who could write poetry, which, I assured her, she would one day see in the papers, and I told her about my dear friend who had a farm – Sam's smallholding. At this point we were joined by a man and a woman from a table near by. The man I had seen before. I did not know his name but I knew that he often looked my way. He talked a lot and he laughed as he talked, but his wife had little to say. He stood a round, and then it was my turn. Someone went to the piano and we all sang. And this was the setting when the door opened and Mollie and her man came in. I was facing the door and I saw her immediately, and with the past lost in the thick vapour of four whiskies I hailed Mollie loudly, shouting, 'Oo! oo! there, Mollie. Oo! oo!' She turned immediately in my direction and after a moment's hesitation she lifted her hand and waved. Then her husband,

119

turning and looking at me for a moment, deliberately took her by the arm and led her to the farthest corner of the room.

Well, who did he think he was? That was deliberate, that was. He wouldn't let her come across, wouldn't even let her speak to me. Who did he think he was, anyway? I threw off my drink.

'What'll you have?' It was the man standing the round again. I looked at him and blinked, and in the act of blinking all my merriness seemed to vanish. I didn't like this man and I didn't like his wife, and I didn't like Mrs Wright. I had spent a lot of money on her tonight and I didn't like her. 'I'll have a whisky – large,' I said to the man.

'You won't, you know, unless you pay for it.' It was the wife speaking, and I turned sharply on her and said, 'I haven't seen you handing out much.'

'Well! Come on, Dickie. That's the limit, that is.' She pulled her husband's arm, and I mimicked, 'That's right – go on, Dickie. Go on before you stand your turn.'

'Now, now.' The man's tone was soothing, and I flung my hand wide and said, 'Oh! get yourself away or she'll hammer you when she gets you in.'

Mrs Wright started to laugh, but I didn't join in. The piano had stopped and people were looking towards our corner, and although the words were whispered I heard a voice saying, 'You shouldn't take it unless you know how far to go. It's shameful. She'll turn nasty now.'

I rounded on the unknown speaker, yelling, 'Yes, I'll turn nasty if you don't mind your own bloody business.'

'Here! here! quieten down.' It was the old woman Wright pulling at me, and I pushed off her hand. Who did the lot of them think they were? They were all looking down their noses at me. I was a bad lot because I'd had two bairns. But there was Mollie over in that corner who had slept with a different man every week for the first year of the war – she had told me so herself – and now she was so respectable she wouldn't look at me – I wasn't good enough.

I was in the middle of the floor before I knew what I was up to and could not stop myself from advancing towards her.

'Hallo, Mollie.'

'Hallo, Christine.'

'Long time since . . . since we met, eh?'

'You'll have to excuse us, we're in company.' It was the husband talking, and I was about to turn on him when Mollie put out her hand towards him and said in the old tone that I recognised, 'Leave her be and let her sit down.'

'Not likely, you're not starting this. I've told you, and on it I stand firm.'

'Oh, firm Mr Arkwright. Oh, goody, goody, Mister bloody Arkwright.' I heard a voice chanting and it didn't seem to be mine.

'Here! here! Now come on.' It was the barman, and he was standing at my side with his hand on my shoulder trying to steer me away. But I flung him off, crying, 'You keep your hands to yourself, I'm sitting here.'

I went to take the seat near Mollie, when, as if risking his life to spare his wife the contamination of my touch, Mr Arkwright stood in front of her. I looked him in the eye for a second, then my arm swept outwards and my hand brought him a slap across the face that resounded round the room and in some way brought me deep satisfaction, so much so that I went to repeat the action with my other hand. Then I was knocked backwards and would have fallen but somebody caught me, and when I was upright again I seemed to be surrounded by hands and faces, and I kept moving my head this way and that to get a look at the man as I yelled, 'Who d'you think you are, anyway, tinpot little greengrocer? Specked apples and rotten oranges in tissue paper.'

'Outside! outside!'

'Take your hands off me.'

'Get!' I was flung through the side door into the yard, and I seemed to bounce off the opposite wall. Then within a second I was back at the door hammering with my fists and yelling, 'You take me money, you've taken it for years, you dirty lot of swine. Who do you think you are?'

Fenwick Houses

Kate, my mother, knew what real poverty meant. She and my aunt Sarah had begged from door to door. She used to tell me of being sent out to beg for bread one day – she was not the only one begging at that time in Jarrow. Her feet were bare and bleeding, the calves of her legs split with keens. At one house a compassionate woman took her in and gave her a pair of boots and stockings, and she went home, forgetting about the bread. Her delight in the boots, although her feet were paining even worse from their pressure on the keens, was short lived, for her mother took them immediately to the 'In and Out'. It was an appropriate name, for you would pawn, say, your man's suit on a Monday to meet the rent and if you hadn't the money to get it out on the Friday you would take in something else to help retrieve it, brass candlesticks, mats, fire-irons, even the stone dish you kneaded the bread in. One thing was always going in to get the other out.

Nearly every day in the summer after I had come from school, after I had run the messages, after I had carried the grey hen to Tyne Dock and back, I would go on the slacks, not to play, but to gather wood. Coal had to be bought. We had no one in the pits and could not often come by a pit-load, so mostly we had to buy the coal from Jackie Halliday. But if you had plenty of wood you could do a baking of bread on that alone; it was quick heating, and if it had tar on it it blazed nicely.

Port Women

Drink or rent arrears drove many a woman to prostitution, and the dockland areas of the Tyne, with their large numbers of transient males with money, were particularly popular haunts. Destitute, Katie Mulholland finds herself living in the bad part of Shields in a house with prostitutes. Lizzie is Katie's mongoloid sister:

She was terrified at coming back home and finding that Mrs Robson had carried out her threat and brought the authorities in. The next step from this would be they'd contact the landlord, and then she and Lizzie would find themselves in the street, with the furniture around them. She had seen so many people in the street sitting helplessly amid their furniture that she had a horror of it happening to them.

Katie stood with her back to the closed door. The Anchor was only a few streets away. It was a notorious public-house, notorious for many things. One of its activities had gained it the name of the 'whore market'.

If only Joe was here. But he wasn't here, and there wasn't a bite or sup in the house, and no warmth, and she was down to her last half-candle. She came from the door as if released by a spring, pulled Lizzie to her feet, guided her into the room and got her into bed, and again she tied her by the waist, this time attaching the end of the rope to the leg of the bed. Then, going back into the kitchen, she took the iron shelf out of the oven – it still retained some heat – and taking it into the bedroom she pushed it under the clothes beneath Lizzie's feet, hoping that the warmth would send her to sleep and ease her crying. She could hardly see her face in

For some families on Tyneside at the turn of the century, boots were a mark of status, dignity even. Their absence was not uncommon.

Mary Ellen would come to the back door stammering 'K...K...Kate. Would you l...l...lend me y...your boots to po...pop into Jarrow?' Kate lent her the boots so often that at last she told her to keep them.

122

'At one point the cab stopped and while her driver had a loud altercation with someone in front of him she put her face close to the window and was appalled at what she saw. Filthy children, some in their bare feet; women, their bodies bulbous with old clothes to keep out the cold, but all with raucous voices yelling and shouting against the hold-up in the street. They looked like creatures from another planet.' Martha Mary Crawford

the dim light of the room, but, bending close to her, she said, 'I won't be long, Lizzie. Be a good girl.' For a minute longer she stood and stroked the lank hair back from the bulging brow; then, going into the kitchen, she rapidly donned her outdoor things and went out of the house.

She hated to be out on the streets after dark. Although some streets were lit by the new gas lamps there were alleys and dark corners where things were known to happen.

The noise from the Anchor greeted her long before she reached it, and she paused outside the double doors before pushing one open and half stepping inside. And then she could go no further. Through the light of the oil lamps she saw a seething mass of people, mostly men, and mostly sailors. Two faces turned towards her with lifting eyebrows and drooling lips, and when two pair of

arms came out to her she sprang back, pulling the door with her, and, dashing to the end of the building, she hid round the corner. Here she stood panting. She couldn't go in there . . . Yet, perhaps her duties might keep her behind the counter. She could ask him. She'd have to ask him.

She moved along the wall to where there was a side door, and from behind this, too, there issued the sound of men's laughter. This was still the bar, likely the best end. She must find a door to the house. But there was no light farther on. She was about to grope her way along the wall beyond the door when it opened and a huge figure stepped into the yard. The next moment a hand was placed on her shoulder and she was swung round, and in the light from the doorway she looked up into an enormous bearded face. The eyes looking out of it were moving over her, the expression in

This depressing nineteenth-century picture of men scavenging for coal on the tips brings to mind Sarah in The Blind Miller, *imagining her impoverished family 'wallowing, choking, in a sea of mud, mud like that which filled the huge timber pond at Jarrow Slacks.'*

Scavenging for coal: The coal carts used to come from the gas works in Jarrow – high carts driven by horses and filled to the top with large lumps of coke. Near Morgan's Hall was a double stretch of tram lines . . . it was at places such as these, where the cartwheels wobbled over the points, that the loose pieces of coke rolled onto the road. At first it was no disgrace . . . it was the beachcomber instinct, but me granda wouldn't come with me, though he'd help me carry the bags of coal back when I went to the tip.

them like that of the two men in the bar. She watched the red lips in the fair beard part, and a deep voice which she knew immediately was not English, said, 'Ah-haa!'

She stammered, 'Please . . . I . . . I want to see the barman. I'm after a job . . . Please.' She tried to pull herself away from the man, but his hold on her tightened and, bringing his face down to hers, he said in precise clipped English, 'A job is it? Oh, min skjoun, I could give you a job. Ah yes.' His head went back and he laughed.

'Look, give over, you. Let me go.'

Still peering at her, he said, 'Stop trembling. You frightened? Why do you come here if you're frightened?'

'Please, I . . . I just want to go. I want to go home.'

'You want to go home?' He was laughing at her again, his face seeming to expand to twice its size. 'All right, min skjoun, we will go home. Ah yes, how pleased I'll be to go home with you.'

'No, no!'

'Aha! Yes. Yes.'

At this moment the door was pulled wide open and another man appeared. He, too, was a sailor and spoke in a foreign tongue, and the bearded man answered in the same tongue, and when the second man emerged into the yard Katie found herself pulled from the wall and pushed forward. And now the bearded man called over his shoulder to the other man, who shouted back apparently in reply. Then they were in the street.

'Which way?' He still had his arm about her, gripping her firmly and forcing her to walk, but when they reached the flare lights outside the pie and pea shop he stopped and peered at her again, saying now, 'Why do you tremble all the time? Why go to the Anchor if you tremble?'

'I . . . I went for work; they . . . I heard they wanted a barmaid.'

Again his head went back and the street rang with his laughter, of which the passers-by took no notice. A drunken Swede laughing with a woman in the streets at night was nothing new. 'You a barmaid in the Anchor! Ah!' He grabbed her face in his big hand and pressed her jaws in as he said, 'You'd be eaten alive. Do you want to be eaten alive? . . . No, no.' He answered himself. 'You're frightened of being eaten alive. Why did you want to be barmaid in the Anchor? There are other works you could do.'

'My . . . my sister is sick. I've got to look after her; I can't go out durin' the day.'

'No one else to look after your sister? No parents?'

She shook her head.

'You married?'

Again she shook her head.

'You live by yourself?'

'With . . . with my brother.'

'Why does your brother not work for you then?'

'He's on strike. He's away lookin' for work . . .'

Before she had closed her mouth on her words she knew she had made a mistake, and he lost not a minute in making use of it. With a nod of his head he said, 'So. So he's away. Well, we go home then?'

'No!' Her voice was harsh now. 'No, no, I tell you. No!'

He did not seem to take any heed of her protest but went on, 'What do you want money so badly for you go to the Anchor?'

When she didn't answer he brought his face down close to hers and said on a surprised note, 'You sulten . . . hungry?'

She closed her eyes for a moment but still didn't speak; and when she opened them she did not look into his face but at the top brass button of his uniform, and some section of her mind registered the fact that he was a captain. This seemed to explain the way he talked, for although a foreigner he used his words like the gentry did.

'My God! That's right, isn't it? You're hungry. Come, come.' He now took her by the hand as if she was a child and pulled her through the doorway of the pie and pea shop, and there, in a voice that seemed to shake the ramshackle place, he cried, 'Pies! Half a dozen. Hot. No, one dozen; I could eat half a dozen myself. And peas, two pints.'

'Where's your can?' said the man.

'Can?'

'Aye, sir, yer can't carry peas in a bit paper.'

'That one there, I'll buy it.'

'It'll cost you fowerpence, sir.'

'Fourpence it is. And fill it to the brim.'

The man beside the counter now wrapped up the pork pies in a piece of newspaper, and when he pushed the parcel across the counter the captain, picking it up, thrust it into Katie's arms.

As she held it against her breast she could feel the heat of the pies through the paper and she had a desire to grab one out and thrust it into her mouth. She also had the desire to take to her heels and fly; and she saw her chance as he was paying the man. Once outside the door she could be away up one of the dark alleys and safe, and the pies with her.

She was backing to the door when he turned round, and like someone chastising a child about to do a mischief he turned his chin to the side, while his eyes remained on her and gave that telling exclamation of 'Ah-haa!' Then, thrusting his hand back towards the counter and the man, he received his change and without looking at it thrust it in his pocket. Then his hand groped towards the can; he picked it up and came towards her, and after looking at her hard for a second said, from deep in his throat, 'We go home now, eh?'

He held her with one hand and carried the can of peas with the other, and like this they went through the warren of dimly lit streets and past the black alleyways until they reached the end of Crane Street, and here, pulling him to a halt and her voice full of pleading, she said, 'Please, please don't come any farther.'

'You don't want me to come to your home?'

'No.'

'You're lying. You want me to come.'

'I don't, I don't, I tell you.' She was hissing at him now. 'I just

Drunkenness was a significant feature of life. A national inquiry in 1899 into 'The Temperance Problem and Social Reform' shows by far the highest number of drunkenness offences in Northumberland and Durham. As today, drunkenness occurred across the classes but of course its long-term effects were felt most strongly in the families of those nearest the breadline.

127

want you to leave me alone. Don't you understand? Just leave me alone. You can have the pies . . . here.' She thrust them at him. But he ignored her action and said, 'I don't believe you. But, look, we're on the waterfront and near the Middle Gates. There'll be one of your polis men there. Shout. Go on, shout, and they'll come and order me off . . . Go on.'

She stood breathing deeply and peering at him. She had thought of that herself. She had thought, if I shout the polis'll come. But as afraid as she was of this great bearded man, she was more afraid of the polis. It was when she thought of being afraid of him that she realized she was only afraid of him because of what they would say in the house, her taking a man up there, and what Joe would say if he found out.

She said lamely, 'We . . . we could walk and eat these as we went.' She patted the bundle of pies.

'But I don't want to walk, I want to go to your home. I want to know where you live . . . Besides, it would be very uncomfortable eating peas while we walked.' He gave a small laugh now. 'Come,' he said. 'This is your street?'

When she didn't answer he took her arm again, and like someone under escort she walked up the street with her head bowed.

There were people about, but they took no notice of her or her companion. Again, what was unusual about a sea captain walking this street with a woman?

Before she opened the door softly she paused and was about to say to him, 'Be quiet,' but she felt that if she did he would let out his big laugh and raise the house.

As soon as they entered the hall Lizzie's wailing came to her, and she hurried forward up the dark stairs; and when he stumbled after her she put her hand out to steady him, and he gripped it and held it until they came to the top landing. And there she whispered, 'Stand still; you . . . you might knock the bucket over.' As she groped for her key in her coat pocket he said, 'What is that noise?' She didn't answer but unlocked the door, and when she opened it it came to her that here was another chance of escape, she could bolt the door in his face. Yes, and have him bellow the house down. From the little she knew of him she could well imagine him doing just that.

She groped her way towards the table, put the pies on it, then moved cautiously towards the mantelpiece and instinctively her hand found the candlestick. There was no glimmer left in the fire to light the candle, so, going back to the landing, she whispered, 'I haven't a light.'

Despite public condemnation by the Church and other bodies there was much tacit acceptance of prostitution as a fundamental part of one culture. From its formation in 1835 up to the early twentieth century, the Newcastle police had instructions to turn a blind eye. As readers will reveal, Katie Mulholland's unjust imprisonment for prostitution tells another story, namely the ease with which a rich man could influence the Law.

Prison conditions may have been less barbaric than in the previous century, but in 1850 two inspectors criticised Newcastle gaol that in their opinion 'instead of being a school of reformation, it serves as a school of corruption'. Katie's experience in Durham prison certainly corroborates that:

On the morning of Katie's release the sun was shining though the air was bitterly cold, and here and there, as if they had strayed from the pack on its way farther north, a snowflake glided down.

The big woman with the huge breasts looked at Katie as if she was loth to let her go, as indeed she was. She had not found such an outlet for her sadistic tendencies for many a long day, but do what she might she couldn't rouse this one to the kind of retaliation that might lengthen her sentence. Purposely now she led her down the stone corridor and through the sacking room where Jinny Fulton and her crowd were gathered, plying their needles. She led the way between stacks of hessian and piles of sail canvas, and almost to the foot of Jinny Fulton herself, and when Jinny cried out 'Aw! Here comes Lady Go-Lightly to say goodbye to us poor creatures' she did not reprimand her. She only slanted her gaze towards her and twisted her lips into the semblance of a smile, which smile told Jinny that she had her permission to go ahead, and she went ahead. She thrust her arm out and drove the long curved steel needle she held in her hand through Katie's skirt and into her calf. Because of her petticoats only the point penetrated, but Katie screamed out and Jinny Fulton, putting her head back, roared; then, gathering a dobble of spit into her mouth and taking direct aim, she fouled Katie's skirt. The wardress stopped and, without reprimanding the prisoner who had committed the offence, said to Katie, 'Wipe that off. You don't want to go out like that, do you?'

Katie had nothing with which to wipe off the filth from her skirt except her fingers; so, bending her knee, she rubbed the skirt against the stone floor, and this brought a howl of laughter from Jinny Fulton and those nearest to her. But all the women in the bag room didn't laugh. There were those that looked at the Mulholland girl with pity, and one here and there with admiration, for they knew that they couldn't have stood what she'd had to stand without doing murder.

'Tickle your Swede for me.' This, followed by a mouthful of obscenities, seemed to push Katie through the door and along another passage and into a room where a woman sat behind a table. This granite-faced individual turned a book towards her, and after she had signed her name, which action seemed an offence to this woman as it stood out against a line of crosses, she was waved away.

It was as she stood at the wooden door and watched the tormentor of her mind and body slowly putting the key into the lock of the small inset door that she thought that her legs would collapse beneath her, that she would never have strength to step through the little door in the gate and into the world again.

But she was almost pushed into it because the door banged so quickly on her heels that it grazed the leather of her shoe. And then she was standing on the rough pavement of Stone Street, blinking.

A Fleeting Sense of Security
I also look back to periods of calmness, like short rests between battles, and these rests held flashes of happiness; quiet evenings in the kitchen when I would sit curled up on the corner of the big steel fender before the roaring fire reading a comic, or my 'conscience-pricking book' as I came to look upon the annual that the caretaker's daughter of Simonside School, by the name of Taylor, had lent me. It was the first real book I'd ever been able to peruse, and I couldn't bear the thought of giving it back to her. And when Kate took me away from the School it was an easy thing to pretend to myself that I had forgotten all about the book. But for years after I couldn't pass that girl and look at her because I remembered that book.

Very often when I sat reading the saliva would be running free in my mouth because finny-haddie might be cooking in the oven, or there might be panhacklety sizzling in the big black frying pan on the hob. The wind would be whirling down the chimney, and the gas mantle making little plop-plopping noises. Me granda would be sitting at the centre table as usual, cheating himself at patience, and, of course, to his hand would be a pint mug of beer, into which he would thrust Dennis* every now and again, after having heated it in the heart of the fire.

I cannot see me grandma on these nights, only our Kate and me Uncle Jack. Sometimes Jack would be sitting opposite me reading the paper while Kate stood at the other table near the window ironing or baking.

And later, during the War and after, I have a picture of Kate sitting at the corner of the table reading the newspaper aloud, me granda nodding occasionally or stopping her to question some point. Every night during the War she read the paper to him; always first going to Philip Gibbs's despatch from France. This was all brought back clearly when I heard recently that Sir Philip Gibbs had died. How his every word had been awaited in that kitchen in 10 William Black Street, for Jack was in France most of the War. Sometimes the kitchen would ring with laughter when Kate read aloud such books as, *Handy Andy*, or *Wee McGregor*, or *Tales of an Irish County Court.*

And there were nights when I'd be bathed before the fire. A mixed joy this because I couldn't stand anybody looking at me. So a towel had to be rigged up to protect my modesty, and when later, clothed in my nightie, I would stand between me granda's knees having sips of beer from his pint pot, I would experience a happiness bred by a fleeting sense of security.

This could be me granda cutting the top off his egg before giving it to me to eat. The top of his egg usually went two-thirds of the way down the egg . . . I often wondered why they couldn't give me an egg to myself.

*The family name for the poker

131

But the feeling of security would be wiped away when, perhaps the very next day, I would be sent to borrow. I hated to ask any one for the loan of money. And most of all I would hate going up to my Aunt Mary's. I would knock on her shiny front door because very often she kept the back door locked, and after one look at her face I would lower my lids and deliver my begging message.

Reading this, people might wonder what became of the close-knit working-class family that is part of the mythology of the North, the kind of mining family that I described in *Tilly Trotter* as the Drews. Well of course such family warmth existed, perhaps especially in mining families whose pitwork would have been in shifts, which meant they'd rarely have the opportunity to gather together as one unit. When they did it was a special event. Most of my neighbours in the New Buildings worked in the shipyard or on the trams, but when later I worked in the laundry at Harton many of my friends came from mining families. Me first lad, a fellow called Mickey Moran, was a pitman. Here is Tilly entering a world she had never herself enjoyed.

It was a two mile walk to the Drew's cottage. It lay to the north of the estate, and was reached by an angled bend that led off the coach road. The cottages were situated on the very boundary of the Sopwith estate and within half a mile of the pit. There were sixteen cottages in the two rows. The Drews' home was in the end cottage of the second row and when Tilly entered it on this hot steamy Sunday afternoon, it appeared to her like a small cramped box after the spaciousness of the Manor. Not only was it small and cramped, but it had a mixed odour which she likened to the smell that emanated from soot and soap-suds, the last soap-suds in the poss tub at the end of the day's wash, an arid, body sweating odour. The small room seemed crammed with people and she stood just within the open door as Katie introduced her, speaking first to a big woman whose bony frame seemed devoid of flesh. 'Ma, this is Tilly, the lass I told you about.'

The woman stopped cutting slices of bread from a big loaf on the end of a table which was surprisingly covered with a white tablecloth, and she paused for a moment and smiled at Tilly as she said, 'Well, come in, lass, come in. That's if you can get in. But, as they say, never grumble about being crowded until you can't shut your door. You're welcome. Sit down. Get your backside off that cracket, our Arthur, and let the lass take the weight off her legs.'

When Arthur, a grinning boy of twelve, sidled off the low stool, then stood with his back against the whitewashed wall near the small open fireplace, Tilly wanted to protest that she didn't mind standing, but feeling very awkward all of a sudden she sat down on the low cracket and looked shyly around the sea of eyes surveying her. Some were looking at her from under their brows, others straight at her. She was wondering why they were all crammed into this room on this rare and lovely day when she was given the answer; it was as if she had asked for it.

Continuing cutting the bread, Mrs Drew said, 'Sunday, we're all

The scene of the Drew family at tea in
Tilly Trotter *is based on my own*
experience of friends who were miners . .

A row of single-story miners' cottages
(each with a tiny room up in the roof),
built around the middle of the nineteenth
century and situated at the top of High
Street, Jarrow.

together for Sunday tea. Rain, hail, sun or snow, 'tis one time in
the week I have me troubles all around me at one go.'

'Aw, Ma. Ma!' The same protest came from different quarters of
the room.

'Do you like workin' up at the big house?'

'Yes; yes, thank you.' Tilly nodded to Mrs Drew, and the big
woman, scooping up the slices of bread in handfuls on to a large
coloured flat dish, said, 'Well, it's one thing, you get trained to be
quick in big houses, not like this lot here.' She pointed to a tall
young woman and a smaller one who were taking down crockery
from the hooks on an old black-wood Welsh dresser, the back of
which Tilly noticed in some surprise was forming a kind of high
headboard to a double iron bed along the edge of which were sitting
two young boys and a youth.

'Oh, Ma. Ma!' It was the same laughing protest.

'Are those griddle cakes finished?' Mrs Drew now looked towards
a plump child who was kneeling before the fire turning pats of
round pastry which were resting on an iron shelf, which in turn
was resting on top of a flattened mound of hot ash.

Before the child could answer, Sam Drew, bending over his

Left:

Women at the poss-tub, early 1900s. In those days a man went out to work and that, in his mind, was enough; the house and all in it was the woman's task, and it lowered a man's prestige if he as much as lifted a cup.

'Mary Ellen had pulled the posstub outside the washhouse and brought pan after pan of hot water from the fire to half fill it. She had put a scoopful of soda into it and now she was sossing two unbleached sheets up and down in the steaming water. Her back was bent over the tub. Her face was covered with steam and she was intent on her work, so she didn't hear the trap . . . there he was this man whom she had loved from a child, this Roddy Greenbank.' A Dinner of Herbs

sister, said, 'She's been scoffin' 'em, Ma.'

The small girl, her face red from the heat of the fire, sat back on her hunkers, crying, 'Oh, our Sam! our Sam! I've never touched one,' slapping out at her brother as she said so. And he slapped playfully back at her; then looking at Tilly, he said, 'This lot must look like a menagerie to you.'

She smiled but could find no reply to this. He was right, they did look like a menagerie.

'Well, if you've got a good memory I'll start at the top and work downwards. That one over there' – Sam pointed to a short, thick man sitting at the edge of the table – 'that's me big brother, our Henry, twenty-four he is, an' married, lock an' chain you know.'

Ignoring his brother's clenched fist, he went on, 'Then there's me next.' He thumbed his chest. 'Then comes our Peg, that one who's slow with the crockery.' He pointed to the taller of the two girls moving between the table and the delf rack. 'And then Bill. He's seventeen, him sittin' on the bed, the daft-looking one.'

'I'll daft you, our Sam, if you don't look out.'

'I'm lookin' out, so get on with it.' Sam grinned at his younger brother, then said, 'And his two daft companions, there's Arthur there on the left, he's twelve, and Georgie, he's the one that looks like a donkey about to bray, he's ten.'

'Oh, our Sam!' This came from different parts of the room now.

'Then there's our Katie, who's not right in the top storey. . . .'

'Oh, you wait, our Sam!'

'And the best of the bunch is Jimmy there. He's a natural scarecrow, aren't you, Jimmy? A penny a day he can earn standin' in the fields.'

'Oh, our Sam! Our Sam!'

'And then there's my Fanny.' He bent and rubbed his fingers in the thick brown hair of the kneeling child, saying, 'She's seven, aren't you, Fanny? An' she's goin' down the pit next year, aren't you, Fanny?'

'Now you shut your mouth, our Sam!' It was his mother turning on him now, no laughter in her face. 'Don't joke about her goin' down the pit. She's not seein' top nor bottom of the pit except over my dead body.'

'I was only funnin', Ma.'

'Well, don't fun about that; the pit's got the rest of yous, but they're not gettin' her. Nor Jimmy there. There's two of you I aim

135

to give daylight to.'

'Aye, Ma; aye, you're right' – Sam's voice was very subdued now – ''tis nowt to joke about.'

Mrs Drew had stopped pouring out mugs of tea and she now looked at Tilly; but for some seconds she did not speak. When she did her voice, although low, held a deep note of bitterness as she said, 'The pit took four of mine in seven years, me man included, so you can see me reason for stickin' out for two of them, can't you?'

'Yes; yes, Mrs Drew.'

'Well now, that said, let's eat.'

It was, Tilly imagined, as if the tall gaunt woman had suddenly turned a knob somewhere inside her being and switched off the bitter memories, for now her voice was jovial again as she cried at her daughter, 'Peg, bring the china cup, we've got company.'

When Peg brought the fragile china cup and saucer to the table and handed it to her mother, Mrs Drew took the saucer between

'Girls were playing the summer game of bays, hopping on one leg, their bare foot pushing the clean-cut bottom of a glass bottle from one chalk-marked paving square to the next; boys in groups according to their ages, were playing chucks in the gutters; and here and there a bare-bottomed young child crawled on the hot pavements.' The Tide of Life

136

her finger and thumb and gently placed it on the table; then looking at Tilly, she asked, 'You like your tea with milk, lass?'

'Oh yes, please.'

'An' you can have sugar an' all if you like.' This was from the upturned face of Fanny. They all laughed and there was a chorus: 'And you can have sugar if you like' in imitation of the small girl, and she, swinging her head from side to side, exclaimed, 'Aw yous! you're alway scoffin', yous!'

'And now we're all here we'll start. I said, we're all here' – Mrs Drew now looked again at Tilly as she placed the china cup and saucer before her – 'except there's my Alec. He's on a double shift – it's the water down there – he'll be dead beat when he does come up. Shouldn't be allowed, twenty-four hours under at one time! and he only a bit of a lad.'

'He's eighteen, he's older than me an' I've done a double shift.'

'Oh listen!' Sam held up his hand. 'Hero Bill's done a double shift.' He leant towards his younger brother now, saying, 'Aye, but it wasn't in water standin' up to your neck.' Then, his tone altering, he said, 'Somethin's got to be done. By God! somethin's got to be done.'

'Now! now!' It was his mother's voice again. "Tis Sunday, we've got company, no more pit talk.'

Since only nine could be seated at the table, two of the younger boys, Arthur and Georgie, remained seated on the bed, and when their mother ordered them to come to the table to get their shives, thick slices of bread with a piece of cheese in the middle, she looked from one side to the other as they approached and said, 'You don't deserve nowt either of you; 'tis a wonder you're not in jail.'

'Why, what have they been up to?' Henry, the married son, said, turning his head towards them. 'What's this? What you been up to, you two now?'

When they didn't answer he looked at his mother and she, evidently trying to suppress a smile, made her voice sound harsher than ever as she said, 'What have they been up to? Just tried to burn the Mytons' place down, that's all.'

'*What!*'

There were splutters from different members at the table. Some of them choked, so much so that Katie had to be thumped on the back before their mother went on, 'They were scrumpin' apples an' one of the gardeners caught them, an' being kind to them instead

Oh, for the eternity of childhood time
When the morning was New Year's Day
And dinner-time was high summer
And evening was autumn
Falling into December and bed.

of taking them up to the house an' then callin' the polis, he thumped them well and roundly, bumped their heads together, kicked their backsides and set them flyin'. And what do you think they did last night as ever was?'

'Well, what did they do, I'm waitin'?' Henry asked.

Again the table was convulsed with laughter, and it was Sam

138

We played ma's and da's
Those years ago:
Ma's apron and skirt,
Da's shirt and old bowler;
Round the top corner
In the chimney breast
We played at houses,
In which the test
Was birth.

who now said, 'They stuffed straw up half a dozen drainpipes, you know the old trick, an' set fire to them.'

'No!'

'Aye.'

'At the Myton place? Oh my God! I wish I'd been there. Eeh! you young buggers!' He turned and looked towards the bed where the two boys were sitting with their heads hanging but with their shoulders shaking with laughter.

'And not content with that' – the mother nodded at her eldest son – 'they went back into the orchard and helped themselves to apples, not windfalls this time but from the trees. My God! when

King Street, the main shopping street in South Shields; 1880.

'In King Street the gas lamps were ablaze. People stood under them in groups, while others gazed into the shop windows. Saturday night was a popular night for window-gazing and there was no hurry to buy even if you wanted to; the supplies never ran out and most of the shops were open until ten o'clock, some later.' The Gambling Man 1880

Katie Mulholland in South Shields market (circa 1860): 'She knew exactly what she was going to buy: a quarter stone of potatoes, some pot stuff to make broth, a scrag end of mutton, a quarter-stone of oatmeal, a half-stone of flour and some yeast, some pigs' fat, two ounces of tea, some bacon ends, half a pound of treacle if it was still tuppence, and a quarter-stone of salt, also at tuppence if they wouldn't split it and let her have a pennorth . . .'

Far Right:
Children playing ball behind Croft Terrace. Kate worked up Croft Terrace; the way they are dressed shows that this is not a poor area.

140

In the late nineteenth century there was little variety in the shops and far fewer proprietary brands than today. Basic stuffs, like butter and sugar, would be made up in a shop and sold in weighed amounts from casks or kegs. Soap was soap and not, at that time, presented in all manner of perfumes or packets.

In the early 1880s, however, two massively expensive advertising campaigns – for Hornimans tea and Holloways pills – began to change all this. Their impact was revolutionary and felt even in the corridors of power, Gladstone himself being attacked in Parliament for advertising himself like Hornimans tea.

they told me that I was sick. To try a second time! God! they're lucky they weren't caught. Anyway' – she grinned now – 'three good stones of them they brought in. As they said, they could have brought a cartload 'cos everybody was too busy pullin' the burning straw out of the drainpipes.'

'They'll end up in Australia those two.' It was Sam now nodding towards them.

'They'll never live to reach Australia.'

As Tilly watched Mrs Drew's head move slowly back and forward there was rising in her a swirl of merriment such as she had never felt in her life before, and when Mrs Drew ended, 'Swing they will, the both of them, from the crossroads an' we'll all have a field day,' the laughter burst from her throat. It surprised not only herself but all those at the table, because they had never heard anyone laugh like it. It was a high wavering sound that swelled and swelled until, holding her waist, she turned from the table and rocked herself. She laughed until she cried; she couldn't stop

141

laughing, not even when Katie, herself doubled up with laughter, put her arm about her and begged, 'Give over. Give over'. Nor when Sam lifted her chin and, his own mouth wide, cried, 'That's good. That's good.' And he kept repeating this until he realised her face was crumpling and that the water running down it was no longer caused by merriment; and so, straightening up, he looked round the table and raised his hand, saying, 'Enough is enough.'

The noise in the room gradually subsided, and Tilly turned to the table again and, her head bowed, murmured, 'I'm sorry.'

'Sorry, lass? You've got nowt to be sorry for. We've never had such release in this room for many a long day. It's good to laugh, it's the salve for sores. Aye, it's the salve for sores. Drink your tea, lass.'

Gratefully now Tilly drank her tea. Then she looked at the sea of

142

A glimpse of South Shields market where Thrift Street and King Street meet. Many would wait until last thing Saturday to get cheap meat that was going bad.

'. . . She next went to the bacon stall, and her searching eyes coming to rest on some scraps, Katie pointed to them and asked for a pound.

"That lot throopence hapenny, lass," the man said.

"Thank you." She nodded and put her hand into the bag for her purse. Then, her two hands tearing the bag open, she let out a yell that made the stall-holder jump and those nearby turn and gape at her.

"The purse! the purse! It's gone. Oh, my God, it's gone."'

Katie Mulholland

I remember that everyone had hats. I had a Henry Heath felt hat that a woman Kate worked for gave her. I would wear it even to Mass and clean it with salt and flour.

Thrift Street, 1890s, near the docks and leading to South Shields market.

faces about her, warm, caring faces, and she thought she had never felt such closeness as there was in this family. Most of them spent their lives underground, even the girls; but there was a happiness here that she envied, a happiness here that she longed to share. She looked across the now silent table at Mrs Drew as she said, 'It's lovely tea, lovely.'

Nearly every night after tea, and when I had been for the beer, I went out to play for a while. Winter or summer we would play round the street lamps, or outside Cissie Affleck's shop. There were certain parts of the

Children, obviously well dressed, skating on the river.

'The people seemed to be deluded into thinking this clean, white world would remain . . . As he stood there John began to feel something of this mass joy. The whole scene, which seemed to have been dropped from another world, where only light laughter ebbed . . . He watched Christine gliding gracefully in small circles near where Katie, Molly and David were sliding with other children. She looked little more than a child herself, a dark, elfin, slip of a child.' The Fifteen Streets

Cissie Affleck's shop in Philipson Street. Nearly every night after tea, and when I had been for the beer, I went out to play for a while. Winter or summer we would play round the street lamps, or outside Cissie Affleck's shop.

New Buildings we selected for play at certain times of the year, as also we did our games. In the winter, towards Christmas, it was usual to gather around the shop, for then, Cissie would be putting the Christmas decorations in her window, and if you were in the Christmas Club you could stand for hours pointing out what you were going to get. A shop with real scales, and bottles, and a counter; a doll . . . a black doll perhaps, or boxes of chocolates, or a long gauze stocking filled with an assortment of useless things. And in between gazing and planning we would skip or play tiggy, or Jack, Jack, shine your light.

In *Kate Hannigan* Rosie Mullen was Annie Hannigan's best friend. Rosie was two years older than Annie, but much shorter. She was a replica of her mother, being dumpy and fat, with small, bright eyes and a round face. Her dark hair stuck out in two-inch plaited points from behind her ears. She looked ugly and quaint and likeable, and Annie had a deep affection for her. . . It was half past eight on Christmas Eve morning when Annie, sitting in the back-yard lavatory of the Hannigan's house, heard a scramble of feet in the Mullen's yard next door. Their back-door banged and her own opened, and a plaintive voice chanted up the yard 'An-nie! are-ya-comin' out? . . . An-nie! Are-ya-comin' out?' Together, the two girls set off to take Nancy Mullen out in the pram:

Rosie grinned broadly, and, taking hold of Annie's hand, dashed

145

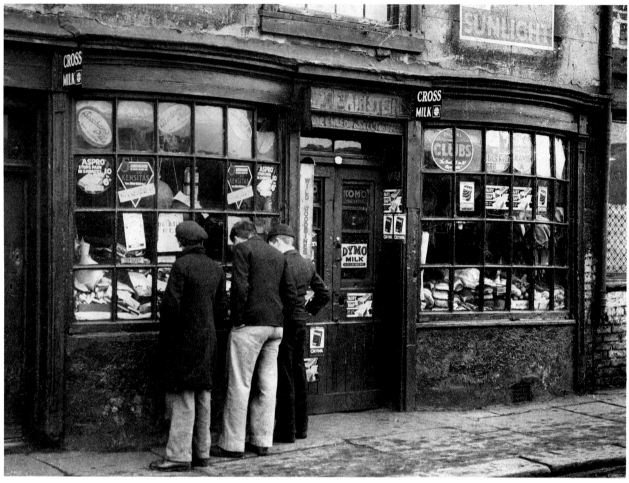

with her into their backyard, seized the big, dilapidated pram, in which a two-year-old child lay sucking a dummy, and pushed it out into the cobbled back lane, down which they hurried, the pram tossing about like a cork on the ocean, past seven back doors with their accompanying coal and oozing lavatory hatches, round the bottom corner, across a piece of waste land where children were already playing among mounds of dirty snow and wet, brown grass, and into the front street of the houses opposite their own. About half way up, one of the houses suddenly changed its pattern;

A general dealer in the Mill Dam, 1930s. 'Mr Tollett sold practically everything and there was always somebody wanting something from half-past seven in the morning until eight at night, ten on a Saturday . . .' Pure as the Lily

above its window a large, yellow tin placard said, DRINK BROOK-BOND'S TEA, and a gay old gentleman, on another piece of tin, asked you to look at him to see how fit he kept on ALLY SLOPER'S SAUCE. The house window itself held tier on tier of bottles of sweets receding away from the gaze of the beholder to dim regions beyond, while, balancing on the front of every shelf, were boxes of hearts-and-crosses, sherbet dips, everlasting stripes, scented cachous and jujubes. In front of the window were large jars of pickled cabbage and pickled onions, and seven-pound jars of loose jam and lemon curd. Among these, at crazy angles, were placed Christmas wares of 'Shops with real scales', dolls in the minutest of gauze chemises, work-boxes, miniature boxing-gloves and tram-conductor sets of hat and ticket puncher. Paper-chains hung in loops from the ceiling, together with huge red and green paper bells, of a honeycomb pattern. From the chains and bells, held by fine threads, dangled swans, balls, dolls, ships and fairies, all in fine glass and painted a variety of colours.

Annie and Rosie pushed the pram against the wall and joined two other children, who were endeavouring to get a first-hand view by hanging on to the high window-sill by their elbows and sticking their toes into the wall . . . 'Ooh! ain't they luverly?' said Rosie, gazing in rapture at the display.

147

Courting and Cavorting

In the summer, we would usually gather on the open space before the terrace, or on the slack bank and the timbers. The big timbers were tied together with sleepers to which ropes were attached allowing each timber some leeway. When the tide was high and the timbers were floating you ran over each one, pressing it down into the water and jumping on to the next before your feet got wet. This was called playing the piano. Or we'd make tents and play houses, or gather round Richardson's top corner and into the chimneypiece and play shops, or bays on the pavement, what others call hopscotch. And then there was diabolo, and scooters, and

In Shields there were the most beautiful girls. I don't know what it was, whether it was the sea air or what, but their complexions were beautiful.

'I love a lassie,
A bonny, bonny lassie;
She's as pure as the lily in the dell . . .'
Pure as the Lily

rounders, and hot rice, and . . . knocky-door-neighbour. Some nights we would get dressed up and go singing in procession round the five streets.

We were only following our elders in this, for like a spring fever, there would come at certain times of the year among certain women of the buildings, among whom were Kate and Mary, a madness, a jolly madness, that would force them to dress up in any old clothes, and singing and beating tin cans, parade around the five streets. I've seen Mary leave her washing and Kate her baking and, getting into the men's clothes, go dancing round the doors, and she solid and sober. There was a primitive weirdness about this which I recall whenever I hear the Kerry Piper's song.

Sundays were a sort of respite to me, but boring to everybody else in the house, because, not having best clothes, they couldn't go out. I connected Sundays with big dinners, everybody going to bed in the afternoon – and Cissie Affleck, because nearly always I watched Cissie and her young man taking their weekly walk after Church on a Sunday afternoon.

149

You could almost tell the time from Cissie and Mr Maitcham passing along the slack bank opposite the end of our street on a Sunday afternoon after chapel Sunday school. I can see them now. He was a tall well-dressed, superior looking man. You couldn't put the prefix lad or boy to Mr Maitcham. I think he must have been about thirty at that time and Cissie in her early twenties. There they would walk, keeping a specified distance apart; sedately, even regally they would pass by the New Buildings. I cannot ever remember Cissie casting her eyes across the road to where, at the corner of Philipson Street, was her shop. No, this was Sunday. A day for Church and courting, a prim kind of courting. You didn't wear your heart on your sleeve in those days. Couples didn't fling their arms about each other in public, even go as far as kissing in public, that was left to the darkness of a back lane, or better still some place up the country, and courting in the front room was only sanctioned by the, morally speaking, broad parents, and this, as was well known, led to a quick wedding and evoked the remark 'Well, what d'ya expect. It was askin' for it.'

But I could never connect the front room or a quiet spot up the country with Cissie and Mr Maitcham, and as for the back lane, never.

A little later, I managed to give time to falling for a lad. There were, I remember, Willie Birket and Tot Lawson, but I made headway with neither. Tot had dreamy eyes but they didn't look at me and in an endeavour to turn them in my direction I gave bullets to his sister Ruby to pass on to him. They had no effect on his eyes. But when I was nineteen he sought me out and he became my lad, for a while.

150

These children, pictured in 1890, would have come from families living one to a room. They'd have had to go to a central tub in the town for a wash; only the better families had their own baths.

'Katie bent right down now until her face was on a level with his. She wanted to take her handkerchief and wipe his running nose. His hair was black, but white-streaked with nits . . . As she gazed pitifully at the children she realised that in an odd way her early years had been good.' Katie Mulholland

In my school days I cannot remember any lad ever giving me a bullet, I was the one who proffered taffie or bruised fruit. On one classic occasion I spent my little hoard on a deceiving male. His name was Eddie Youlden. He sat behind me in Standard Four, and I thought he had made a song up about me that he kept singing down my neck. It went:

K-K-K-Katie,
Beautiful K-Katie,
You're the only g-g-girl
that I adore.
When the m-moon shines on the cow shed,
I'll be waiting at the k-k-k-kitchen door.

I'd passed him bags of bullets before I realised I was being deceived. Never trust a ginger headed man.

Conditions of Life

All of the health statistics for Tyneside compared unfavourably with national averages and with the record of other industrial areas. When the national infant mortality rate was 32 per 1,000, the Jarrow figure was more than 62 per 1,000. Why was the local record so bad?

Certainly overcrowding played a big part. Overcrowding had been defined in 1891 as more than two adults to a room. Children under ten counted as half and babies under a year old not at all. Under this definition a two-roomed dwelling could contain any combination of adults and children between four adults and no children, and one adult and six children (plus any number of babies), without being considered overcrowded. Still, in 1921, 14,782 (42.3% of the population) lived in overcrowded conditions in Jarrow.

Our house was hardly ever without lodgers. Sometimes they would sleep on the feather bed in the bedroom with me Uncle Jack. Then me granda would sleep in the brass bed in the front room, me grannie on her couch opposite him, and Kate and I on the saddle in the kitchen. But invariably it would mean that the beds would be turned round, me granda and me grandma sometimes having the feather bed in the bedroom, and four lodgers sharing the two beds in the front room. For one short period I remember Kate and I slept at Mary's, while the saddle in the kitchen was taken up by Uncle Jack. At another period there were five men sleeping in the front room, one on a shake down.

In the nineteenth century, sanitation was as inadequate in rural areas as it was in the townships. *The Girl* is set in the fictitious village of Elmholm, but both its geographical position (two-and-a-half miles south of Allen-

If a coal cart came down the alley, the driver would yell and you'd have to run out and take in the washing or lift it up with a prop. The coal was delivered outside the backyard in the alley, and Kate would shovel it inside.

Despite health acts in the 1870s food retailing was still very much a matter of caveat emptor. In Tilly Trotter Widowed, Noreen Brentwood, pregnant by Tilly's son, works in Proggles of Newcastle: 'The lamps fixed to the walls on each side of the table were so placed that they illuminated only the table itself and the double oven fireplace exactly four feet from the end of it. Perhaps this was as well for they shut out from Noreen's gaze a regiment of cockroaches and fearless rats that infested the margin of the basement . . . The two cats that should have been parading the premises were so satiated with food that they slept.'

dale) and this description of its state in the 1850s attest to reality:

It consisted of forty-five houses. These included the two short rows of miners' cottages, which were situated behind the houses on the right hand side of the village green if you were journeying from Allendale towards Sinderhope. They had been built some fifty years previously to house the overflow of miners then employed in the lead mines and smelting mills. They were low two-roomed stone dwellings with mud floors, except where flagstones had been laid down; and at first the sanitary habits of their occupants had been similar to those which prevailed in the town of Allendale itself; their middens* had been in front of their front doors, to the disdain of the artisans in the village who kept their middens at the back of their houses, or better still at the bottom of their gardens. But time had wrought change so that now not only were all middens to be found behind the cottages but for most of the year

*dry lavatories.

Two-room Northumberland cottage, 1910. Picturesque as it looks, in the nineteenth century of Tilly Trotter such cottages were far from ideal. In the little mining villages through Northumberland and Durham, poor sanitation and ill-health was as much a problem as in the Tyneside towns.

'Beyond the stretch of moorland lay a huddle of houses known as Rosier's Village. They were mean, two-roomed, mud-floored miners' cottages housing the workers in the mine that lay half a mile beyond . . . Even when he was well past the village the stench of it still clung to his nostrils.' Simon Brentwood in Tilly Trotter

the villagers all lived peaceably together, except on days such as fair days, or the Friday after the pays. This was the day on which the miners received their accumulated pay. Then the rowdiest among them fought, cracked each other's heads, and beat up their women. The return to normal wouldn't take place until work started again.

The village proper was shaped like a pear, the road from Allendale entering it between Ralph Buckman's blacksmith's shop

*Near Langley in Northumberland,
around 1890.*

and Will Rickson's house and builder's yard before dividing to pass round both sides of the green, joining up again to leave the village where, like the stalk of the pear, it narrowed between the wall of the churchyard and Elmholm House.

The cottages and houses making up the village were of various designs and sizes. Ted Loam's was a two-storied dwelling, the ground floor of which he used as a butcher's shop.

Two others that stood apart belonged to Walter Bynge the stonemason and Thomas Wheatley the grain chandler who, although his main business was in Allendale Town, used his ground floor, too, for the sale of flour and pulses in times of necessity.

But most of the inhabitants were either farm labourers or drovers who, however respectable they were during the week, would invariably, like the miners, become mortallious on fair days, at weddings, christenings, funerals, and occasionally on a Saturday night.

In *The Glass Virgin*, the middens are 'a series of big holes in the ground and a number of mounds'. But in East Jarrow at the turn of the century, real progress had been made! In our house the lavatory was a dry one – a misleading term – with a long wooden seat with a hole in the middle and, if you kept the lid on, it was a wonderful place for musing and meditation. Once having made yourself comfortable you looked out through a space between the top of the door and the framework on to the grey, sloping, slated roof that covered the wash-house and the staircase of the upstairs house, and if you were lucky you saw a grey bird hopping about – we called them grey birds because we didn't know their real names. Here you were shut in and became lost in a world apart, a secret world. That is, if the lid was on. If it wasn't and you fell into a state of musing, which often happened, you could be aroused by the back lane hatch being lifted and the scavenger rudely thrusting in his long shovel. Many a time has this catapulted me from the seat to hide my face against the door, leaving my bottom exposed.

From time immemorial the streets of Newcastle and Jarrow would have been loaded with horse muck, attracting flies that spread disease, and although Public Health legislation in the 1870s extended the scope of sanitary authorities, house sanitation remained primitive well into the twentieth century. One tends to forget that improvements in sewerage or the water supply – and utility operations of any kind – cost money. Today we are accustomed to central government as Lady Bountiful, but then any progress came from the rates, from the local people.

In the following piece, Katie Mulholland describes the awful conditions in what was regarded as a well-kept, working-class home in the 1860s:

'Ma! Ma! What's come over me. You know what I forgot? . . . Me pay.' She swiftly undid the two buttons of her dress, unloosed the tape that tied her bodice, then thrust her hand inside the neck of her chemise and unpinned the calico bag. Her breath was coming quickly and she gabbled now, 'You wouldn't believe it. That's all I've thought of for days, getting me wages, and I couldn't get home quick enough, but since I come in the door I haven't thought a thing about it. Would you believe it?'

She bent her slender body towards Catherine and pressed the calico bag into her hands, and Catherine slowly took the four shillings out, looked at them, then swifly she opened her arms and drew her daughter to her, and as swiftly she pushed her away

'*The only time Annie got a violent distaste for it was when the men unexpectedly lifted the back hatch to clean it out with their long shovels. Then a revulsion for it would overcome her. She didn't like the scavengers, nor would she follow the cart with her companions, shouting:*

Cloggy Betty, on the netty
On a Sunday morning . . .'

Kate Hannigan

A woman, in the late nineteenth century, carries two buckets of water, steadied by a wooden frame. Disease was a constant possibility.

'"Ty . . . typhoid? God! how . . . how did we get that? Is it about? I've never been further than the town. Never heard nobody's got it . . ."

Dr Arnison turned and pointed to the bucket standing on the table.

"The watter?"

"Aye, the water . . . Where do you get it from?"

"She draws it mostly." He now jerked his head towards Hannah, then demanded, "Where did you get it from?"

Hannah looked at the doctor as she said quietly, "I always put the bucket under the ripple that comes out of the bank, never into the stream."' The Girl*

again. Unclenching her fist and holding out her palm with the money in it, she said in a voice that was cracking slightly, 'You must have a shilling back every month.'

'A shilling, Ma! No, no, I don't want a shilling.' Katie's voice was high and she shook her head from side to side. 'The threepence will do. Mrs Davis has got a half a crown saved up for me, now; I don't want a shilling.' She pushed her mother's hand away, and so quickly that the money spilled on to the floor, and immediately she was on her hands and knees picking it up. One of the shillings had rolled into a mud-filled crevice between two of the stones, and when she dug her finger in to get the coin she disturbed the earth and a strong obnoxious smell rose to her and filled her nostrils. The smell in the house was always worse in the summer when the water from the middens seeped under the foundations and oozed upwards. In the winter the rain dispersed it more quickly.

When the four coins were retrieved they all laughed. Katie now opening the back door, stood under the lean-to and rinsed her fingers in the wooden tub of water that stood on a bench attached to the wall.

One of the major health hazards was the water supply. In the nineteenth century the sources of supply lay in the river, in wells, and perhaps most safe of all in rainwater gathered domestically in barrels. In *The Dwelling Place* Matthew actually invents a system which pumps water out of a burn to be carried to sluice out the water closets. But it doesn't save him.

In 1846, when William married an apothecary's daughter from Shields, Matthew built him a fine house, standing in a half acre of land within a quarter of a mile of the mill itself. It had a large kitchen and a parlor, three bedrooms and a garret, and besides the washhouse, coal-house, and stable there was, of course, the new sanitary arrangement – even better this one, for the effluent didn't flow back into the river as it was too far away to pipe it, but into a huge cesspool; nor was their fresh water supply drawn from the river but from a well that Matthew had caused to be sunk at the bottom of the garden.

It was around this time that Matthew became really conscious of the danger of the river water, for it was into this that the effluent flowed, that cattle paddled and went to drink, that cats and dogs were thrown, and it was from this also that most of the hamlets and the villages drew their water supplies.

157

The fact that the river was fast running in parts failed now to convince him of its purity, for all along its length it was being used as a dump for filth.

It was in 1844, when typhoid was sweeping both sides of the river from South Shields to Gateshead and from North Shields to Newcastle, that Matthew's mother and grannie were taken, and also Nellie. Nellie had been thirteen and bonny and bursting with health, but she had been snuffed out like a tallow-candle in the wind, whereas Annie, who had always been weakly and who, too, had lain with the fever, survived. There was no accounting, they said, for the workings of God. All man could do was to bow before His will. Matthew had let his pass, and concentrated on the river.

But in 1849 when his only daughter, the one child that Cissie had given him, died of the cholera at the age of eleven, he did not let it pass, but cursed God. He cursed Him in private and in public; he cursed Him to the face of his great friend, Parson Hedley . . . And he cursed Him to the damnation of his own soul, so said the righteous when, two years later almost to the day, after rising up from the laden Christmas table, he died.

He had left the table and staggered to the settle because of a violent pain in his chest, which he said wasn't like wind for he had hardly commenced to eat. An hour later, still sitting on the settle, strangely enough where the miller before him had drawn his last breath, he died, and more strangely still, of the same complaint. . . .

There are many reasons given for Tyneside's poor housing and health record compared to other emerging industrial townships of the nineteenth century. Perhaps, in the end, it was simply a question of priorities: expansion, not health or hygiene, was the main priority of these 'frontier' towns. It was the lure of rich new coalfields, for example, that provided the impetus for a healthy water supply:

For years men had failed to discover whether coal lay beneath the apparently impenetrable magnesian limestone layer of the East Durham plateau. The solution, after much costly failure, came with the development of powerful steam pumps. This equipment then proved equal to the task of bringing clean water from deep underground for drinking.

Only with this breakthrough in the 1850s did the drawn-out development of a decent domestic water supply begin in earnest: first to a tap that served five or six homes, then to a tap for every backyard, and finally, in the twentieth century, to people's homes.

158

Strife

STRIFE

What did I want from life?
Gaiety, riches, happiness,
Not strife.
Why not strife?
Again I say why not strife?
For at this stage of your age
The only wisdom you have gleaned
Has been sucked from strife:
Fighting through trammel,
Through fear, sickness, pain,
All generated by strife,
Has taught you that life,
To be a vital thing,
Must be bred on strife.
It is the yeast to knowing, growing,
An understanding of the decades
Allotted to your share,
Of the being in you you cannot touch,
  but hear
And fear to know more
  in case you see yourself bare.
Strife has been your friend;
Do not desire to finish your last days
  alone.

In 1877 those who were enlightened by reading newspapers discussed among other things such topics as Disraeli proclaiming Queen Victoria Empress of India and seeing to it that she had the adulation of Indian princes and African chiefs. But for the ordinary man and woman in towns such as South Shields, there were other happenings that struck nearer home, very much nearer home.

The sea which provided most of the inhabitants with a livelihood also created havoc and disaster. There was that awful night in December last year when three vessels were wrecked and the sea, still unsatisfied, had engulfed and destroyed another two later in the day, and all under the eyes of horrified townspeople who could only watch helplessly. Even though the Volunteer Life Brigade did heroic work, many lives were lost.

Such tragedies had the power to unite the townspeople, at least for a time. Rich and poor alike mingled in their sorrow until the poor, once again forgetting their place in God's scheme of things, protested against their lot. And how did they protest? They protested through societies called trade unions.

Since the first national union of the Amalgamated Society of Engineers had been founded in 1851, in every town in the country where skilled workers were employed trade unions had sprung up, to the fear and consternation of the middle classes who looked upon them as a network of secret societies, whose sole purpose was to intimidate honest citizens, plot to confiscate their property, cause explosions and mob violence and bring the country to total revolution if they were allowed to get the upper hand.

The County of Durham was a hotbed of such people. They agitated in mines, in steel works, in shipbuilding yards, in factories, and it was even whispered they tried to inveigle young women into their ranks; and not only those, let it be understood, from the common herd, but women of education and property.

The Gambling Man

One such woman of education and property was Theresa Rosier, who had been reared in the very cradle of capitalism by the powerful and influential mine owner, George Rosier, a man capable of declaring that he'd see his striking workforce 'gnaw their arms off . . . before they get the

159

better of me'. She appears to us, first, in the opening page of *Katie Mulholland*:

Theresa took after her father, at least outwardly; whom she took after inwardly they had yet to discover, for whoever heard of a mineowner's daughter going to a chartist meeting.

[The Chartists championed the social and economic grievances of the working class through petitioning for political reform. Feargus O'Connor was an extremist leader of the organisation.]

The Rosiers had thought they had heard the last of Chartists in 1855 when that madman O'Connor had died; but there was an element trying to revive itself in Newcastle and their own

The Black Middens, rocks at the mouth of the Tyne, and the hard sands outside Shields harbour created a high risk of disaster. Adding to the risk, after 1850 when competition appeared from steam colliers, the old fashioned sailing vessels could no longer afford adequate maintenance or crews.

'The river always rose with heavy rains, but now she could see the dull leaden grey of its waters was covering the bank, and it was running fast.' Martha Mary Crawford

daughter had attended a meeting and dared to voice her views at the dining table. That any girl of seventeen should talk back to her father was unheard of, but that she should bring into the open a matter that was like a gaping wound in his side was so monstrous that she had feared on that particular occasion that Mr Rosier would collapse. And if this wasn't enough, her own brother had espied her, three miles away on the fells, talking to groups of evicted miners from the village, trouble-makers, men who were

more like savages and brutes than human beings. At the sight of his sister degrading herself Bernard's rage had been almost as great as his father's. To use his own words he had thrown her into the carriage. Mr Rosier had confined his daughter to her room for a fortnight, and she, her mother, had had to bear the brunt of his tongue. What, he had demanded, had she bred him, a viper? A viper indeed.

Theresa doubted whether she would have come to her present way of thinking at her age without the tutoring and guidance of her governess.

'The man pointed his thin dirty finger at John. "We'll have to hang together, that's the solution. The bloody unions will have to find out whose side they're on. Why aren't they up in London doing somethin'? There'll be riots afore long, you'll see."' The Blind Miller

162

'He was excited about the march on Monday, the march from Jarrow to London, the march of protest against starvation, and he had talked of nothing else for weeks.' The Blind Miller

Ainsley had been a forcing house, like the one over there near the greenhouses where Mr Wisden, the head gardener, performed miracles on plants with a stove-pipe. Ainsley had been her stove-pipe, and she thanked God for her . . . Ainsley had taught her to see things as they really were.

She had been five years old when Ainsley came into her life. She could remember the day when she first saw the tall, thin woman and realised that Ainsley was plain-looking. That was before she became aware that she herself was saddled with the same complaint. Ainsley was thirty when she came to Greenwall Manor. She was forty-two when she left it, on the day following their secret, exciting visit to the meeting on the Newcastle Town Moor, when the cavalry came and rode into the thousands of people, and

163

they had run with the rest and almost been trampled to death. It was there they had been seen by Mr Careless, a magistrate and friend of her father's.

Ainsley had been turned out in disgrace and without a reference. For who could give a reference to a governess who had corrupted a young mind? That's what her mother had said. Her father had said much more and his language had been much stronger, for had not the woman made him a laughing-stock by inveigling his daughter to attend Chartist meetings, and making her an open sympathiser with the rebel and scum in his own pit?

Ainsley had refuted nothing her employer had accused her of, and she had dared to stand up to him and say that she was proud she had enabled one of his family to think for herself, and that he, too, should be proud that he had one intelligent person among the dunderheads in his household.

She had known what it was to die when she saw Ainsley being driven away from the door. She hadn't been allowed any word with her; she was locked in her room, but she had hammered on the window and Ainsley had lifted her joined hands towards her. They said, 'Be strong. Be strong.' She had tried to be strong, but it was

'"There's going to be a short service in Christ Church for the marchers afore we leave . . . As for May, she neither believes in God . . . or man." He stressed the last word. "She says it's a lot of damned hypocrisy, the men going to the church before the march, for ten to one there hadn't been a man Jack of us inside a church or chapel for years . . . and I suppose she's right in a way . . ."'
The Blind Miller

Left:
*The Jarrow March, October 26th, 1936,
also showing Miss Ellen Wilkinson,
M.P., leading the marchers into Luton.*

*'The name mostly on John's lips
was that of Ellen Wilkinson. Sarah had
never seen Ellen Wilkinson. She didn't
think of her as a woman, not an ordinary,
normal woman. In fact any woman who
was in Parliament could, of course, not be
ordinary. As for being normal, well,
women had their place, hadn't they, and
it wasn't really their place to yell their
heads off among a lot of men in
Parliament.'* The Blind Miller

Above Right:
*It wasn't just the men who rose up
against their masters, as is shown by
this picture of striking fish curers, nor
was it only women from the workforce
who protested. Prototypes for those
twentieth-century champions of female
suffrage led by Emily Pankhurst found
vehicles for expression in both the
Chartist and Union movements.*

difficult without Ainsley's support. She had begun by proposing setting up a weekly class in the village to teach the miners to read and write. When her mother had recovered sufficiently she had said, 'Child, do you think a miner would go down a mine if he could read and write correctly? Do you want your father's business to collapse? Do you want us to starve? Never let such a proposal come to your father's ears, it could cause him to have a seizure.'

These women were, not least in their courage, prototypes for those twentieth-century champions of female suffrage led by Emily Pankhurst.

People ask me what I think of the feminist movement today, and I have to disappoint some of them by saying that I do not agree with the way the movement tries to denigrate men, to take their manliness away.

Certainly my women characters are strong, they always come through, but that is because they are me. I have had to be strong all my life, from the time I was a child I have had to contend with fear: I feared God, hell and damnation, and the priest's admonitions from behind the grid of the confessional; I feared Kate's drinking to an exaggerated extent and feared going the same way as her; and then, for ten years, I had to contend with the breakdown. Now, I am capable of doing everything that I make my characters do: good, bad or indifferent. I am quite capable of doing the worst things possible.

But I would never condone a matriarchal society. I have always worked with men and I have always preferred to do so, though the men I work with are associates, not bosses. I will not have bosses!

Them vrs. Us

It might be expected that in the later part of the nineteenth century, the working class was all set to rise up as one against its industrial masters. But in fact the only example of working class solidarity came during ten days in the middle of May, 1926 – the occasion of the General Strike.

Of course many strikes did take place and some were marked with considerable violence, but through inter-union conflict and squabbles over demarcation lines (between boilermakers and shipwrights after the revolution wrought by the John Bowes, for example), the unions consistently failed to present a unified front, or even to convince the

'"To hear our Katie talking about the unions you would think their members had been bred in monasteries, all the men are so good, honest, upright individuals, all fighting their wicked masters. Mind, I'm not saying that some of the masters don't deserve that title and they need to be fought . . ."' The Mallen Girl

Some of the 93 Boldon Colliery Putters arriving at South Shields County Court, to answer breach of contract summonses. Moves to educate working men posed a threat to some leading industrialists: 'Theresa had begun by proposing setting up a weekly class in the village to teach the miners to read and write. When her mother had recovered sufficiently she had said, "Child, do you think a miner would go down a mine if he could read and write correctly? Do you want your father's business to collapse? Do you want us to starve?"' Katie Mulholland

majority of workers that they should join them. In the great engineering strike of 1871, for example, only about ten per cent of the striking workers actually belonged to unions.

This conversation between Katie Mulholland's brother Joe and the older man, Mr Hetherington, shows the mixed feelings among the workers and hints at the inter-union chaos.

They remained silent for some minutes until Joe, trying to turn the conversation, said, 'What do you think about the movement, Mr Hetherington?'

'What do I think about it?' Mr Hetherington took a bite out of a meat sandwich. 'I think it's comin' to a head, lad.'

'You think there'll be a strike?'

'It's as near as damn it, but none of us wants it.'

167

'Have they put the petition to the old man?'

'Aye, but things are different now.' Mr Hetherington put his head back and looked up at the tangle of gear attached to the grimy roof. 'They've changed; the whole place has changed since it went over into a company. I've seen the day when you could go to the old man an' talk to him. Aye, even me. Many's the time he's stopped by me side an' said, "What do you think, John? Is it an improvement?" He was always out for improvement, makin' things better and better.'

'Well, he still is, isn't he?'

'Aye, yes, but at a price. He hasn't got the hundred per cent backin' of the men he used to have in the old days. You can't get at him, or any of them up top for that matter; they're workin' from London now instead of inside the works here, although the bloody place is so full of offices and staff now we'll soon have to move the blast furnaces.'

Joe laughed at this but continued to look at Mr Hetherington – he liked to listen to the older man talking – and Mr Hetherington went on, 'See what they've done to the puddlers. Given them a ten per cent cut, and the whole country has accepted it like sheep – that is, all but North Staffordshire. They're standin' firm and

168

they've come out.'

'Do you think wor puddlers'll support them, Mr Hetherington?'

'No, lad, I don't. There's too many unions, too many heads of unions, too many bosses, too many under-bosses. It's every man jack for himself, or his own little band, instead of them all joining up together. After all, we're all steel men. But God knows we don't want any strikes; I've seen enough of them in me time.' On this Mr Hetherington rose to his feet, saying, 'Well now, here we go, lad. Let's see those rivets flyin'.'

And all day Joe helped the rivets to fly until the buzzer went at half-past five. He had entered the boiler shop in the dark and he left it in the dark. But that didn't trouble him; he had seen the daylight through the grimed windows of the shop, and at dinner-time he had sat on the river bank where the skeleton ribs of a ship were rising from the keel, and with his mates he had talked ships, talked 'Palmer's' with as much pride in the firm as if he was one of the shareholders getting his ten per cent.

Palmer's men might fight, and argue, and talk against the bosses, even against the old man himself, but they were Palmer's men, and underneath it all, proud of the title.

It wasn't always easy for the union bosses in the mining industry either. For when new coalfields were opened up (for example in East Durham in the 1820s and '30s and on the Durham coast in the 1900s), groups of workers, each accustomed to widely varying working conventions and conditions, would converge on these important new sites from many different places. The workers' different conventions and conditions were absolute tinder for internal industrial disputes, and posed a fundamental distraction from the overall solidarity of purpose.

Outsiders like to brand all workers in the North-East with similar personalities, needs and aims, as members of one group of like-minded people called the working class. Out of that comes the myth that the real conflict was a class conflict: strife between 'them' and 'us'. In fact the struggle was as much 'us vrs. us' as it was 'them vrs. us'. Take a look at *The Fifteen Streets*; the magnifying glass of the novelist cannot lie. If it did, who would believe what my characters do and say?

There were those who did not live in the fifteen streets who considered the people living there to be of one stratum, the lowest stratum; but the people inside this stratum knew that there were three different levels, the upper, the middle, and the lower. All

A keeker supervising sorters.

'*Mark Bunting, the keeker as he was called by the men, was the man who checked the corves of coal hewed by the miners, he was the man who had the power to cut a man's wages by as much as half if the seven-hundredweight basket the miner sent up from the black bowels of the earth should show a deficiency of two or three pounds . . . The keekers worked on a commission basis; the more corves they found faulty and could pass as free to the owners the more money they themselves made.*

'*Mark Bunting needed protection; . . . It was not an uncommon thing for keekers to be found in the ditches with their heads split open.*' Katie Mulholland

lived in 'houses' either upstairs or down; but in the lower end each house had only two small rooms, and upstairs or down the conditions were the same – the plaster on the walls was alive with bugs. These might only appear at night, to drop on the huddled sleepers, but that strange odour, which was peculiarly their own, wafted through the houses all the time, stamping them as buggy. No one went to live in the lower end unless he was forced. To the middle and upper fifteen streets the bottom end was only one step removed from the workhouse, for its inhabitants were usually those whose furniture had been distrained or who had been ejected from their former houses for non-payment of rent.

There were three nightmares in the lives of the occupants of the middle and upper fifteen streets. And these were linked together: they were the bums, the lower end, and the workhouse.

In the middle houses there were four rooms . . . boxes, generally, but boxes that were divided, giving privacy of a sort to one or two extra beings. The upper end had only three rooms to each house, and these were either up or down. Here, water was not carried from the central tap in the back lane but from a tap at the bottom of each yard. This stamped the area as selective, automatically making it the best end.

170

Upstarts

Not only did these more subtle social divisions exist, but if anyone tried to cross a demarcation line he would very likely be vilified for being an upstart. Like Angus in *The Round Tower*, I was an upstart and was called an upstart. Here, Angus is about to rise in the world but will find it more difficult than buying a few smart shirts:

As the back gate opened there came the sound of a train whistle and it seemed to pipe Emily Cotton into the house. She came in backwards, thrusting her thick, firm buttocks against the door and from her arms she dropped on to the table an assortment of garments, exclaiming 'There! What do you think of that lot?'

'Oh, Mam! Look at the bread.' Rosie retrieved the loaf from underneath the clothes, then swiftly began picking up one article after another. Holding a jumper up in front of her, she said, 'Oh, this is all right. What did you give for it?'

'Threepence.'

'Here, I got you a couple of shirts; they'll do for work for you.' Emily threw two garments towards her son and he caught them, and without looking at them he threw them on to a chair, saying, 'I've told you, Mam. I don't like wearin' other blokes' gear.'

'You were bloody glad to wear other blokes' gear, let me tell you, once on a time.'

'Well, I'm not any more, Mam; so don't get them for me.'

'God!' Emily Cotton lowered herself into a straight-backed chair and lifting one foot slowly up on to her knee she stroked her swollen ankle vigorously, and it was to it she addressed her remarks as she said, 'Talk about out of the frying-pan into the fire, I've spent most of my bloody life with upstarts. That lot along there; their noses in the bloody air so much they have to have their necks massaged. And now I come to me own house and me son tells me that he's got too damned big to wear another bloke's shirts. Let me tell you,' she lifted her head to him, 'you'll never be able to buy shirts of that quality in your lifetime. Let me tell you that.'

Angus stared at his mother for a moment. Then, the corner of his mouth moving upwards, he went towards her and, leaning forward, put his big hands on her shoulders and brought his face down within an inch of hers and said, 'Emily Cotton, that's where you're wrong. One of these days I'm goin' out and I'm goin' to buy six of the best bloodiest silk shirts in all this bloody town, and I'm goin' to wear them for work just to let them see.'

Maggie Rowan: '*George Rowan stripped himself of his pit clothes with a fierceness that suggested that each article was burning his flesh.*' It was odd the things I clutched at to make our family superior and I remember this as one of them: our men washed in the scullery and closed the door!

Religious Divisions

And there were other divisions, which were always much more powerful than class and which gave scope for the most terrible cruelty and bigotry.

Me granda was a Catholic who never stepped inside a church door, but who would strike a blow for the Pope, yet at the same time scorning and decrying the Richardsons and the McArthurs, close neighbours, who were strong practising Catholics. Pulling them to shreds almost daily, he would hold them up as a sample of everything that was bad. He despised them as

The temperance movement was strong in those days. Shops would open selling cocoa in an attempt to reform people's drinking habits.

A variety of temperance societies were established by the end of the nineteenth century, often allied to churches and chapels. This culture offered a demonstrably advantageous alternative to the one which expressed itself in drink, prostitution, irreligion and poverty, and it gave its participants a leg-up in society irrespective of class. 'Chapel people had power, they could get people done out of their jobs, she had heard of it happening.'
The Tide of Life

he despised all churchgoers, yet it was he who insisted that I was to go to a Catholic School.

I was the only one who ever dared to argue with him, but one day I had to run for it. I was about thirteen at this time and I was quite concerned because of the fate of my Protestant friends, for I had a lot of nice Protestant friends and the fact that they were all going to end up in hell worried me. It had been hammered into me that there was no hope for the Protestants, simply because they were Protestants. If they were sensible and changed their coats then they could be assured of eternity in heaven; if not, it was the devil and hell for them. From an early age I developed the faculty of seeing two sides to everything and one night, after listening to a particularly bitter haranguing against the Protestants, my imagination running wild, I saw most of the neighbours in a state of undress being forced to sit on hot grid-irons – because that is what happened to you in hell – and my mind protested and said it wasn't right. The following day was Sunday and on my return from the first session of praying for me granda's soul I passed the Salvation Army standing outside the line of bars opposite the Dock gates, openly proclaiming their allegiance to God. I saw them as a courageous group of people and I knew that I wouldn't have the pluck to stand in the open and acknowledge my God. This filled my mind all the way home and when I got indoors I answered the unintentional brain-washing of years by saying, without any preliminary lead-up, 'I like the Salvation Army, they've got pluck.'

Betty was a pet hen. She was twelve years old, she had rheumatics and couldn't walk but could still lay eggs. When she died me granda couldn't eat her, but he wasn't going to lose on her so he sold her to one of the Arab boarding-house keepers in Corstorphine Town.

I can see his face now. It seemed to stretch at all angles until it covered the whole fireplace and was as red as the blazing coals that were cooking the gigantic Sunday roast.

'What did you say?' His voice seemed to come up through the floor boards. I ignored the wild signalling of Kate from the scullery. She, I know, thought I had gone clean doo-lally-tap, but nothing could stop me.

'The Halleluyahs aren't afraid to praise God in the open.' I went on, 'And another thing, they don't go to Church and then come out and get drunk.' Of course the last bit didn't apply to him because he got drunk without going to church.

'GET OUT!'

'You'll not frighten me like you have everybody else, so you needn't think . . .'

Kate saved me by dragging me by the scruff of the neck into the scullery, and from there pushing me into the backyard, the while hissing at me, 'Have you gone stark starin' mad? What's come over you? Stay out for a minute.'

As I stood at the bottom of the backyard I heard him yelling, 'Salvation Army, now, is it? Did you hear her? Begod! we'll have her comin' down the street next knockin' bloody hell out of the big drum, or sitting at the

174

Corstorphine Town 1895, the Arab quarter in South Shields on the banks of the river.

'Talk to an Arab! She had only to be seen doing that and . . . Once your name was coupled with an Arab you were taboo.'
Rose Angela in Colour Blind

harmonium at the street corner leading the lot. You'll see.'

And you know, I think he was a bit afraid of what I might do if driven too far, so for a while, at any rate, there was no tirade against the Protestants.

In such a community as this, innocent people got hurt. In *The Blind Miller* it was Sarah whose only sin was to love a chapelite, David Hetherington. But as Ma Ratcliffe takes great comfort in pointing out: 'Stink-pots like the Hetheringtons couldn't be expected to walk this way with wedding rings.':

All along Sarah had known it would come to nothing – what hope was there for a Catholic and a chapelite? It was a greater barrier than a social one. The Hetheringtons might live in the fifteen streets, but the gap between her family and them was as wide as between a prop man in the docks and one of the managers living in his big house down Westoe end in Shields.

Just as often the hurt would rebound on the bigot. In *Fanny McBride*, as we have already seen, the redoubtable Fanny eventually rejects her favourite son, Jack, for marrying a Protestant, and spends the rest of her life regretting it.

All the neighbourhood had been laughing up their sleeves at what

An Arab procession through the streets.

In Colour Blind the priest tries to correct
Rosie's view of Arabs: ' "Look at me,
Rosie, for I have something to tell you . . .
Has no one ever told you that God is
colour-blind?"

"Colour-blind . . .? No, Father." Her
eyes were stretched to their widest.'

was going on, and not one of them daring to tell her. And they were
wise, for she would have laid out anyone who dared to come and
say that her lad, her Jack, was courting a Hallelujah on the sly; for
whoever heard of a Catholic taking up with a Salvation Army
piece?

Divisions of Race

The Arabs were introduced to Shields in the crews of sailing ships in the
nineteenth century. By the First World War as many as half the crew of a
ship might be Arab. As a child I took their presence for granted and didn't
register the difference between Arabs and us especially because, from the
age of seven when I started at St Peter's and St Paul's School, I would go
through the docks each day and see a multitude of nationalities waiting to
be taken on. If they weren't Arabs they were Swedes or Negroes or
Russians – those big, burly Russian Captains.

Not once did anyone handle me, even though at the time there was a

176

The Mill Dam Riots in 1931.

'"There's always been trouble down there," she went on. "Look at that Saturday a few years back, when the Arabs rioted around the shipping office and stabbed them three policemen."

"You couldn't only blame the Arabs for that," Cavan put in sharply; "it were our blokes agitating them not to sign the P.C.5. form that did that, together with those bloody Arab boarding-house masters who bleed them dry . . . It was the white agitators and the black masters who caused the shipping trouble, I'm telling you . . ."' Colour Blind

tremendous fuss about the white slave trade – girls being picked up and whisked away.

But among our people were those who relished the luxury of condescension in a community where there were few luxuries of any kind. Race, like class and religion, was an opportunity not to be missed.

In this extract from *Colour Blind*, Bridget, a Roman Catholic, is pregnant by James, a Protestant Negro, whom Bridget has married in a Registry Office, thereby transgressing virtually every tenet of so-called respectable society!

A bairn coming. Kathie held her head between her hands. A black bairn. For it would be a black bairn, she was sure; there was too much of him in comparison with Bridget's whiteness. The child would be black both inside and out, and her Bridget would have to push a black bairn around the streets. Mother of God! How could a daughter of hers stand up under the shame of it? She rocked her head with her hands. But Bridget didn't seem to be ashamed: there she was, away now in Shields, walking openly with him in the broad daylight! Hadn't she watched her go down the street with never a look to right or left, her head held high as if she had something to be proud of? What had come over her? Why had she done it? Kathie beat the top of her head with her fist. Would the

177

good God tell her why she had done it?

Something of the same question was passing through Bridget's mind as she faced the look of ill-concealed scorn in the eyes of the shop assistants. She had watched her husband put down the five pounds deposit and sign his name with a proud flourish on the form which was an open sesame to a choice of oil-cloths, of beds and bedroom suites, of half-sets of china and Nottingham lace curtains. Never had she dreamed that she would be able to set up house with thirty pounds' worth of furniture. She should be mad with the joy of it; but there was no spark of joy in her, only pain and pity, and gratitude and abhorrence – the pain and pity and gratitude were the feelings that the bulk of towering blackness evoked in her; the abhorrence was for herself and the thing she had done.

When they left the shop it was her husband who showed her out. Taking the door from the hand of the shopwalker he stood aside to allow her to pass. But the closing of the door did not shut out the tittering from the shop, and its sound brought an angry flush to Bridget's cheeks, and a higher tilt to her chin. They laughed at her because he treated her like a queen! If she had married one of them she would have been made aware of her inferiority for the remainder of her life, and if she had married one of her own class never would she have known the meaning of worship – not to speak of consideration; never would she have known what it was to be loved as this man loved her. Then why was she ashamed of him? Why did it take all the rallying of her forces to brave the streets with him at her side?

When they were together, closed in by four walls, with no eyes upon them, the shame would fade, and then a strange tenderness for him would fill her. Even at times a feeling she thought might be love for him would sweep over her. This often happened in the night when he woke her with his loving, for even with his passion, which lifted her into realms hitherto unknown, his love-making never lost the adoring quality that gave to it a gentleness. But she wished again and again that he would not show this gentleness to her in public, for it was this as much as anything that brought the guffaws and smiles of ridicule upon them. She wanted to tell him, but she could not bear to hurt him. She had soon found that she could hurt him with a look or a word; and she knew that she must never do this . . . she must never hurt him more than she had done by marrying him. She did not blame him for marrying her – if she had been in her right senses it would never have come about – Matt had always warned her . . . Matt . . . She shuddered. She had Matt to face yet. Oh God, give her strength for the day when Matt would speak to her, and drag from her the reason why she had done this thing . . .

As they turned into Dunstable Street James spoke a cheery 'good evening' to a small group of men standing at the corner. They answered him in low growls, turning their heads away and becoming engrossed in each other's conversation.

And Bridget felt a desire to stop and shout at them, 'He's as good as you – he's better than you. He wouldn't let his wife trail round the bars after him to get what was left of his pay; nor yet have his beer if the bairns went naked – you lot! What are you, anyway? . . . Scum . . . scum.'

She was shivering when they entered the empty house; and James, all concern for her, said, 'I know you got chill, honey – come, we go to your home – there's big fire there . . . You love me, Rose?'

She nodded.

'Always?'

She nodded again.

'No other man, ever?'

She shook her head.

'Not when I'm away at sea, like some white women?'

'No, no, never that!' Her protest was vehement.

His enormous lips slowly traced the outline of her face. The moving black blur filled her with such conflicting emotions that she became faint under them. His unfinished words ran into one another, forming a lulling drawl. 'Rose love . . . my beautiful Rose. No other woman in world like you. . . You marry me 'cause you love me. You don't mind colour, and our baby . . . my baby, she be a girl; we call her Angela, eh? like angel . . . Rose Angela.' His fingers moved down the waist-band of her skirt and pressed gently on her stomach. 'I feel her heart-beat . . . she'll be like you, Rose . . . white and beautiful with long limbs and . . .'

The sound that checked his words was of someone breathing. They both remained still, pressed close against each other for a second longer, listening to the hiss of the indrawn breath. James turned slowly, but Bridget almost jumped into the centre of the kitchen at the sight of the priest standing in the front-room doorway.

If it had been an ordinary man, James would have demanded 'What the hell you up to eh?' before, perhaps whirling him through the air into the street. But a priest to him was not a man, so he said with laughing irony. 'Why, sir, you near scared me white.'

The priest looked from James to Bridget, and the expression in his eyes bore down her courage. Her head drooped and the old childhood fear of him overcame her.

'I told you to bring him along to the vestry.' Father O'Malley might have been speaking of an animal, and his words seemed to have been pressed thin in their effort to escape his tight lips.

'I . . . I didn't tell him, Father.'

Aloneness

Later Bridget imagines 'that once inside the fifteen streets she would find a measure of peace and protection among her own kind; but when she thought this, the enormity of her crime in all entirety had not been brought fully home to her . . . it needed the return to her own class to do this.' God help you if you earned exclusion from the community and dared to remain in it. Illegitimacy was not unheard of in the Tyneside of my youth but it provided a tempting challenge for the bigoted poor. One day one of the girls in Philipson Street was having a birthday party. I hadn't been invited but I knew I would be. I knew I was going to that party because hadn't all my playmates been invited? There they were now, all going towards this particular backyard door. But the funny thing about it was that they all passed me without even looking the side I was on. I might have been a brick in the wall for all the notice they took of me. They had their best dresses on; some had pinnies over the dresses. They all wore nice hair ribbons, and each carried a little parcel.

When the last one had gone in I still hadn't moved, but when I thought I heard Kate's voice calling me I went swiftly down the back lane, keeping close to the wall, past the low lavatory hatches, past the higher coal hatches, until I came opposite this back door. And there I stood looking towards the upstairs window. And as I stared there came into my body a riot of feelings, anxiety, disappointment, urgency, all churning round a sort of breathless desire. I stood with my mouth open, panting. I had to get into that party, it was imperative that I got into that party, because I had never been to a party except once when I was five when I went to a birthday party in Mrs Lodge's in Leam Lane. But I only remember that occasion because my Aunt Mary had put some pearl beads on me, her own beads and I had snapped them, and I got a spanking for my pains. We had parties, I have described them, but this party was different. It had been talked about for days, even weeks. There were going to be lovely cakes on

It was in the spring of 1929 I left the North, sad yet hopeful; sad because I told myself I was never going back. I had finished with the North and all it stood for.

the table, all kinds of lovely cakes, and then games and carry-on. I had to get into that party.

I knew what had happened. Mrs X had forgotten to ask me . . . I knew it wasn't girls who picked who were coming to their parties, it was their ma's who said, 'You can have that one, and that one, and that one.' I knew I had only to attract Mrs X's attention and I would be in at that party.

I could see the outline of figures moving backwards and forwards behind the lace curtains so I set about attracting the attention of one of them. I jumped up and down, I did a lot of Ooh, ooh, oohing! because I knew that if any one saw me they would tell Mrs X and she would come to the window and say 'Aw, there's little Katie McMullen. Why, come on up, Katie. Fancy me forgetting about you. Come up, hinny.'

But my antics attracted no one to the window. The back lane was empty. There was no one in the whole wide world for me to speak to. There descended on me a feeling of desolation, of aloneness, it wasn't to be borne. I ran across the back lane, pushed open the yard door, went up the stone steps to the staircase door and knocked.

At this point memory dims. I seem to see one figure after another coming to the top of the stairhead and looking down. Then the hostess herself came towards me. I can see her face now, round, flat-looking, full of self-importance. But she deigned to bend towards me as she whispered, 'You can't come up. Me ma says you can't.'

Perhaps I was foolish enough to ask 'Why?' I don't know but I do remember her next words.

'Well, me ma says you haven't got no da.'

Children need no preliminary lead-up to vital statements, they simply make them. I turned from her, closed the door quietly, went down the stone steps, out of the backyard, across the back lane and up our backyard.

I am not sure whether I am the first person to use this word 'aloneness' to mean something quite different to 'loneliness', but I tried to capture what I mean in *Fanny McBride* when, at the end, the whole family stays away except for Philip, the son whom Fanny never really liked because he was an upstart. The image I recreated there I owe to a great friend of mine called Mannie Anderson, a Jewish doctor from South Shields. After I left the North and began to write I would be invited back occasionally to give talks, and would stay in Shields with Dr Anderson. What impressed me about him was his sheer dedication to the patients in the Infirmary: in the middle of the night, if necessary, he would go to them and comfort them. And one day he told me that what saddened him most of all were those patients who had big families but for whom no visitors would ever come. At visiting time in the ward they would just sit there staring into space, knowing no one cared. His description stayed with me and touched a strong spring in myself. I understood what those patients felt and I knew I had to bring it out in my work:

When Philip stood looking down on her, she pulled herself to her feet saying nothing, then angrily pushed the chair to one side and shambled to the light which she switched off before saying shortly, 'Get yourself to sleep!'

Without a word now he went into his room, and in the firelight she groped her way to the bed and, sitting on its edge, she began to rock herself back and forward, back and forward. And after a while her rocking ceased and she was about to slide to her knees on the floor and implore God of His mercy to take this lonely longing from her heart when her whole body was consumed by a furious anger. It rushed through her like a torrent sweeping a gorge. The anger cried out against God, against her entire family, against this son [Jack] that she loved more than anything on earth. What had she done to deserve such treatment? Hadn't she given him everything? With every ounce of her flesh and every fibre in her heart she had given to him, depriving the others of love to give to him, and what thanks had she ever got from him? But she had never wanted his thanks, only for him to laugh with her, joke with her, tease her, as if she was a bairn or lass, and for that small return she had given him everything, her life, the whole of her life. Damn and blast him! he was an ungrateful swine . . . an unforgiving swine. Blast him to hell! . . . She hoped . . . she hoped . . . There was a great lump in her chest like a weight of iron. It rose, pressing itself upwards into her throat. She gripped her neck to suffocate the sound that was endeavouring to escape, then as the tears spilled from her eyes she turned and pressed her face into the pillow. So intense was her emotion that it seemed to her that she was crying through every pore of her body, for the whole of her huge bulk was aching with a queer ache like a cramp, and as a cramp will converge to one spot all the aching gathered itself into a knot in her side where the wind usually was, and so intense did the pain become that it even stilled her crying, and she slowly straightened herself up, her hand gripping at the flesh under her breast. She tried to call out to Philip, but there was no sound in her throat.

She knew she was in her chair by the fire again, but she couldn't remember moving from the bed. The pain had stopped. It had been shoved away by a blackness that for a brief moment terrified her and checked her breathing. She was now lying in the blackness. It was as if a mighty hand had been placed over her mouth and eyes and even over her inward sight for she could see nothing, not even in her mind.

Slowly the fear of the darkness left her and she lay in it, almost calmly, waiting as she had been doing all night, and for days and weeks past, waiting, waiting. And when at last the darkness slowly lifted and she was able to glance once more about the firelit room, she noticed a very odd thing, so odd that, to put it still in her own words, her heart nearly shot out of her mouth, for sitting in the other armchair right opposite to her, literally dead to the world, was herself.

With a strange lightness upon her now she rose from her chair and moved nearer to the great, slumped figure and stood staring at it in a kind of awe for a moment. Begod! she wasn't a pleasant sight, not a bit like she thought she was. She stroked down her apron, as if in an attempt to put a semblance of tidiness on herself, and the thought struck her that it was . . . queer . . . it was, that she could do this, make herself tidy . . . yet that other one of her was not affected by it. As she raised her eyes and looked slowly around the familiar room, with every detail clear and distinct before her eyes, although there was nothing but the dim light of the fire to show them up, it came to her with a sort of great pity, overwhelming pity, that she had died, died in that spasm of pain

183

and anger and doubt, and all her waiting was over, all the recriminations, all the worries of being left alone. Everything she had tired herself out with these past months had been a useless waste of good time.

The 'Escape'

This feeling of aloneness grew into a concrete thing. Hard and painful, this feeling of rejection was to gather to itself, as time went on, shame, anxiety, remorse and bitterness. But even as a teenager it exercised a positive power in me, a power which, at twenty-three years of age, was to enable me to escape the North-East altogether.

When I was thirteen I had an accident in the school yard which left me immobile for some time. I remember the day when I stood on my two feet alone once more. I can see myself limping out of the bedroom and leaning for support on the white scrubbed kitchen table and looking through the window down the length of the yard. The yard door was open and I could see into the back lane, and there passing was Florrie Harding and Janie Robson and as I watched them I said to myself, 'I'll never play with them again.' I did not know childhood had left me, but I remember saying to myself 'What are you going to do?' and that this question was accompanied by an odd feeling in my chest. It was a mixture of many feelings, the feeling that I had when I went to the pawn, and when I carried the grey hen; the feeling I had when I humped the coke sack on my back; the feeling I had when I passed some of the other girls on the road with their nice clothes on while I was wearing an old costume coat of Kate's that reached to my knees and bulged out like a balloon from my hips – the feeling I had of being different.

But on this day I resolved to do something about it. I said 'Well, I can only do two things, I can write and I can do housework.' There was no lack of ideas or even complete stories, the impediment was the mere matter of grammar and spelling. This, as I have explained in my introduction, I rectified as soon as possible. And so it was some ten years later that I left the North and all it stood for. Hopeful because I was going to make something of myself. In my case I carried notes from Lord Chesterfield and a page torn from a cheap magazine. I still have that page.

> I will succeed I simply cannot fail,
> The only obstacle is doubt.
> There's not a hill I cannot scale
> Once fear is put to rout.
> Don't think defeat,
> Don't talk defeat,
> The word will rob you of your strength.

Right:
'I will succeed I simply cannot fail; the only obstacle is doubt.'

At the age of twenty-three I got the post of laundry manageress in the workhouse at Hastings . . . if my fate was to work in a laundry then I would one day manage the biggest in the country. I also became the owner of The Hurst. You might wonder how a laundry manageress earning £3 a week could buy a fifteen-roomed gentleman's residence, but I had been preparing for this from the days when I had carried the grey hen instead of taking a tram, and so saved a ha'penny. This was hidden in the rafters of the lavatory where the plaster was broken, and if Kate knew about it she never raided my bank.

'I will succeed', this phrase repeat
Throughout the journey's length.

The moment that 'I can't' is said,
You slam a door right in your face.
Why not exclaim 'I will' instead,
Half won then is the race.
You close the door to your success
By entertaining one small fear.
Think happiness, talk happiness,
Watch joy then coming near.

But the truth is that you cannot escape your roots. There is a need to come back. It's in most people, but it's much stronger in the North-East than many areas.

The politicians in the South find it difficult to understand why the people of the North will not leave their homeland if they cannot get jobs. If a child in the South does well at school he'll make light of the decision to move away in search of a job. Certainly this was the case in Hastings: if a boy had big ideas he'd move to London, no problem about it. But people up here, they might hate each other within the family, they might hate each other from one town to the next, but if anything happens it's the North-East against the rest.

To Tishy, who was in her first year as a teacher at the secondary modern, the solution was to move away, get out of the North-East. 'The trouble with us in this corner of the globe,' she said, 'is that we are too insular. Metaphorically speaking, everybody in the North-East has the chummy back lane, back-to-back mentality. People won't move. If they do it has to be within easy reach of the town in which they were born. If they go farther afield they develop symptomatic phobias.'

The Invisible Cord

The day I went up to the New Buildings, East Jarrow, and saw William Black Street was no more, a deep sadness overwhelmed me. I stood on the rubble where the kitchen had been, that kitchen in which all the emotions of life had been enacted, and memories flooded back to me. But in that moment the most vivid one, strangely enough, was of my granny.

I've talked a lot over the years about Our Kate and me granda, but not much about me granny perhaps because she died when I was seven years old, but on this particular occasion memories of her came flooding up so poignantly that the tears rolled down my face and I went back to the car and wrote down the vivid impression I had got of her.

185

Me granny sat in a wooden chair
She had a stiff face, wrinkles and straight black hair,
But if I ever needed comfort I found it there.
Between her knees each day she'd have me stand,
And look me head for nits, and I'd play the band
Until she said, 'Here's a bullet
Mind you don't choke yourself
It'll stick in your gullet.'

I went home sad, my mind filled with nostalgia for the days that had been, for the days that I once ran away from, from the North as it once had been – when I was little Katie.

Eventually, upstart that I was, I had to face the fact that I wouldn't write a word that anyone would really want to read until I threw off the pseudo-lady and accepted my early environment, me granda, the pawn, the beer carrying, the cinder picking, Kate's drinking, and of course my birth, for it was these things that had gone to make me. Also, to own to being a Northerner and all this implied. It was this cathartic outlook that set the pattern for *Kate Hannigan*, my first novel.

I once wrote a piece called *Time and the Child*, which seems to sum it up:

The day I went up to the New Buildings, East Jarrow, and saw William Black Street was no more.

I can smell my memories of childhood. The smell of real manure from a farmyard, as opposed to that from chemicals, recalls the scene of a farm outside Shields. I was on high ground. There were rocks and the sea to the left of me, and there away in the distance was a field of corn, red corn.

On closer investigation I found that the edge of the field was rimmed with fragile flowerheads, hundreds and hundreds of them. Kate later told me they were called poppies. I thought the name didn't suit them somehow, they should have been called flamers; and there was no incongruity in the fact that this is what me granda called the people next door.

Perhaps it's old age creeping on or galloping on but I find my mind going back to these days to episodes in my childhood, more and more.

Here I am seventy-one and I know that inside I am still very much the child, the child that was Katie McMullen of East Jarrow, only the facade is the woman and it hasn't the power to control the child. Somehow I can't ignore the power of the child I once was and still am. I am still hurt as she was hurt. I still laugh as she laughed. I still have the secret insight that she had, the insight that recognised sorrow and loneliness in others, the insight – that was in me before I suckled milk, for, as our Kate said, if I in her womb had been aware of what she was suffering during those nine months that she carried me, then I should surely have been born mental.

Well, I must have been aware of her pain for I nearly went mental, didn't I?

I find that time is galloping away now; it isn't dawn before it's dusk. The hours leap into days and the days disappear into weeks, and I can't remember what I did in them. The pity of it is, my mind at this stage is clearer than at any period of my life, and I long for time, long time, the time of childhood, in which to expand and grow again.

You know, we are what our early environment makes us. I believe that is true. All through our life those early years colour our thinking. No matter how thick the veneer, heredity has a way of kicking itself through the skin. When the race is almost run and the two ends of the circle are meeting you see the child coming towards you, and you go back into his time more and more. You can recognise his thinking more so than when at twelve, thirteen or fourteen you left him behind. The knowledge of his magic is fresh before your eyes, for in his time of being there was no growing, there was no age. You knew people did what they called dying and although they were put into the earth they had gone into the sky; but you were here, there'd be new bread for tea, it was Saturday the morrow and there was no school. Sunday, you'd have to go to Mass. On Monday . . . When was Monday? There was no such thing as Monday, not on a Friday night. Monday wouldn't appear until late on Sunday night when you were dropping off to sleep. And Sunday was a long, long way off. It came after Saturday. But tonight was Friday and tomorrow you would go to the penny matinee at The Crown. What greater joy could anyone ask for?

In that time I can smell baking day in the kitchen. I can see the kitchen as if it were set out before me. There's me sitting on the fender, Kate bustling all around me.

'Move your backside out of that,' she says.

I shuffle along the steel fender away from the black-leaded oven door, quickly past the fierce blazing fire built up in a slant you know to keep the heat against the oven, and when I reach the far end of the long fender I say, 'A . . .w!' for the steel is always cold between the end of me knickers and the top of me stockings.

I watch her lift the sneck of the oven door and pull out the oven shelf on which there are four loaf tins; she plonks the shelf onto the fender, dextrously upturns the loaf tins that are as black as the oven itself, gives three taps with her knuckles on the bottom of each tin, nods towards the oven as if acknowledging her debt to it, then looks at me and says, 'Have you got your yule-doo ready? Come on, look slippy if you want to put it in. I haven't got all day.'

I can see myself coming out of my dreaming, jumping to the table, picking up the much fingered piece of dough I've shaped into a man – perhaps this time he has currants for his eyes, mouth and nose, and a row for his coat, or perhaps this time funds were too low for currants and his face was featureless and his suit without buttons. I can see me laying him tenderly on the hot plate. I want to straighten him out, but Kate's voice will have none of it.

'Don't make a meal of it, not yet anyway. Out of me road!'

The oven door bangs on my yule-doo, Kate straightens her back, dusts the palms of her hands loudly against each other, blows a strand of hair from her sweating brow by thrusting out her lower jaw and puffing upwards, then she looks down on me and says gently, I can hear her saying it gently, 'Well, that's done, we'll have a sup tea, eh hinny?'

'Oh aye, Kate. Aye, yes.'

The smell of new bread slides me back into eternity, the eternity that was childhood; the eternity of pain and fear and that sick feeling in my chest caused by fear; the fear that me granda would make a big hole in his pay by dropping into the North-Eastern pub before coming home.

The fear that he might have had a very good week and so they'd all have a drop too much, and there'd be divils fagarties later on.

The fear there'd be no money on Monday for the rent; and I'd be kept off school to go to Bobs – Bobs was the pawnshop.

The fear that I'd have to miss Mass on Sunday 'cos me boots weren't decent.

The fear of facing the headmistress on the Monday and admit I hadn't been to Mass. Oh, that fear outdid the one on purgatory, hell and damnation.

But, as I said, there were moments of wonder when all these fears were forgotten – in that everlasting time by memories of flamers in a field, and the smell of new bread in that kitchen that served so many purposes, and the memory of which will stay with me till I die.

I wrote in my introduction, 'Isn't it strange that from the wider world into which I escaped I have to return, like the eel to the Sargasso Sea, to die where I began, among my ain folk.' As a child in Jarrow I would go to seven o'clock mass on Sundays at St Peter's and St Paul's, but in this my eighty-first year I no longer have superstitions about life and death. I see death as a long sleep, and if it isn't a long sleep it'll be a nice surprise.

In the last few years the blood disease which has been with me all my life has brought me to the depths and I have been ready to let go. On January 18th, 1975 I wrote the following: I felt very ill yesterday. The feeling continued into the night; I couldn't sleep. My siamese twin self-pity, was in charge. This was a real bout of mental exhaustion. For months now it has been a fourteen hour day, seven days a week, up at half-past six in the morning trying to get through my ever growing mail; the day allotted to the phone, visits from agents, editors, photographers, interviewers and, just recently, the BBC Unit. I tell myself it can't go on, but it does.

188

The truth is that you cannot escape your roots. There is a need to come back.

When the race is almost run and the two ends of the circle are meeting you see the child coming towards you, and you go back into his time more and more.

Lying there in the dark last night with Tom by my side I asked myself what I wanted, and strangely the answer was – joy.

Some months ago I felt so bad, bleeding so badly, that I made the decision to give up writing altogether. Believe me I have to be bad to do that. I was in a desperate state, feeling that I was about to let go. And I went to this place, and I said to whatever was there that I was tired and just wanted to give up and let go.

But as I said it I thought, why do I ask? Because I know from experience that I will never get the answer that I want. Never do I get the sympathetic answers: 'Yes, you're right. This is what you should do. It's about time you thought about yourself.'

Instead it was as if someone had come to my side, and then went for me – 'You're going against your nature. All right, if you give up, you'll give up and you'll go. You'll go very quickly because it isn't your nature to give up. Your character is to fight. As you once wrote, strife is your meat and drink; you've got to fight.' And again it went for me, and said: 'Tomorrow morning get out of this bed. No matter what you feel like, get out of this bed. You needn't put your clothes on, just put a dressing gown on, and DO something. Start checking what you have written. Get onto the tape.' [I always start my books on tape].

And I said, 'But I'm too ill to get up.'

And the voice said, 'We know how ill you are, but you tell Tom of your decision.'

And I said, 'I haven't made a decision.'

'But you have . . .'

And this went on for about an hour.

The next morning I told Tom exactly what had happened. I told him the exact words because it was still so fresh, and Tom said, 'Yes, that's right, you know, this is what you should do.'

I could hardly stand on my feet but I got up and stayed up for half a day. And when I got back into bed, as always with my tape recorder beside me, I mumbled into it, 'Sarah, I'm not sure where I was in this story, but start a new chapter.' [It had been three months since I had written a word of it.] And then, 'I know what has to happen. Start a new chapter . . .' And from then, it went on. . . .

This morning I don't feel any joy but I have an idea for a story which is the next best thing.

Lord, beckon me to joy:
My mind is weary
My body sick;
Who can I employ
To ease my spirit
And lift my heart
And give me strength
To combat this strife
And the energy
To work at life?
Lord, beckon me to joy.

I have no hobbies:
No more do I knit,
Play the piano or paint;
My mind abhors the needle,
My fingers irritate the keys,
I see no colours, no trees.

Then what do I do
With my days?
I write,
And part of the night.
O Lord, beckon me to joy.

Epilogue

The author describes her novels as 'readable social history interwoven into the lives of people', but that disguises her art. It is precisely *how* history is woven into the lives of people that sets apart talented writers in the genre from the rest of the field. Many historical novels are full of history and empty of character; some others are peopled by characters who would be more at home in the twentieth century.

Catherine does not write historical plots to order; thank goodness, she would not know how to. Her talent is as creator, as life-giver to real characters who are made to exist in our imagination. Her readers know what it is to be ensnared by a master storyteller, to be led breathless from one scene to the next. But she achieves this through the most complete presentation of character: we believe in her people and can imagine what they would feel in any situation. As the *New York Times Book Review* recently said about *The Black Velvet Gown*, 'Mrs Cookson treats her characters and their problems as Thomas Hardy or Elizabeth Cleghorn Gaskell would – that is, omnisciently.' Their stories cannot help but unfold.

Whence do her people come? Today, in the fine and tasteful surroundings of this millionairess's Langley home it is hauntingly possible to catch a glimpse of the little girl from Leam Lane, held hostage in a 'fortress of pain wherein she was a child'. She stands centre stage in the kitchen of the house in William Black Street, listening, absorbing and – incredibly, aged seven – feeling responsible for the lives and relationships of a granda, a grandma, an uncle called Jack, and a mother we now know as our Kate.

'Everything that happened in that kitchen,' she says, 'everything I thought, everything that I have written since seems to have been bred in that kitchen.'

The South Tyneside Council plays host to thousands who come, even from America, to the environment that engendered her people: to see the plaques at William Black Street, St Peter & Paul's, the Workhouse (now the General Hospital), Rory's boatyard or Westoe Village where he first called on Charlotte Kean with her father's slum rents, or Shields Market that once witnessed Mrs McGrath's vicious assault on Tilly Trotter's infant son, or Jarrow, where Bede's ancient church contains a table made by the hunger marchers of the '30s, and which is redolent today with memories of Palmer's great shipyard and the long, remarkable life of Katie Mulholland. And now in South Shields' Ocean Road Museum, that kitchen itself: 'the hub, the heart of the matter, the axis about which revolved the lives of my people, be they what they may...'

Rory's boatyard, off Wapping Street, today.

Significantly, *Catherine Cookson Country* provides in the passages from her writings a map of the author no less than that of the area and its people, but only the full scope of her novels can illustrate the complexities of the woman. The part of her character most commonly to the fore in Katie Mulholland and Tilly Trotter has largely been subsumed, though two other characters are still embattled within her: Mary Ann, the 'holy innocent', and Miss Brigmore, embodiment of high moral principles (though happily flawed). In the continuing battle Mary Ann as the little liar still maintains the upper hand, just as she did when Catherine was a child: 'It was me granda who first told me I was a writer. He didn't actually say I was a writer, not in so many words ... I can see myself running up the backyard and into the kitchen and going straight for him where he sat in his chair, crying, "Granda! you know that little man you tell me about, the one that sits on the wall in Ireland no bigger than your hand, you know him? With the green jacket and the red trousers and the buckle on his shoes, and the high hat and a shillelagh as big as himself, you remember, Granda?"

"Aye, what about him?"

"Well, I've seen him, Granda."

"Ya have?"

"Aye, Granda. He was round the top corner."

"He was, was he? And I suppose he spoke to you?"

"Aye, Granda, he did."

"And what did he say?"

"Well, he said, 'Hello, Katie.'"

"He said, 'Hello Katie,' did he? And what did you say?"

"... I said, 'Hello, Mister, me granda knows you.'"

He wiped his tash with his hand while raising his white eyebrows, then he said: "You know what you are, Katie McMullen, don't ya? You're a stinking liar. But go on, go on, don't stop, for begod! it will get you some place .. Either into clink or into the money!'"

The philosopher, the moralist, the teacher loom large, but the natural storyteller is still in the lead.

Catherine's belief that she inherited from her father genes which somehow set her apart from the hopelessness around her not only fostered the strength to work hard but also, in rare moments of freedom, to strive to better herself. Her father 'provided the norm at which I aimed. Without that side of me,' she believes, 'I may not have become a writer.' This selective self-image 'pushed and pulled' her out of the early environment of poverty and stigma, and she left the North-East. It is impossible to read of Sarah's impoverished family in *The Blind Miller* 'wallowing and choking in a sea of mud like that which filled the timber yard at Jarrow Slake', and not wonder what it took Catherine to perform her own rescue from the mire.

In Hastings the angst that her 'escape' produced possibly hastened the breakdown that lasted ten years. Whether it was this, the unremitting work, the trauma of the loss of her children in childbirth, the inner turbulence aggravated by her growing disaffection with Catholicism, or a combination of all that lay at its root, it was neither the Church nor even Lord Chesterfield who drew her slowly up from the hell into which she had fallen, but Tom Cookson.

With Tom's help she began to accept her roots and 'throw off the pseudo-lady'. What emerged was a true novelist of the spirit, yet far from the Romantic tradition.

In *The Mallen Litter* Catherine writes: 'Neither the events of the world nor the struggles of the working class towards emancipation touched Brook House and its inmates during these years. Mrs Dan Benshaw occupied herself mostly with reading the works of the Brontë sisters, never Dickens or Mrs Gaskell.' It is nigh on certain that Catherine and Barbara Bensham would not have seen eye to eye had they met, and who knows perhaps they did!

The saying that you cannot tell a book by its cover has never been more literally true than in her case. There is nothing sentimental about her writing; Catherine is unrelenting in the strong images she employs to cast her spell. They are born of her formative years and her struggle to realise herself. No one who has read even one of her books (and there are few who can have stopped at one) can visit Tyneside without hearing the sounds of the steelworks, the hubbub of the now silent docks, or the voices of her characters as they once passed through the halls of her imagination and now live in ours.

As the traveller crosses the Tyne between Gateshead and Newcastle, nature and the works of man combine to excite our wonderment and awe. This is the gateway, you feel, to the capital of another kingdom, but it is also the focal point of Catherine Cookson's country: the Tyne is its binding factor, the reason for prosperity in its heyday and now imbued with the moods and tempers cast upon it by Catherine's tales, tales which ring true for readers from all over the world. Catherine's insight into the lives of ordinary people is so exceptional that she is translated into seventeen different languages and read in all English-speaking countries, but as she says, 'Human nature is much the same the world over.'

The integrity of her spirit, now assured by the reunion with the environment that inspired it, is today enhanced by her determination to give spiritually, emotionally and financially to those in need. Her warmth and generosity permeate her books and are very probably another factor in their extraordinary popularity. On her eightieth birthday, the date on which this book is first published, she is as indefatigable as ever. In hospital one day for a distressing operation, she is back in her beautiful home the next, propped up in bed by pillows, not languishing but embarked upon yet another novel, destined like all the others to become a bestseller.

192